The Literary World
of San Francisco & Its Environs

THE
LITERARY WORLD
of San Francisco & its Environs

by

DON HERRON

Edited by Nancy J. Peters

CITY LIGHTS BOOKS
San Francisco

Cover photograph: Jack and Charmian London on the rigging
of *The Snark*. Courtesy, Russ Kingman

Grateful acknowledgment for lines from *Desolation Angels*
by Jack Kerouac, © 1960, 1963, 1965 by Jack Kerouac:
G. P. Putnam's Sons.

"Dashiell Hammett Tour" is a registered Trade Mark and Service Mark of Don Herron

Cataloging in Publication Data

Herron, Don.
    The literary world of San Francisco & its environs.

    Includes index.
    1. Literary landmarks—California—San Francisco.
2. Literary landmarks—California, Northern.
3. American literature—California—San Francisco—History and Criticism.
4. American literature—California, Northern—History and criticism.
5. San Francisco (Calif.)—Description—Guide-books.　6. San Francisco
(Calif.)—Intellectual life.　7. California, Northern—Description and travel—
Guide-books.　I. Title.
PS144.S4H47　　　1985　　　917.94'610453　　　84-19870

ISBN: 0-87286-157-0

Designed by Nancy J. Peters & Kim McCloud
Maps by Kim McCloud
Mezzotints by Northern Lights
Typesetting by Richard Brown

rot
10 - 21 - 86

CITY LIGHTS BOOKS are edited by Lawrence Ferlinghetti &
Nancy J. Peters and published at the City Lights Bookstore,
261 Columbus Avenue, San Francisco, California 94133

CONTENTS

Introduction vii
Market Street 1
South of Market 18
Civic Center 21
Dashiell Hammett 29
Union Square 40
Nob Hill 52
Russian Hill 58
Polk Gulch 70
Pacific Heights 75
Fisherman's Wharf 80
Mark Twain 87
Telegraph Hill 95
North Beach 106
Jackson Square — Chinatown 121
The Mission 132
Haight-Ashbury — Fillmore 143
Other City Sites 154
Jack London 163
Points East 177
Points South 197
John Steinbeck 214
Points North 228
Photo Credits 242
Index 243

INTRODUCTION

The lure of San Francisco began with gold and the onrush of the Forty-Niners, creating almost overnight a city unique in America. In the one-hundred-thirty-five years since the first argonauts sailed into port, San Francisco has become one of the world's favored places, famous for its views, restaurants, weather, culture. In 1920 the visiting journalist H. L. Mencken summed up part of this special appeal in the comment, "What fetched me instantly (and thousands of other newcomers with me) was the subtle but unmistakable sense of escape from the United States."

Thousands of other writers have stopped in this city, from Mark Twain who came from the alkali wastes of the Washoe to further his career as a journalist, to Ambrose Bierce, Bret Harte, Dashiell Hammett, John Steinbeck, Kay Boyle. Poet Lawrence Ferlinghetti decided that perhaps he moved here in 1951 because San Francisco is adjacent to the best wine country in America. Jack London and Robert Frost were natives. Shirley Jackson was born here on December 14, 1919. The elusive B. Traven claimed San Francisco, among other cities, as his birthplace. Walter Tevis, famous as the author of *The Hustler* (1959), was also a native—his science fiction novel *The Man Who Fell to Earth* (1963), about the reactions of an alien stranded uncomfortably on earth, is based on Tevis' feelings as a boy when his family moved from cosmopolitan San Francisco to live in Kentucky.

The old Platt's Hall on Montgomery Street, now site of the Mills Building, saw Oscar Wilde, Hans Christian Andersen, W. D. Howells, Lowell, Emerson, Whitman, and other major writers lecture. Anthony Trollope is one of many visiting authors who made the required visit to the Cliff House—and came away, as did Mark Twain, not greatly impressed. It's said that when Agatha Christie, Queen of the Murder Mystery, came to town she made a business-like side trip to the botanical gardens in Berkeley's Tilden Park to examine a rare poisonous plant.

The attraction of these writers' homes and haunts, for many of us, is irresistible. In 1870 California's own Joaquin Miller left for England to place a laurel wreath on Byron's neglected tomb, to see sites associated with Burns and Scott, to track in London the steps of Browning, Bayard Taylor, and Tom Hood. The great Chicago bookman Vincent Starrett (who as a young reporter broke the story that the Literary Lion of 1800s San Francisco, Ambrose Bierce, had disappeared into Pancho Villa's Mexico) recalls meeting the mystic writer Arthur Machen in London in 1924. As they strolled down a lane, Machen pointed to a plaque marking a home of Thomas Hood, Sr., and exclaimed "All over London!" (One of these London literary plaques on a dwelling place of W. B. Yeats compelled Sylvia Plath to take a five-year lease on the flat, where she committed suicide.) The L.A. writer Charles Bukowski mentions discovering John Fante's novel *Ask the Dust* (1939): "Fante was my god and I knew that gods should be left alone, one didn't bang at their door. Yet I liked to guess about where he lived on Angel's Flight and I imagined it possible that he still lived there. Almost every day I walked by and I thought is that the window Camilla crawled through? And, is that the hotel door? Is that the lobby? I never knew."

The Literary World of San Francisco gives you the addresses, and maps out areas easily toured on foot. With a current S. F. Municipal Railway map and a California state map you may also tour outlying sections.

Of course, several important literary sites — such as the Rincon Hill house where Henry George wrote *Progress and Poverty* — are gone now, and it is impractical to mention *every* writer who has drifted through, or even *all* the apartments where Allen Ginsberg has crashed. I'm convinced that every corner grocery has its literary anecdote. Certainly almost every house built before (and sometimes after) 1920 maintains a "tradition" that Stevenson, Bierce or London "slept here."

This guide concentrates on still-standing buildings, on authentic locations. Thus, you'll find listed commercial concerns such as Jack London Square or Cannery Row which have true connections with London and Steinbeck, but not the "Mark Twain Hotel" on Taylor Street (earlier the Linden and then the Don Hotel, where Billie Holiday was busted for drugs in 1949), or the "Robert Frost Retirement Center" at Jackson and Gough, or the neatly-named "O henry's" restaurant and bar on Union (though O. Henry did write "East is East and West is San Francisco"). And I've skipped the "Bret Harte district" in Hunter's Point and the "Bret Harte Junior High School" in Oakland as well. A majority of sites in this book are now private homes, but the houses of Eugene O'Neill, Robinson Jeffers, John Muir, Stevenson, London, and some other writers — as well as cafes, hotels, and bars — are open to the public: more than enough to give you a feel for the writers' eras and lives.

Sources of information are mentioned, catch as catch can, within the text. Bill Kostura has provided major research assistance into his favorite area, Russian Hill, and helped track down sites for Steinbeck, London, and literary Carmel, as well as the house where Frank Norris died. Nancy J. Peters found many of the sites for North Beach and Telegraph Hill, Chinatown and the Mission, and Stan Old was of great help with the East Bay. Russ Kingman of the World of Jack London Bookstore mapped out London's Oakland for me, and Mickey Friedman's excellent book column in the *Examiner* provided many leads. Lawrence Ferlinghetti, Gary Snyder, Allen Ginsberg, James Henry, Geraldine Monosoff, Steve Eng, Ray Nelson, Richard Lupoff, Donald Sidney-Fryer, the late George F. Haas, Fritz Leiber, Margo Skinner, Donna Mathews, Gordon De Marco, Richard L. Tierney, Betty Zarn, Robin Gajdusek, Amy Beason, Bruce Taylor, Alejandro Murguía, Paul Yamazaki, George Leong, GGNRA historian James P. Delgado, Jack "The Trivia Man" Kelly, and John C. Moran of the F. Marion Crawford Memorial Society all contributed information. I'd like to acknowledge their help, and that of many others (such as the anonymous postman of Telegraph Hill) in researching this book — which will take you back to the days when Mark Twain covered San Francisco on his reporter's beat, through bars and back alleys familiar to Jack Kerouac, over hills cloaked in night-fog where the shadow of Sam Spade still walks the city streets.

— Don Herron

MARKET STREET

The Ferry Building, 1914

On a Saturday night the city joined in the promenade on Market Street, the broad thoroughfare that begins at the waterfront and cuts its straight path of miles to Twin Peaks. The sidewalks were wide and the crowd walking toward the Bay met the crowd walking toward the ocean. The outpouring of the population was spontaneous as if in response to an urge for instant celebration.

Every quarter of the city discharged its residents into the broad procession. Ladies and gentlemen of imposing social repute; their German and Irish servant girls, arms held fast in the arms of their sweethearts; French, Spaniards, gaunt, hard-working Portuguese; Mexicans, the Indian showing in reddened skin and high cheekbone—everybody, anybody, left home and shop, hotel, restaurant, and beer garden to empty into Market Street in a river of color. Sailors of every nation deserted their ships at the water front and, hurrying up Market Street in groups, joined the vibrating mass excited by the lights and stir and the gaiety of the throng. "This is San Francisco," their faces said. . . .

(Nineteenth Century Market Street)
Harriet Lane Levy, *920 O'Farrell Street*

In young San Francisco the major thoroughfare was Mont-gomery Street on the waterfront. The three-million-dollar Mont-gomery Block built by Henry W. Halleck in 1853 was the most ex-pensive construction in the West. Commerce, law, and the arts all flourished on or near this street, and its fame was international. When the French writer Jules Verne rushed Phileas Fogg and his imperturbable valet Passepartout through our port in *Around the World in Eighty Days* (1873), he had them briefly caught up in the "Camerfield-Mandiboy election" and the political climate that stormed up and down Montgomery.

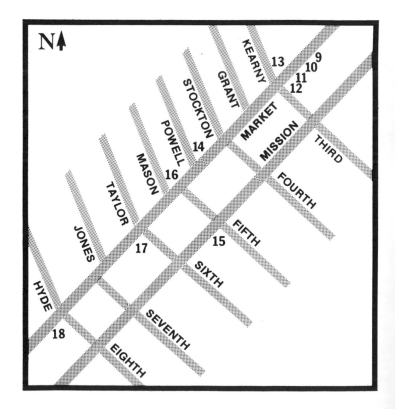

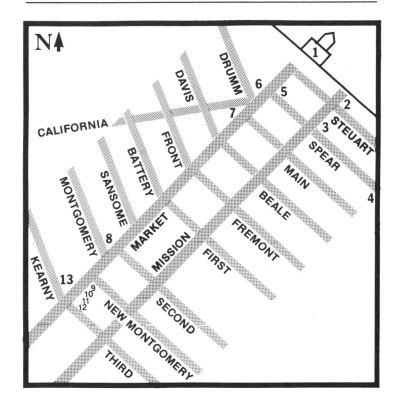

By the mid-1870s, however, another street came to prominence. Landfill had pushed the waterfront several blocks east of Montgomery, and buildings that outstripped the old Montgomery Block were underway. The day the five-million-dollar Palace Hotel opened its doors to guests in 1875 was the day Market Street finally shed its reputation as a wide, workable but commonplace sort of avenue to become a place with glamour. With the construction of roofs over the South Pacific Coast and Central Pacific ferry slips at the foot of Market in 1876, San Francisco had its first "Ferry Building," and the railroad companies of the day quickly put in streetcar and cable lines leading to this portal to the East. Market became the most traveled street in the city, and was the first to be repaired and reoccupied after the fire of 1906.

Today Market is still the spine of downtown San Francisco. A walk of some ten blocks up its brick-paved sidewalks will give you a varied look into the city's literary history.

Begin this tour at Market
and the Embarcadero, in the
Ferry Building. Buses or
trolleys eastbound on Market
with "Ferry" as the destination

sign will get you within half a block; so will any of the Muni streetcars which now run under Market Street to the Embarcadero Station terminal. Parking may be found close by in the garage of Embarcadero Center Four, a highrise at Sacramento and Drumm Streets.

1 FERRY BUILDING   This famous structure with its Moorish clock tower was designed by A. Page Brown and Willis Polk. Opened in 1895, an estimated fifty million people passed through its halls every year until 1937, when the new Bay Bridge opened a path above the waves from Oakland to San Francisco.

In the late 1800s Ambrose Bierce walked through this building *en route* to points East, or returning, as did Jack London, Ina Donna Coolbrith, Charles Warren Stoddard, Gertrude Atherton, W. C. Morrow, Charles Caldwell Dobie, Gelett Burgess, Frank Norris—the list is comprehensive: *every* writer, every mobile man, woman, and child of the time, traveled these halls.

It is said that George Sterling drafted many of his early poems aboard the ferry boats, riding west from his job as secretary in his uncle's real estate and utilities office in Oakland to enjoy the Bohemian nightlife of San Francisco. From across the Bay the clock tower dominated the city's skyline, rising like a colossus on the waterfront, and winds carried the rich aroma of coffee from the Hills Brothers warehouse south of Market to passengers standing on the rocking decks. By the time of Sterling's death by suicide in 1927 he was recognized as San Francisco's poet laureate, one of the most famous personalities in the city. The ferry system would have yet another prime decade as the major means of transit across the Bay. Today Sterling's fame has dwindled, and the Ferry Building is dwarfed by dozens of skyscrapers rising against the clouds.

Yet what skyscraper can ever overshadow the romance and excitement of those days when ferries plied the icy fog-bound Bay? What scene set in some modern office building will ever compare with a scene like that in "The Tenth Clew," a story in which Dashiell Hammett's short fat Continental Op is prodded onto the open deck of a westbound ferry by a man with a gun?

> The deck was deserted. A heavy fog, wet as rain—the fog of San Francisco Bay's winter nights—lay over boat and water, and had driven everyone else inside. It hung about us, thick and impenetrable; I couldn't see so far as the end of the boat, in spite of the lights glowing overhead. . . .
> I went on until I reached the rail.

Then the detective is sapped and thrown overboard, and from out of the blanketing mist,

> from every direction, in a dozen different keys, from near and far, fog-horns sounded. . . . After a while I picked out the moaning, evenly spaced blasts of the Alcatraz siren. But they told me nothing. They came to me out of the fog without direction. . . . I was somewhere in San Francisco Bay, and that was all I knew, though I suspected the current was sweeping me out toward the Golden Gate.

*From the Ferry Building walk
south one block to Mission and
stop at the first address on that
street, an old French-style
structure at 1-21 Mission
known as:*

2 THE AUDIFFRED BUILDING   Built in 1889, the Audiffred once
housed a Norwegian mission called the Seven Seas Club on the second floor and the legendary Bulkhead Saloon on the first. History records
the weird harmonies created by the sounds of hymns, coming from the
mission, mixed with the crashes, curses, and groans created by brawlers
in the Bulkhead. The Audiffred and the Ferry Building are the only structures in this part of town that survived the 1906 fire. Soldiers dynamited
many blocks to create a fire break between the burning city and the
wharves, so that ships with emergency supplies would have a place to
dock. As they set out their charges for the Audiffred, the bartender ran out
of the Bulkhead with a proposition: a keg of whiskey per man, and a
wagonload more, if they spared the saloon. The dynamiters moved on
and the city-fire never reached the building—though a blaze in 1978
gutted the Audiffred seventy-two years later.

Now the building is "restored" in a style much more elegant than the
way it looked in the early 1950s when Lawrence Ferlinghetti first came to
San Francisco after several years in Paris, and rented a loft here from the
famous abstract-expressionist painter, Hassel Smith. To this enormous
room overlooking the Bay, heated with a wood stove, Ferlinghetti went
several days each week to write and to paint. At that time he was contributing criticism to *Art Digest*; his biographer Neeli Cherkovski points out
that "Ferlinghetti was greatly influenced by the abstract-expressionists."
His theories of art and poetry were to merge, so that the visual presentation
of the poem on a page became as integral an element of his poetry as the
words he used. Other locally famous artists who had studios here
included Frank Lobdell, Martin Snipper, and Howard Hack.

*Move up Mission past Stewart.
Filling the south side of this
next block is the:*

3 RINCON ANNEX   This branch of the U.S. Postal Service has at least
two literary associations worth noting. If you go inside the building
you'll notice twenty-nine panels of an epic mural by artist Anton Refregier,
which was commissioned by the Roosevelt administration's WPA and
unveiled in 1948. With the rise of McCarthyism in the 1950s this art
became "highly suspect": Refregier was known to have left-wing, even
Communist connections. Protests against "subversive themes" in his
portrayal of conquistadores, Indians, vigilantes, bridge-builders, and
founders of the United Nations— an overview of San Francisco's history—
became loud in 1951 and again in 1955. Lawrence Ferlinghetti in his job
as art critic vigorously defended Refregier's work, stating that the murals
were "the latest battleground of intellectual and artistic censorship." Sup-
porters of the murals won the issue, and the uncensored panels still en-
liven a trip to this post office.

For eight years Lawrence Swaim worked a regular shift in this building, working on his fiction on the side. Swaim was a union official here, and drew on his experiences for his first novel published in 1977 — about a man working in Rincon Annex. The book has one of the most appropriately "San Francisco" titles ever used: *Waiting for the Earthquake.*

Step outside the post office and consider for a moment one of those neighborhoods lost in history, an area once the only "respectable" place to be born, where an internationally famous writer experienced a pivotal moment in his life:

4 RINCON HILL Carted away for landfill, leveled in the name of progress, Rincon Hill today can be seen in a cut-away shoulder of earth here and there, holding up access ramps to the Bay Bridge. The best look at the remains may be found along Harrison Street in the vicinity of Fremont, First, Ecker, and Second Streets, but in its day Rincon rose up from the foot of Mission, with rows of houses climbing to its crest.

On October 30, 1857, Gertrude Franklin Horn — a great-grandniece of Benjamin Franklin — was born in one of those buildings.

> I was born on Rincon Hill, a slight elevation south of Market Street and covered with roomy houses in pleasant gardens, two or three of which lingered there until the fire of 1906. Rincon Hill, South Park at its feet, Folsom and two or three other streets near-by, and, in the north, running up the hill, Stockton Street and its immediate western neighbors, were the only places in those days where one could be born respectably.

After an unsatisfying marriage to a rancher's son named George Atherton, she began a literary career as Gertrude Atherton that would last almost six decades — from her early articles for the San Francisco *Examiner* and the publication of her first book *The Doomswoman* in 1892, when she was thirty-five, to her death at age ninety-one in 1948, with several dozen books written over the years.

One of the most powerful literary ghosts haunting our streets is the tubercular, starved figure of Robert Louis Stevenson, who came halfway across the world to California in pursuit of a married woman, only to find himself stranded in San Francisco without immediate hopes of a union with Mrs. Fanny Osbourne, and without a job. Between breaking his fast for 10¢ in the morning and eating a later meal at the extravagant cost of 50¢, carefully doling out his last dollars, Stevenson walked the town, a thin apparition in longworn clothes, with a drooping mustache and a small goatee under his lower lip, his hair several inches longer than the style of 1879 and 1880 thought fashionable.

On a walk up Rincon Hill he attracted the notice of Charles Warren Stoddard, who invited R.L.S. into his "plover's nest" at 3 Vernon Place near Second Street for tea. It was the first of many visits with Stoddard, a newspaperman who had published his early poetry under the name "Pip Pepperpod" and who went on to a long literary career as an editor on the *Overland Monthly*, Mark Twain's secretary in London, and author of several books — the most famous of them *The Lepers of Molokai.*

Stoddard's enthusiasm for the South Seas—the mementos of his travels in Hawaii and other islands on display in his rooms—kindled a like fire in Stevenson. "It was in such talks," R.L.S. recalled, "that I first heard the names—first fell under the spell—of the islands." He left that initial visit with copies of Melville's *Omoo* and Stoddard's book of verse *South Sea Idylls*. In after years, a beloved and world-famous writer, he spent his last days on Samoa, where he was called *Tusitala*, the Teller of Tales.

Stoddard mentioned R.L.S. climbing up the decrepit, shaking stairway to his place in a new and enlarged edition of *In the Footprints of the Padres* (1911):

> He used to come to that eyrie on Rincon Hill to chat and to dream. . . . The little glimpse that Louis Stevenson had of it in its decay gave him a few realistic pages for *The Wrecker*.

At the next street, Spear, turn right and go one block onto Market. Pause, look back to the Ferry Building to your right, the imposing mass of the Hyatt Regency Hotel across the street, the other large buildings looming up near-by:

C. W. Stoddard

5 THE FOOT OF MARKET STREET In the science fiction classic *The Blind Spot* by Austin Hall and Homer Eon Flint, first published in 1921, the action begins "On a certain foggy morning in September, 1905," when "a tall man wearing a black overcoat and bearing in one hand a small satchel of dark-reddish leather descended from a Geary Street tram at the foot of Market Street, San Francisco. It was a damp morning; a mist was brooding over the city blurring all distinctness." This man is the Rhamda Avec, and before the novel is over he will draw a professor from U.C. Berkeley and several others to a house at "288 Chatterton Place" in the city, plunge them into occult mysteries, and through the gate between dimensions known as the Blind Spot.

Less the stuff of adventure, but at least as weird, is Stephen Schneck's novel *The Nightclerk: Being His Perfectly True Confession* (1965). The nightclerk, J. Spenser Blight, weighs 617 pounds and is "one of the most physically repellent men alive." Schneck writes:

> Down at the end of town, at the bottom of Market Street, the monstrous Travelers Hotel occupies a full city block. A very special, zoned-off city block, outside the laws of nature as well as most municipal ordinances.

Where this block might be in which Blight performs his sweaty duties is a matter for the imagination. Perhaps where the Hyatt stands now? Perhaps on the far side of the Blind Spot?

The Hyatt has attracted attention for its interior architecture—a ceiling twenty stories high, glass elevators rising up the side of the wall to the Equinox, a revolving bar atop the hotel. The films "The Towering Inferno" and Mel Brooks' "High Anxiety" made use of this impressive setting; so did Stephen Englehart's novel *The Point Man* (1981). Englehart wrote for the comics—Marvel, D.C.—for several years, just as writers turned out stories for the pulps in the 1920s, 1930s and 1940s before moving on to book publication, screenplays and television scripts. (Mickey Spillane is the most famous writer to emerge from comic books—he originally created Mike Hammer as a comic book hero named "Mike Danger," but when the idea did not sell to the comics he made a novel titled *I, The Jury* out of the concept, and became one of the best-selling authors in history.)

Go into the Hyatt if you wish—up the elevators (if you're not afraid of heights), but when you come back onto the street find the small plaza where Drumm meets Market—it is next to the turntable for the California Street cable car line. You'll see a large stone pedestal, about waist high, on which is mounted the:

6 ROBERT FROST PLAQUE   Frost was born in this city March 26, 1874, and lived here eleven years. Researchers into Frost's early life now believe his family lived in at least seven different houses, all of them east of Van Ness and north of Market—the area destroyed in the 1906 fire—but disagree about which house he was born in. One biographer says the birth street was Washington between Polk and Larkin; a more recent opinion holds out for 14 Eddy Street. This current plaque and plaza were dedicated on the 104th anniversary of Frost's birth. His reputation as a poet is so strong that crowds of one hundred to two hundred people still turn out in this plaza for the ceremonies held each year at noon on Frost's birthday.

From this plaza (and, yes, it is one of the most un-Robert Frost-like sites imaginable) cross Drumm to where California comes angling down to Market. In 1894 a literary phenomenon was born in San Francisco on this corner of:

7 MARKET AND CALIFORNIA   —where Gelett Burgess, with the brothers Bruce and Robert Porter, threw ropes around a statue of

Dr. Henry Cogswell and brought it toppling off its granite pedestal. Cogswell, called by columnist Robert O'Brien "perhaps the dullest San Franciscan who ever walked down Market Street," was a dentist who came to California from his native New England. He is credited with devising the vacuum method for holding dental plates in place, and for being in 1853 the first dentist in California to use chloroform as an anesthetic.

Whatever his lack of inner fires, Cogswell managed to draw in money faster than the Mother Lode drew miners, and retired from competition with McTeague in 1856 to manage his empire of stocks and real estate. To immortalize himself he donated huge statues, usually of Dr. Henry Cogswell, to more than a dozen cities across the country. These cast-iron statues of Cogswell portrayed the good doctor offering passersby a glass of water — Cogswell was a teetotaler, and drinking fountains were included in the pedestals so that others might follow his example.

Burgess lost his job teaching topographical drawing at the University of California over this incident, shrugged, and continued to rain blows against pomposity by lauching — with Bruce Porter — *The Lark*, a magazine of humorous anarchy. Thus, with a resounding crash of iron and shattered pavement, and the jubilant cries of three men, was the *fin-de-siècle* movement *Les Jeunes* born in this city.

Continue up Market on the north side of the street until you reach Montgomery — some four blocks. An almost forgotten literary spectre lingers at this intersection of:

8 MARKET AND MONTGOMERY In *Science Fiction in Old San Francisco: History of the Movement from 1854 to 1890* (1980) the prominent science fiction historian Sam Moskowitz credits this city with being the first center in America for a science-fiction-and-fantasy literary movement. Stories by Ambrose Bierce, W. C. Morrow, William Henry Rhodes, Emma Frances Dawson, and others appearing in the *Argonaut*, the *Overland Monthly*, the *Examiner* and other local publications constituted the first major body of speculative fiction in this country.

And in the person of Robert Duncan Milne, a Scottish immigrant to San Francisco, Moskowitz sees the world's first full-time science fiction writer. Milne wrote at least sixty stories in twenty years, exploring an immense range of speculative themes: time travel, television, etc. Unfortunately, Milne was a fellow who would have profited by heeding Dr. Cogswell's call for temperance. Shortly after midnight on December 15, 1899, he weaved drunkenly out across Market, here at Montgomery, and was struck by a cable car. He died a few hours later.

The San Francisco of skyscrapers, jets, automobiles, underground train systems, and computers which you see around you is much closer to the one pictured by Milne's fertile imagination than was the city he lived in during the nineteenth century. His best work is collected as *Into the Sun and Other Stories* (1980).

Cross Market, with more caution than Robert Duncan Milne, to the south sidewalk

and continue on a few strides
until you stand at Market and
New Montgomery. On the
southwest corner of this inter-
section is:

Oscar Wilde

9 THE PALACE HOTEL The original Palace Hotel built by William C. Ralston opened its doors for business October 2, 1875, the largest and finest hotel in the West—a "Bonanza Inn." As Gertrude Atherton noted in *My San Francisco* (1946), ". . . no hotel of the past or present could compare with the old Palace. . . . Seven stories high, it surrounded a great central court into which four-horse teams would race at top speed while excited guests hung over the galleries above." Too expensive to serve as a frequent hang-out for the struggling writers of San Francisco's Bohemia, who made do with the red wine and pasta found in North Beach, it soon found its place in literary annals as a hotel where already-famous authors would stay when they toured the country.

On March 22, 1882, the twenty-seven-year-old Oscar Wilde, flam-boyantly clothed in velvet and silk, signed into the Palace as "O. Wilde and servant." A celebrity in England as a spokesman for The Beautiful, Wilde lectured in Platt's Hall, carrying a gigantic sunflower in one hand, an ivory cane in the other, creating an after-hours sensation in the city. At a dinner in the Bohemian Club the six-foot-two-inch, two-hundred-pound Aesthete showed its members how to drink, leaving them under the tables, and then strolled back to the Palace. His declarations for Irish independence and his foppish clothes prompted attack and ridicule in the local press, but Wilde's sharp wit deflected the blows, and cut easily back. As he said to Marya Watson of the *Examiner*—the first "lady reporter" he ever met—". . . not only here but all over America I have been quite amused at the struggle each of the gentlemen have had to write what I did not say; but I have the most sympathy with the writers of the articles which strive to be what is called here in the United States 'funny.' Their hard work has been so apparent."

Later in the 1880s Rudyard Kipling stayed in the Palace, which he called "a seven-storied warren of humanity." Ambrose Bierce, then editor of the *San Francisco Illustrated Wasp*, rejected Kipling's short stories; the *Chronicle* rejected *The Light That Failed*. In his dispatches to the Indian newspaper for which he was correspondent, Kipling got even: "The tale of the resources of California—vegetable and mineral—is a fairy tale. You can read it in books. . . . All manner of nourishing food from sea-fish to beef may be bought at the lowest prices; and the people are well-developed and of a high stomach. . . . When they disagree, they do so fatally, with firearms in their hands, and on public streets. . . . The Press records the fact, and asks in the next column whether the world can parallel the progress of San Francisco."

On May 1, 1895, the first issue of *The Lark* took wing from William Doxey's bookstore on the Market Street side of the Palace. Printed on bamboo-fiber, it was an unusual publication for the day, airy instead of stuffy, light not dense. Gelett Burgess and Bruce Porter, those topplers of Cogswellian statues, started the little magazine "with no more serious intention than to be gay — to sing a song, to tell a story." Contributors to *The Lark* were called by the papers *Les Jeunes* — which translates loosely as "The Young" — and included the artists Ernest Peixotto and Florence Lundborg, architect Willis Polk, printer Porter Garnett, and poet Yone Noguchi. Material by Robert Louis Stevenson was used with permission of his widow, the former Mrs. Fanny Osbourne, for whom Polk eventually designed a home on Russian Hill. (Stevenson's daughter-in-law, Isobel Osbourne Strong, was an employee in Doxey's bookstore, soon known as "The Sign of the Lark.")

The Lark's utter frivolousness became the rage of the season. Possibly Gelett Burgess produced the definitive examples of *Les Jeunes* art with his "Goops," circular little people who adorned the magazine in its heady two years of existence. The "Goops" have been charming readers ever since. Certainly Burgess' very light verse "The Purple Cow" represents the tone of this active San Francisco literary circle:

I never saw a Purple Cow
I never hope to see one
But I can tell you anyhow,
I'd rather see than be one.

In 1898, the year after *The Lark* suspended publication, Romantic novelist F. Marion Crawford came through the city two times to lecture at Platt's Hall, where Oscar Wilde had spoken sixteen years before. Author of *The White Sister, Casa Bracio, The Witch of Prague*, and many other novels, Crawford was a fascinating and popular figure, an American expatriate in Italy, fluent in eighteen languages (he kept his diary in Urdu), scarred from duels in his student days at Heidelberg, a seaman who piloted his yacht across the Atlantic — it is said that he never wrote a novel half so romantic as his own life. His first book *Mr. Isaacs* (1882) was based on his days as a newsman in India and, in sharp contrast to the chauvinistic writings of Kipling which followed almost a decade later, was strongly anti-British rule. Crawford's traveling companion and manager, Major J. B. Pond, records a dramatic incident of their stay in his book *Eccentricities of Genius* (1900):

> "Mr. Crawford, are we in the dining-car? See how these dishes are dancing."
> Mr. Crawford pulled out his watch and said:
> "It's an earthquake, Major. Don't be frightened. I've been in fifty of them. It will only last twenty seconds."

Crawford timed that quake at forty seconds. The one of April 18, 1906, was said to have lasted all of seventy seconds, but it brought down buildings and started the fires that consumed the city — the original Palace was gone. By 1909 the new Palace you see today was open: George Kelham was the supervising architect — he also designed the Russ Building, the Hills Brothers Coffee building, and the main public library in Civic Center.

This newer Palace structure has fewer literary associations, but Sam Spade does go here for lunch in *The Maltese Falcon*, and William Saroyan in *Places Where I've Done Time* (1972) records a job he had when he was nineteen, and an odd encounter:

> I was counter clerk at the small branch office of the Postal Telegraph Company at 651 Market Street in San Francisco, in the famous Palace Hotel Building, in the month of September, 1927. San Francisco was in my blood and bones.

One day "a stocky little man, with pince-nez glasses attached to the top of the bridge of his nose. . . , with a neat little mustache and a neat little Van Dyke beard" came into the office, sat at a table, wrote and crumpled versions of a telegram for about an hour, "and then at last he came to the counter, and I counted the words in the telegram, looked at him, told him the charge, and he went away." The man was the famous Lincoln Steffens, author and muckraker. Saroyan never met him again. He soon transferred to an office at 405 Brannan, worked for another couple of months and quit, getting out of the business world and into writing.

Across the street from the Palace at 650 Market you might notice the Bonanza Inn bookstore, first opened in the Palace in 1948, moved to the current site in 1956. The shop takes its name from the book Bonanza Inn *(1939) by Oscar Lewis and Carroll D. Hall, a history of the Palace. In 1983 the Bonanza Inn published an in-house edition of this book and had a new autographing party for the ninety-three-year-old Lewis, a San Francisco resident who is one of California's most famous historians.*

An alley runs next to the west side of the Palace; it is named:

10 ANNIE STREET In the middle-1970s Annie was christened "Mark Twain Street" in honor of one of the truly great writers connected with San Francisco. This city has been sparing at best in naming avenues after its writers. Book-lovers going up the on-ramp approach to the Bay Bridge named Sterling Street, found on Bryant between Second and First, may hope in vain the name honors George Sterling, the poet-king of Bohemian San Francisco. There is a half-block cul-de-sac dubbed Bret Harte Street on a slope of Russian Hill, running off Francisco Street between Leavenworth and Jones behind the San Francisco Art Institute. But apparently Twain does not have as much clout with our municipal powers as Harte—this alley was renamed Annie Street in December 1980, with the Turk Murphy jazz band—legendary locals—providing entertainment; Annie once housed the famous Dixieland nightspot The Dawn Club.

And Twain is once more among the legions of local writers without a street.

Past Annie at 681 Market you will come to:

11 THE MONADNOCK BUILDING The leftwing gumshoe Riley Kovachs has his office here in Gordon De Marco's hard-boiled detective novels *October Heat* (1979) and *The Canvas Prison* (1982). The political scene for *October Heat* is San Francisco, October 1934, two months after the longshoreman's strike, "Bloody Thursday," and the General Strike in July, with socialist author Upton Sinclair running for governor in the upcoming elections—and about to get knocked out of the race by the first organized barrage of "dirty tricks" in modern electoral politics. Kovachs unravels this Watergate: 1934 scenario, going from waterfront to Nob Hill, meeting such real-life figures of the day as Harry Bridges, Charlie Chaplin, and Tom Mooney, the imprisoned but indomitable symbol of San Francisco's radical labor movement.

The odd alliance between hard-boiled detective fiction and proletarian politics that provides the background for De Marco's books occurs in major figures connected with this city. Dashiell Hammett, who became the master of the form with the fiction he wrote in San Francisco, was imprisoned by the McCarthyites in 1951 for refusing to give them names of contributors to a bail bond fund. Paul William Ryan was a reporter for the Communist weekly *People's World*, published in Berkeley; his articles appeared under the name Mike Quin. "Quin" wrote the definitive account of the July, 1934, confrontation between labor and management in this city: *The Big Strike* (1949). Under yet another pseudonym, "Robert Finnegan," Ryan wrote a series of hard-boiled novels featuring newspaper reporter Dan Banion, begining with *The Lying Ladies* in 1946. His mysteries *The Bandaged Nude* (1946) and *Many a Monster* (1948) are set in San Francisco.

Stop on the southeast corner of Market and Third, in front of the old:

12 HEARST BUILDING The "H" over the doorway identifies this place as one of the publication offices for the Hearst *Examiner*. The saga of the Hearst empire includes a vast roster of literary San Franciscans: Gertrude Atherton, Robert Duncan Milne, W. C. Morrow, Lincoln Steffens, and hundreds more. Ambrose Bierce still remains a century later the literary lion of the pride.

When he took over the "Town Crier" feature in the *News Letter* in 1868 Bierce created the first recognized "newspaper column" in America—or anywhere else. In his Sunday column "Prattles" for the *Examiner* he wielded the knife of wit and the club of odium with an abandon no one could equal, for no one was as cynical and nihilistic as "Bitter" Bierce. The dominant literary figure of the 1800s in the city, he made and unmade artistic reputations; his attacks on society and government were no less feared. He predicted a major earthquake would be a boon for San Francisco's corrupt politicians. It's said that many local nabobs lived in dread of finding their names in his column, and that not all of Bierce's excursions to outlying towns such as Auburn, Sunol, or Santa Cruz were because of his asthma—though they were all "for his health." Some days it was safer to get out of town.

Bierce's horror stories, such as "The Damned Thing," are classics in the field, and his tales set during the Civil War are among the best short fiction in American literature. ("An Occurrence at Owl Creek Bridge" stands as one of the finest examples of stream-of-consciousness writing, fifty years before stream-of-consciousness was "discovered.") His *The Devil's Dictionary* offers such compelling definitions as "BORE, *n.* A person who talks when you wish him to listen" — it will be read as long as cynics draw breath.

In 1913 Bierce achieved additional immortality at the age of seventy-one by going as a war correspondent into Pancho Villa's Mexico, never to be heard from again. Bierce's attitude and mordant appeal are perhaps best expressed by his poem "Dead":

Done with the work of breathing; done
With all the world; the mad race run
Through to the end; the golden goal
Attained and found to be a hole!

Ambrose Bierce

Still on this corner, look down Third. The low-level landscape of the Moscone Convention Center three blocks down is representative of the changes sweeping through this area south of Market. Skid-row hotels such as the Cameo at 389 Third Street, near Harrison, where Jack Kerouac lodged in the 1950s and wrote "October in the Railroad Earth" and "San Francisco Blues," drinking wine and looking out his window on the street life passing by — these hotels are gone forever.

Cross to the north side of the street and stand on the traffic island where Geary and Kearny come into Market. On the island you will see:

13 **LOTTA'S FOUNTAIN** The actress Lotta Crabtree, "the toast of the goldfields," bestowed this fountain on the city in 1875. Fritz Leiber, the wonderful author of fantasy and science fiction, placed a scene here in his novel of supernatural horror, *Our Lady of Darkness* (1977). In a flashback to San Francisco in the early 1900s, Leiber has authors Jack London and George Sterling, as well as a ragtime singer named Olive Church and a man named Fenner, instructed "to approach the fountain by streets that would trace the four arms of a counterclockwise swastika while concentrating in their minds on the four points of the compass and bearing objects representing the four elements — Olive a potted lily for earth, Fenner a magnum of champagne for fluid, Sterling a rather large toy hydrogen-filled balloon for the gaseous, and Jack a long cigar for fire." They are directed by Thibaut de Castries, a wizard who is convinced he can unleash the titanic energies of the city itself, focus these arcane forces, and crumble into ruin an office building on Market Street.

De Castries has reckoned without taking the wild Bohemian nature of his erstwhile disciples into account. They all arrive (somewhat loaded) at the fountain; Jack London touches off Sterling's balloon with his cigar, the sudden hydrogen explosion startles Olive and Fenner into dropping their pot and magnum; and the wizard's spell goes awry—"a small brick warehouse behind Rincon . . . collapsed into a pile of masonry."

But de Castries' spells would linger well into our century, and cause more problems for San Francisco in the 1970s. . . .

Walk along Market towards Grant.

On the south side of this block between Third and Fourth, Hubert Howe Bancroft had built a five-story brick building to house his bookstore and stationery business, which he had first opened on Montgomery Street in 1856. San Franciscans joked about his move from Montgomery to Market: "Bancrofts are going to move their store to the country." But upon settling into the new building in 1870, Bancroft swept into writing and publishing a history of the West from Alaska to Mexico, employing dozens of assistants in his "history factory" over the next two decades. The finished work comprised thirty-nine volumes and Bancroft's collections of books and documents on which the history was based became the foundation for the Bancroft Library at U.C. Berkeley. In San Francisco's Literary Frontier *(1939) Franklin Walker called Bancroft's achievement the "greatest feat of historiography since Thucydides."*

Continue along Market to the Flood Building at:

14 **870 MARKET** The Flood Building is where Hammett worked for the Pinkerton National Detective Agency, and doubtless where the Continental Detective Agency in his stories had *its* offices. In *The Big Knockover,* his first novel-length work, Hammett wrote that "The Continental Detective Agency's San Francisco office is located in a Market Street office building" about seven blocks from the heart of the financial district on Montgomery.

The Flood Building stands on the site once occupied by the grand Baldwin Hotel, built by Lucky Baldwin in 1876, razed by fire in 1898. One tradition holds that Ernest L. Thayer wrote his one immortal poem, "Casey at the Bat," in the Baldwin. And on the corner of Powell and Market, a few steps from the Flood's doorway, Gertrude Atherton lived in an apartment as a youth. As you can see, these buildings are long vanished, as is 14 Eddy, the birthplace of Robert Frost—a Bank of America is on that site today. But the cable car with its turntable still operates, still as much a symbol of San Francisco as it was when Kipling visited and wrote: "They take almost no count of rise or fall. . . . They turn corners almost at right angles. . ., and for all I know may run up the sides of houses."

(A few steps up from the Bank of America office is the doorway for the Powell Hotel, where Charles Willeford lived in 1951 while writing his first novel *High Priest of California*, about a used car salesman on Van Ness Avenue. Willeford, whose later books include *Cockfighter, The Machine in Ward Eleven*, and *Miami Blues*, recalls that in those days you'd see perhaps six or seven people waiting to climb aboard the cable cars at the turntable — unlike the crowds today, waiting in line for hours.)

Go on to Fifth Street. One block down to Mission, if you are interested, will put you at:

15 **THE CHRONICLE AND EXAMINER BUILDINGS** The *Chron-icle* at 925 Mission and the *Examiner* at 110 Fifth Street are today's equivalent of the old "Newspaper Corner" that was formed around Lotta's Fountain by the Hearst Building on the southeast corner of Market and Third, the *Call* Building on the southwest corner, and the *Chronicle* Building at Kearny and Market. (The *Call* and *Chronicle* Buildings still stand along with the Hearst Building, though they have been so greatly built-over that they no longer evoke that early era of San Francisco journalism.) Our dailies today have seen many writers come and go. Some, like columnists Herb Caen and the late Charles McCabe, become institutions, while many more—Count Marco, Kevin Starr, Pat Montandon, Robert O'Brien—write columns for only a few years and move on. The *Examiner* book critic Mickey Friedman followed a tradition that dates back to Bret Harte, writing her first novel *Hurricane Season* (1983) here, but going to Paris to write her second. (Harte soon moved to London when he became successful—many others in the 1800s only made it as far as New York.) A number of local news staffers have published books—John Stanley of the Sunday *Chronicle* wrote the science fiction novel, *World War III* (1976), and co-authored with *Chronicle* artist Kenn Davis the mysteries *The Dark Side* (1976) and *Bogart 48* (1980). Frank Herbert of the Sunday *Examiner* went on to write a number of science fiction novels, including the best-selling *Dune* series.

On the north side of Market, Mason Street was the site of a home for Mrs. Maynard Shipley, one of San Francisco's most prolific writers, who lived for decades at 55 Mason in the:

16 **AMBASSADOR HOTEL** She came to San Francisco from Phil-adelphia in 1918, but began publishing in 1906 under her maiden name Miriam Allen deFord. Hundreds of stories, articles, and poems appeared under her by-line. She wrote fifty of the Haldeman-Julius "Little Blue Books," and books on prison reform and true crime, as well as novels, science fiction, mysteries, poetry, and history. Among her dozens of titles are *Love Children: A Book of Illustrious Illegitimates, Who Was When?: A Dictionary of Contemporaries, They were San Franciscans, Shaken with the Wind, Murderers Sane and Mad, The Overbury Affair, The Real Bonnie and Clyde, The Real Ma Barker,* etc.

Fritz Leiber recalls a local science fiction convention where deFord appeared to take part in a panel discussion. She came to the meeting hall punctually, spoke, and left soon after. She was a bit appalled by the many science fiction writers lingering at the convention for the weekend, signing autographs, trading shoptalk, drinking with the fans. "But how do you get any *writing* done?" she asked, and went back to her work in the Ambassador Hotel.

Continue up Market to:

17 SIXTH STREET In Niven Busch's novel *California Street* (1959) the publisher Anchylus Saxe issues the San Francisco *Day* from his "Day Building" on Sixth—perhaps it is no coincidence that he places it a block away from the *Chronicle* Building at Fifth and Mission.

Also, in a letter of January 10, 1880, Robert Louis Stevenson relates how he "descends Powell, crosses Market, and descends on Sixth to a branch of the original Pine Street Coffee house," where for 10¢ he eats a breakfast of "coffee, a roll, and a pat of butter."

Around the corner on Seventh at Mission is the old main branch of the post office. The Continental Op does some fancy gumshoe work on those marble floors in Hammett's story "The Golden Horseshoe." And the list of writers who have gone into that building to mail their manuscripts East, if known, could well fill a chapter.

Another block up Market past Eighth will get you to:

Black Bart

18 THE BLACK BART SALOON Located in the San Franciscan Hotel, this watering hole was never frequented by Charles E. Bolton, the infamous Black Bart, but it bears his name and sports western memorabilia evoking the day of that poetry-writing stagecoach robber. Bolton, as "Black Bart PO8," wrote one of the great proletarian poems:

> I've labored long and hard for bread
> For honor and for riches
> But on my corns too long you've tread,
> You fine-haired sons of bitches.

(The history room of the Wells Fargo Bank also memorializes with photos and a statue the poet-bandit who victimized their stage lines—Bart's fame rides on, especially in such lines as "So blame me not for what I've done,/ I don't deserve your curses,/ And if for any cause I'm hung,/ Let it be for my verses!")

Before checking out the Black Bart take a look down the length of Market just traveled. One of the most successful self-published books to come from the Bay Area is Ernest Callenbach's Ecotopia *(1975)—it sold many printings by its author and soon went into a mass-market paperback. In this socio-political novel Callenbach pictures the states of Washington, Oregon, and northern California seceding from the U.S. to form the ecologically sane land of Ecotopia. In this imagined future a visitor comes to San Francisco. He is amazed to find a beautiful forested stream running through the city where the broad expanse of Market once carried fleets of cars and trolleys.*

SOUTH OF MARKET

Jack Kerouac near the S.P. switchyards, mid-1950s

The industrial area south of Market Street is worth a brief literary tour, though urban renewal has transformed into vacant lots many of the blocks of warehouses, factories, and blue-collar hotels where writers such as Jack Kerouac lived and worked. In recent years, artists have been moving into spacious warehouse lofts. Experimental performance spaces, galleries, restaurants and late-night bars have sprung up from the Mission to the Bay, attracting punk rockers, gays, artists and writers.

Begin this walk on the southeast corner of Brannan and Third Streets, six blocks south of Market. The 30 Stockton bus southbound, boarded at 4th & Market, or the 15 Third Street bus southbound, caught at 1st and Market, will bring you to this intersection—and, northbound, will take you back to civilization.

A Wells Fargo Bank at 601-605 Third Street stands on the southeast corner. To the left of its front doors you will find:

1 JACK LONDON PLAQUE On January 12, 1953, the 77th anniversary of his birth, the California Historical Society installed this plaque to mark the place Jack London was born in 1876. As the plaque states, "The original home on this site, then known as 615 Third Street, was destroyed in the fire of April 18, 1906." The London home was a two-story dwelling, one of a row of seven houses numbered 615-627; this row began, according to insurance maps of 1887, some 120 feet south of Brannan. Controversy still rages among London buffs, with many insisting the plaque should have been placed on the *current* 615 Third Street—a red-brick building erected in 1908—located next to the bank. You may step off the 120 feet from the corner and make your own decision. But was the *corner* of Third and Brannan in 1876 exactly where it is today? Controversy rages.

Walk one block south on Third to Townsend and turn right. At Townsend and Fourth Streets you will find the:

2 SOUTHERN PACIFIC DEPOT The train terminal you see today is of more modern origin than the one which occupies an honored position on the map of San Francisco's mystery stories. The old terminal extended further east, into the area now occupied by a recreational vehicle park. From that depot Hammett's ubiquitous Continental Op shadowed countless yeggs; and Charles Graham caught "the 5:29 back to Redwood City, Climate Best by Government Test" in Samuel W. Taylor's *The Man With My Face* (1948), one of the best mysteries set in the Bay Area.

Go south on Fourth past King and Berry streets to the bridge crossing the China Basin Channel. On the single pier jutting out over the water you'll see Blanche's Cafe, opened by Blanche Pastorino almost 25

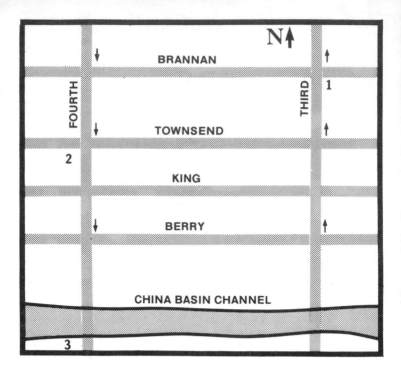

*years.ago, still an interesting
hangout, its walls crowded with
paintings and literary
memorabilia, and frequented
by the many artists and writers
living on Potrero Hill. From the
open-air deck on the pier
behind the cafe you can see:*

3 RAILROAD SWITCHYARDS   These railroad tracks south of China
Basin are where Jack Kerouac worked as a brakeman for Southern
Pacific in 1952 — living for a while with Neal and Carolyn Cassady in
suburban San Jose, for a while in a skid-row hotel in the city. Drinking
sweet wine in his hotel, he sketched his experiences on the job, speed-
writing in an experimental rush, no revision. This spontaneous prose
record of his job as a brakeman on the train from San Jose to San Francisco became "October in the Railroad Earth," published in *Lonesome
Traveler* (1960).

Allen Ginsberg, too, wrote about these switchyards in "Sunflower
Sutra," collected in *Howl and Other Poems* (1956), beginning:

> I walked on the banks of the tincan banana dock and sat down under the
> huge shade of a Southern Pacific locomotive to look at the sunset over
> the box house hills and cry.
> Jack Kerouac sat beside me on a busted rusty iron pole, companion, we
> thought the same thoughts of the soul, bleak and blue and sad-eyed, sur-
> rounded by the gnarled steel roots of trees of machinery.
> The oily water on the river mirrored the red sky, sun sank on top of final
> Frisco peaks, no fish in that stream, no hermit in those mounts, just our-
> selves rheumy-eyed and hungover like old bums on the riverbank, tired
> and wily.

CIVIC CENTER

Fritz Leiber at 811 Geary, 1978

The center for our local government, state and federal office buildings, public library, Museum of Modern Art, and opera and symphony, as well as the birthplace of the United Nations, this area offers a typically wide range of literary associations.

*Begin at Larkin and McAllister.
The 19 Polk will drop you
here—the many Muni lines
which run along or under
Market stop two blocks south,
and there is a Civic Center
BART station. Parking is
available onstreet or in Civic
Center Garage under Civic
Center Park.*

*The huge gray stone building
on the southeast corner is the
main branch of the:*

1 SAN FRANCISCO PUBLIC LIBRARY   After the Old Montgomery
Block, with its many and legendary literary connections, the main
library undoubtedly has seen more of more writers than any other place
in San Francisco. Authors researching projects in the stacks or the history room, speaking at one of the library-sponsored free lectures, or just
coming in to check out a good read must number in the thousands.

Eric Hoffer as a hobo and migrant worker in the 1930s had library
cards in dozens of California towns; when he came to the city he rented
room 208 in 1438 McAllister (now gone) "halfway between the library
and the whorehouse. Both were equally important." Born in New York
City in 1902, Hoffer went completely blind at age seven and mysteriously
recovered his sight at age fifteen. He never attended school, but educated himself from libraries. Ronald Gross, author or co-author of *The
Lifelong Learner, Radical School Reform, The New Old: Struggling for
Decent Aging* and other books, in *The Independent Scholar's Handbook*
(1982) states: "Completely his own man . . . , he shows that serious
thinking can be done quite outside the system of supports that most
intellectuals enjoy. Moreover, Hoffer's philosophy itself affirms an axiom
of independent scholarship: that mental power, indeed genius, are far
more pervasive in our society than we imagine. The life of the mind, he
both demonstrates and contends, is available to virtually everyone."
And Hoffer's life of the mind began in a library, and continued thriving in
this library.

The prolific Miriam Allen deFord also lived within blocks of this building to research her books. Dashiell Hammett, who dropped out of high
school in the ninth grade, walked every afternoon in the early 1920s
from his apartment on Eddy Street three blocks down Larkin to read here.

In the supernatural thriller *Our Lady of Darkness* (1977), Fritz Leiber's
protagonist Franz Westen comes to the library for quick research—he
even *steals* a reference book (this in the days before the electronic
guard system). Leiber himself participated in a reading of poetry by the
California Romantics on November 17, 1982, in the Lurie Room here,
choosing as his selection George Sterling's epic "The Wine of Wizardry,"
which Ambrose Bierce had praised so extravagantly.

When Westen—like Leiber, a horror writer—approached the library
he noticed that the front of the building was decorated "with names of
great thinkers and American writers, which (score one for our side) included Poe." You'll see the names engraved in the granite at about the
second floor level on either side of the front, and you'll notice as well five
statues in the gallery above the main doors. These figures are obviously

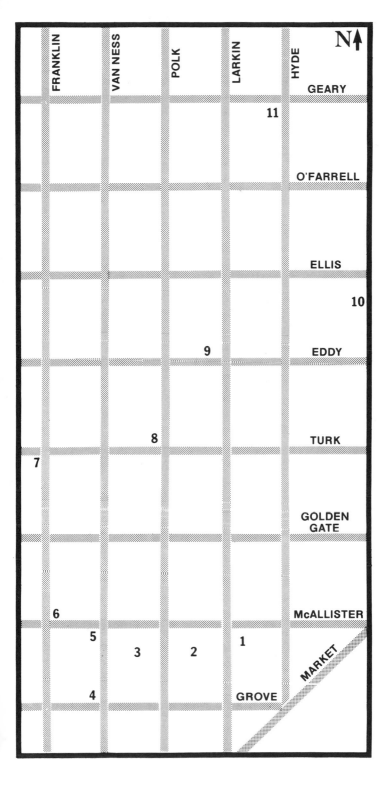

rough, unfinished, especially compared with the fine detail in the rest of the building. They were set up as a temporary measure until the day when they could be replaced by finished statutes of great California authors. The plan somehow was forgotten, and these statues still stand in niches meant for Twain, Bierce, Norris, Harte, Coolbrith, London, Sterling, Steinbeck, and company.

There are many other literary connections, such as the fact that Kevin Starr, director of the library under Mayor Alioto, wrote a regular column for the *Examiner*, the non-fiction *Americans and the California Dream* (1976), and the enormous novel *Land's End* (1979), in which he also set scenes in this building.

From the library head over toward the green-domed City Hall; you're walking across:

2 CIVIC CENTER PARK   Gertrude Atherton wrote in 1946 that the Civic Center was one of the city's "beauty spots": "Here there are really noble buildings. The wide plaza with its fountain, its acacia trees and boxed yews is surrounded irregularly by the splendid City Hall, the Public Library, the Civic Auditorium, the State Building — presented by the Pacific-Panama Exposition of 1915 . . . these are of gray granite and in the style of the French Renaissance . . . a magnificent group."

Enter the Polk Street doors of City Hall. To your left you'll find a large niche containing a:

3 JAMES D. PHELAN BUST   The column supporting this bust reads "native of San Francisco 1861-1930/ Mayor of San Francisco 1897-1902/ United States Senator 1915-1921/ Patriot, Philanthropist, Patron of Arts and Letters." An amateur poet himself, Phelan was a major figure in the literary history of San Francisco and California as the most prominent public supporter of our writers until his death in 1930. When he became senator he created a Poet Laureateship for California — the first Poet Laureate post established in America. Phelan also personally gave money to many writers; he set up a quarterly trust fund for the impoverished young poet Clark Ashton Smith that was paid to the Auburn native until Phelan's death. With his contemporary Albert "Mickey" Bender, Phelan was the major patron for San Francisco writers of his day. His example has been ignored by most politicians since. Governor Jerry Brown was something of an exception, having at least set up an arts council composed of real artists and writers, among them the environmentalist poet Gary Snyder. Governor Brown during his term was also known to show up unannounced at Zen Center or literary events, as he did one night for a poetry reading benefit for *Beatitude* magazine (at the Tivoli on upper Grant Avenue in North Beach) during his last year in office.

Exit through the Van Ness Avenue doors, turn left. On the northwest corner of Van Ness and Grove you'll see:

4 THE SAN FRANCISCO OPERA HOUSE This building and the newer Louise M. Davies Symphony Hall across Grove Street draw in many writers with a taste for high culture. The mystery writer and critic Anthony Boucher of Berkeley was also a big opera fan; he had a huge collection of historic recordings which he played in his "Golden Voices" program which ran for eighteen years over KPFA radio. At each season opening until his death in 1968 you would see Boucher here, decked out in top hat and tails.

The versatile writer Chelsea Quinn Yarbro is another devoted attendee. While she is perhaps best known for her series of stories about the vampire Ragoczy, Count Saint-Germain, which began with *Hotel Transylvania* in 1978, Yarbro also has written non-fiction, occult books, several science fiction novels and collections, historical and mainstream fiction, and a couple of mysteries featuring an American Indian lawyer named Charlie Moon, who works out of San Francisco. In *Music When Sweet Voices Die* (1979), Moon investigates a murder onstage here at the opera.

Go north on this block to the War Memorial Building which houses:

Harriet Lane Levy. By Matisse

5 THE MUSEUM OF MODERN ART — as well as Herbst Theatre. Fritz Leiber sets a scene in *Our Lady of Darkness* in the theatre, and the poet and playwright Ruth Weiss worked part time for a few years at the ticket desk of the museum. Weiss, born in Berlin in 1928, has also worked as a bartender, magician, actress. She came to San Francisco in 1952. Her poetry collections include *Steps*, *Gallery of Women*, *Blue in Green*, *Desert Journal*, and *Single Out*, and her one-act plays, such as the recent "The Thirteenth Witch," have been performed in a number of our theatres. She showed a forty-minute film made from her poem "The Brink" at the San Francisco International Film Festival in 1961.

The museum also preserves tangible mementos of an otherwise lost San Francisco literary connection. Harriet Lane Levy in the fine memoir *920 O'Farrell Street* (1947) gives her recollections of life in the city late in the nineteenth century; however, 920 O'Farrell and 922 next door where Alice B. Toklas was born April 30, 1877, were destroyed long ago. Levy eventually went to Europe with Toklas and became an intimate of Gertrude Stein and her circle. She began collecting work by her new friends Matisse and Picasso, as well as Derain, Degas — assembling one of the most important private collections of French art. In her will Levy left a bequest to the San Francisco Museum of Modern Art of eleven works by Matisse, eight by Picasso, and several other paintings. One of the drawings by Matisse is a portrait of Levy, returned to her native city.

*Turn left on McAllister and go
to Franklin Street. The
apartment house on the
northeast corner is:*

6 580 McALLISTER   In "The Whosis Kid," one of the series of twenty-eight short stories by Hammett about the gumshoe work of the never-named Continental Op, the jewel thief Ines Almad has an apartment here — on a top floor in the rear, at the east end. According to Hammett, this tale was a prototype for *The Maltese Falcon*, one of the stories where he said he had "failed to make the most of a situation I liked." With its scenes of a falling-out among thieves, a tense wait in this apartment for the jewels to turn up (as they wait at the end of the *Falcon* for Effie to bring in the black bird), and the detective caught in the middle, you can see the basic plot which Hammett turned into a suspense classic with the addition of a jeweled falcon from the Knights of Malta.

*Go up Franklin to Golden
Gate. Up the next block on the
west side of the street you'll
see a large building with the
letters spelling:*

7 STATE EMPLOYMENT BUREAU   Earl Summerfield works as an interviewer here in Evan S. Connell's *The Diary of a Rapist* (1966), the only one of Connell's novels set in San Francisco, though he has lived in this area for many years. Summerfield stalks through the city after his workday is over, trying to overcome his hesitation about doing "things I should have done but was afraid to do," trying to get something out of his life, even if it's by force.

Head east on Golden Gate. You can't help but notice the huge Opera Plaza development on the north side of this block, which occupies lots where a row of Victorians stood through the 1960s. The suspense writer Joe Gores worked out of 760 Golden Gate for nine years as an operative of David Kikkert and Associates ("Auto Repossessions, Skip Tracing, Collections, Adjustments"). His major series of modern San Francisco mysteries is about the "Daniel Kearney Agency" — a fictional DKA which also works out of the no-longer-standing 760 Golden Gate. Titles: Dead Skip, Final Notice, and Gone, No Forwarding.

Up Polk a block to Turk,
on the northwest corner, in the
fabulous old California Hall
building, you'll find:

8 THE RATHSKELLER   Daniel Kearney eats a meal in this restaurant in *Gone, No Forwarding*, and in recent years the Maltese Falcon Society has held its meetings here. Speakers have included Hammett biographers William F. Nolan and Diane Johnson, mystery writers such as Stephen Greenleaf, real cops and ops, and Tiny Boyles, a six-foot-three-inch, 389-pound professional bounty hunter ("He could make a glass eye weep.") whose exploits have been the basis for a series of paperback novels. The society begins its meetings with an official toast borrowed from Sam Spade, when he raises a glass to police homicide inspectors Dundy and Polhaus and says: "Success to crime."

Turn north up Polk, then east
on Eddy. Near the end of this
block on the north side you'll
come to:

9 620 EDDY   Dashiell Hammett and his wife set up housekeeping here after their marriage July 7, 1921, in a $45-a-month furnished apartment. Their first daughter Mary Jane was born October 15 that year; when their second daughter, named Josephine after her mother, was born May 24, 1926, they soon moved into a larger apartment in this same building.

In this place Hammett wrote about half of his one-hundred-odd short stories, including the early Continental Op tales "Arson Plus," "Slippery Fingers," "Zigzags of Treachery" and others. His wife said he wrote directly on the typewriter, going through draft after draft until he had his first stories to his satisfaction. In the first, smaller apartment, he wrote at the kitchen table; in the larger apartment he set up a writing table in the living room. They lived here until late summer 1926, making this Hammett's longest residence in San Francisco.

Continue on Eddy past Larkin
to Hyde, if you wish to plunge
solidly into the fringes of:

10 THE TENDERLOIN   Bordered loosely by O'Farrell or Geary to the north, Larkin or Polk to the west, Mason to the east, and Market to the south (with some cultural spillover into Skid Row on Sixth Street), the Tenderloin is the roughest area of downtown San Francisco—though the construction of more large hotels on Mason and the immigration of many families from Southeast Asia are changing the flavor of the neighborhood. You get classic Tenderloin scenes in such novels as Lawrence Swaim's *The Killing* (1980) and Joe Gores' *Interface* (1974), though most reviewers found Gores' realistic treatment of the streetlife appalling—people don't act or talk *that* way! (These reviewers obviously never walked through the Tenderloin by day and certainly not by night.) The Market Street edge of the action is well covered in Don Carpenter's *Hard Rain Falling* (1966), and of course you can find a few literary sites in the area which do not have the seamy, violent atmosphere writers usually evoke, such as the old Longshoreman's Hall at 150 Golden Gate in the Syufy Building, where Eric Hoffer was working in the period when he wrote *The True Believer* and where Allen Ginsberg gave a reading of "Kaddish."

Turn north up Hyde. In the 500 block, Stanley McNail has kept an apartment for several years. He is known for writing one of the best collections of horror poetry, Something Breathing. *His most recent book is* Your Haunted Tape Recorder, *a manual on recording paranormal voices.*

At Geary turn left to:

11 **811 GEARY** Fritz Leiber moved into apartment 506 of this building in January 1970, and lived here until 1977, when he moved to another residential hotel further down the street. Born December 24, 1910, in Chicago, Leiber began writing in college under the encouragement of his correspondents H. P. Lovecraft and Harry Fischer. With Fischer he created the Sword-and-Sorcery heroes Fafhrd and the Gray Mouser— Fafhrd, tall like Leiber; the Mouser, short like Fischer. His first published story, "Two Sought Adventure," about the pair appeared in 1939, and over six volumes concerning "the two best swordsmen in Lankhmar" have appeared since— *Swords Against Death*, *Swords and Ice Magic*, etc. Under Lovecraft's spell Leiber began writing horror stories for *Weird Tales* magazine, and also branched out into the science fiction pulps. Now one of the most acclaimed authors in the fantasy and science fiction field, Leiber has won the Grand Master of Fantasy Award, the Life Achievement Award from the World Fantasy Convention, and six Hugos, the Sci-Fi Oscar.

In this building he wrote his supernatural horror novel *Our Lady of Darkness* in 1974 and 1975. The hero of that book, Franz Westen, also lives in 811 Geary in circumstances very similar to Leiber's at the time. The description of Westen's apartment is Leiber's quarters exactly pictured, and every place mentioned in the book, every building, every bus line, every step, may be found or followed out. All the action occurs in two days in the mid-1970s, with flashback scenes to old San Francisco where authors George Sterling, Jack London, Dashiell Hammett, and Clark Ashton Smith appear as characters. *Our Lady of Darkness* won the best novel of the year award from the World Fantasy Convention, but Leiber's 1943 supernatural novel *Conjure Wife* is more famous— the idea is that every woman in the world is a witch, secretly controlling men's destinies. It is very popular among feminists. Other fine titles among Leiber's forty-odd books are the Sci-Fi novels *The Wanderer* and *The Big Time*, both Hugo winners.

DASHIELL HAMMETT

Dashiell Hammett, 1940s

"Frankly, I can conceive of better writing than the *Falcon*, and a more tender and warm attitude to life, and a more flowery ending; but by God, if you can show me twenty books written approximately 20 years back that have as much guts and life now, I'll eat them between slices of Edmund Wilson's head."

— *Raymond Chandler in a letter, December 12, 1945*

Samuel Dashiell Hammett lived in San Francisco from summer 1921 to fall 1929. During those eight years he wrote most of his fiction, the now classic novels such as *The Maltese Falcon* and *Red Harvest*, pioneering an authentic American style for the murder and mystery tale — creating in his rented rooms in the Tenderloin and on Nob Hill the modern hard-boiled detective story.

Born May 27, 1894, in St. Mary's County, Maryland, Hammett was the son of Richard Thomas Hammett and Annie Bond Hammett. His middle name "Dashiell" derives from his mother's French family, De Chiel, who Americanized the spelling when they moved to the States. He was raised in the cities of Philadelphia and Baltimore. At the age of fourteen he quit the high school where he had briefly enrolled, to get a job and help support the family. Hammett never went back to high school. He did not attend college.

Hammett worked as a stevedore, messenger, freight clerk, and operated a nail machine in a box factory. His long series of such short-lived jobs bored him. Often he did not show up for work on time. As he later wrote in a letter to *Black Mask* mystery magazine where most of his fiction appeared, "after a fraction of a year in high school . . . I became the unsatisfactory and unsatisfied employee of various railroads, stock brokers, machine manufacturers, canners, and the like. Usually I was fired."

When Hammett was about twenty-two he answered another employment ad in the Baltimore paper. The job: hire in as an operative for the Pinkerton National Detective Agency. Hammett hired in. It was a deciding moment for popular fiction. Over the next five years he traveled America as a Pinkerton man. In Washington, D.C., in the early days of World War I, he shadowed a man suspected of being a secret agent for Germany, and who became the model for Caspar Gutman, the fat man in *The Maltese Falcon*. In Pasco, Washington, he nabbed an oily little guy who had been forging checks; this criminal appeared as the perfumed rogue Joel Cairo in the Sam Spade novel. In Stockton, California, working out of the San Francisco office, Hammett arrested a holdup man the newspapers called the "Midget Bandit," who became the model for Wilmer Cook, the young gunman traveling with Gutman who threatens to "fog" Sam Spade if he doesn't "lay off."

Hammett came to San Francisco to marry Josephine Dolan, a nurse he had met while hospitalized for tuberculosis in 1920. He had contracted the disease during the year he spent in the army in 1918, and it would recur frequently in the next decade, forcing Hammett to quit his job with Pinkerton a few months after their marriage on July 7, 1921. Originally they had planned to return to Hammett's native Baltimore, but once Hammett had a taste of life in San Francisco, Baltimore seemed considerably less attractive.

Reading the pulp magazines of the day, Hammett realized that most of the mystery writers knew nothing about real detective work. He figured that he could do just as well, if not better, with a detective story, and decided to become a writer. He landed a job writing advertising copy for Samuel's Jewelers on Market Street by day. By night he began to work on his hard-boiled fiction.

In San Francisco, Hammett was first published. About half of his stories take place in this city, including the novels *The Big Knockover*, *The Dain Curse*, and *The Maltese Falcon*. He finished *The Glass Key* after leaving San Francisco for New York late in 1929, and wrote *The Thin Man* in New York City in 1933; otherwise, all his novels and the majority of his approximately one-hundred stories were written in his apartments on Eddy, Hyde, Monroe, Post, and Leavenworth streets. His longest series, three novels and twenty-eight stories concerning the casework of an unnamed operative for the Continental Detective Agency, is set largely in this city. So, of course, are the adventures of Sam Spade.

And Nick and Nora Charles, even though they are in New York when the thin man is murdered, are also residents here.

Hammett's San Francisco stands as one of the great literary treatments of a city — it has been compared with Joyce's Dublin and Dickens' London for its evocation of place and time, the days in the 1920s when night-fog cloaked the hills and a certain fat man was afoot. In the Continental Op tales, the nameless detective goes to every neighborhood in the city and encounters every level of society, from bankers with wandering daughters in Pacific Heights mansions to cheap gunmen living in furnished rooms in Tenderloin hotels who do their drinking in North Beach speakeasies. In *The Maltese Falcon* Hammett created a plot line as glamorous as San Francisco itself, adding new luster and legend to the city. Sam Spade in snapbrim hat and trenchcoat, stalking through the fog, is as firm a part of San Francisco's lore as the 1906 earthquake and fire is of her history. No other novel has excited so much interest here, or sent so many people scurrying over the hills as they shadow Spade's movements in his search for the fabulous figurine of a mysterious black bird.

Separated from his wife and the two daughters born during their years in the city, Hammett was in New York by 1930, but soon traveled to Hollywood — he traveled frequently between New York and Hollywood over the next twenty years. In Hollywood, winter 1930, he met Lillian Hellman, then the twenty-four-year-old wife of screenwriter Arthur Kober; they began a relationship that would last until Hammett's death.

The Thin Man and six short stories by Hammett were published in 1934; no other novels or stories appeared in his lifetime. He did write continuity for the comic strip *Secret Agent X-9* in the mid-1930s and scripted a few Hollywood films, contributing polished dialogue and plotting for the first three *Thin Man* movies and writing the 1943 film adaptation of Lillian Hellman's play "Watch on the Rhine." This last screenplay was nominated for an Oscar. Hammett's best efforts in literature after 1934 were made as a reader of Hellman's plays: he gave her detailed criticism, suggested plots, and in the case of "The Autumn Garden" contributed a major speech in the last act.

Money rolled in, from radio shows — "The Adventures of the Thin Man," "The Adventures of Sam Spade" starring Howard Duff, even a show featuring a detective weighing 237 pounds known as "The Fat Man." ("The Fat Man" probably had the most appropriate sponsor in the history of radio: Pepto Bismol!) In 1945 Hammett's stories for the pulp magazines began appearing in paperback under the editorship of Ellery Queen, beginning with *The Adventures of Sam Spade, The Continental Op*, and *The Return of the Continental Op*. From his Thin Man characters alone Hammett earned more than a million dollars — and he spent most of it, on women, drinking, gambling, and on donations to leftist causes.

In World War II Hammett joined the army as a private. He had all his teeth pulled so he could serve overseas in a combat zone, and he spent the war in the Aleutian Islands and Alaska, leaving the service in September 1945.

By the early 1950s Hammett's leftwing politics began to draw heavy attention from McCarthy and his forces. Hammett had given thousands of dollars to various causes, signed petitions, talked at rallies. He agreed to act as chairman for the bail bond fund of the Civil Rights Congress. Four communists released on bail from that fund skipped out, and Hammett and other people connected with the fund were called to court and asked for names of contributors to the bond trust. Hammett refused to give names. He was sentenced to six months in prison for contempt of court.

After he was imprisoned the Internal Revenue Service determined that Hammett owed unpaid back taxes, plus fines, amounting to approximately $140,000. Hammett's radio shows went off the air because commercial sponsors in the McCarthy era were afraid to be connected with a "communist writer." The last *Thin Man* film had appeared in 1947, and a 1951 movie based on "The Fat Man" radio series was the last movie based on a Hammett character in his lifetime. Another collection of Hammett stories, *Woman in the Dark*, appeared in 1952; the next collection, *A Man Named Thin*, would not see print until 1962.

When he came out of prison in 1951, Hammett faced a bleak final decade, not alone because of finances. His health was declining. In the last few years he was a near invalid. From 1957 until his death he lived with Hellman in her New York City apartment at 63 East 82nd Street or her place on Martha's Vineyard. Hammett died in Lenox Hill Hospital in New York City on January 10, 1961, of cancer of the lungs. At his request, he was buried in Arlington National Cemetery.

In the mystery field Hammett is recognized as the second most influential American author, second only to Edgar Allan Poe, who created the detective story in the sense we know it today. His influence has spread far beyond the bounds of the detective novel; now he is more often placed in the company of William Faulkner, Ernest Hemingway, and other major authors.

Yet perhaps Hammett's most lasting accomplishment is that he did what only a handful of writers have done: he created an authentic mythic figure of popular culture in the person of Sam Spade, San Francisco's — and America's — hard-boiled detective.

DASHIELL HAMMETT TOUR

Begin this walk through the city gumshoe by Sam Spade on the northeast corner of Geary and Hyde Streets, six blocks west of Union Square. You may reach this intersection via the 38 Geary bus westbound (the 38 eastbound will drop you one block south at O'Farrell and Hyde). Head north on Hyde.

You are treading one of the most authentically 1920s, Hammett-era parts of San Francisco. The skyline looking north and south is very much the one Hammett would have seen as he ascended this rise to his apartment. The west side of the block, in particular, has seen little change since the days Hammett lived in the neighborhood. This area burned in the fire of 1906, but most of these buildings were built soon after, to house people for the 1915 Panama-Pacific Exposition — the big fair announcing that San Francisco was back on the map.

The first stop on this tour, the four-story brick building on the southeast corner of Post and Hyde, however, was erected in 1917:

1 891 POST Hammett moved here, into the Charing Cross Apartments, after separating from his family late in 1927. He stayed throughout 1928, but moved to 1155 Leavenworth on Nob Hill in

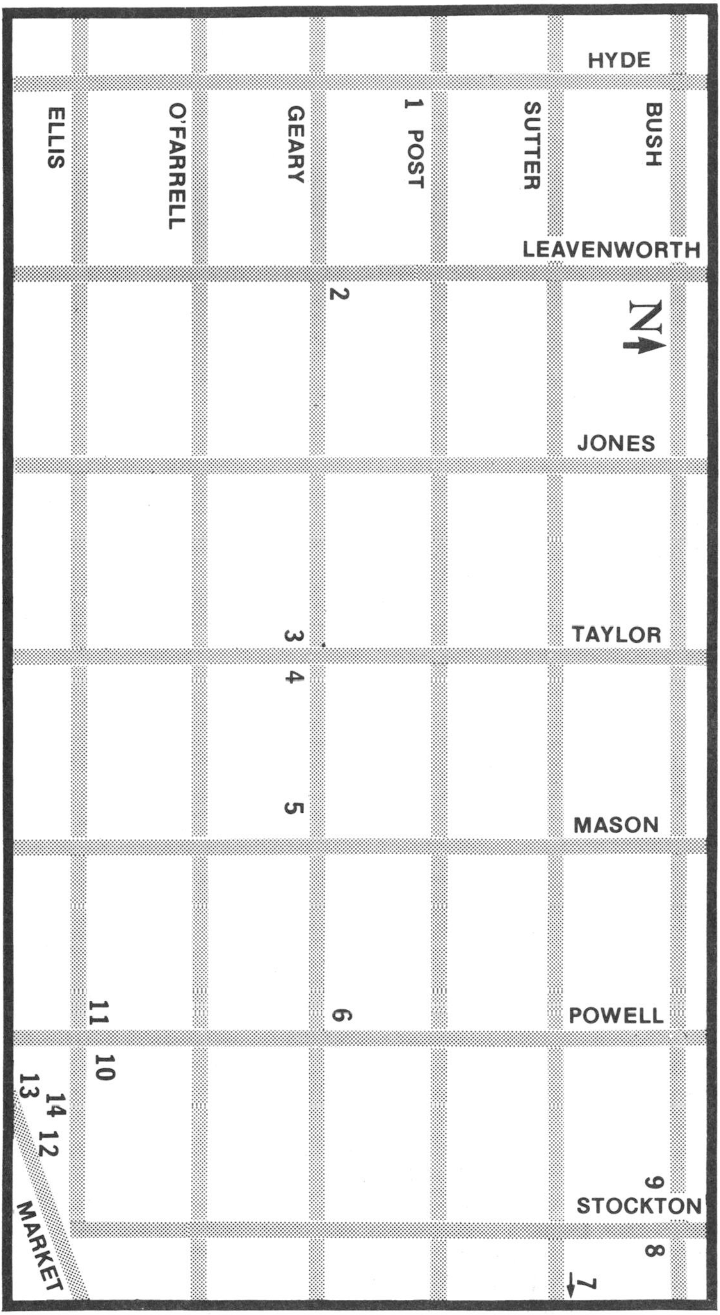

HYDE

ELLIS O'FARRELL GEARY 1 POST SUTTER BUSH

LEAVENWORTH

2

N

JONES

3

TAYLOR

4

5

MASON

11 6

POWELL

10

13 14 12

9

STOCKTON

7 8

MARKET

March 1929. He completed *Red Harvest*, finished the serial version of *The Dain Curse* which appeared in four issues of *Black Mask*, and started his next novel. In the new book he decided to drop the short fat Continental Op, who had just slugged and shot his way through *The Big Knockover*, *Red Harvest, The Dain Curse*, and over twenty short stories. Hammett created a new detective: Sam Spade.

The Continental Op, Hammett said, was modeled on Assistant Superintendent James Wright of Pinkerton's Baltimore office who gave Hammett his training in detective work. The Pinkertons worked out of the Continental Building in downtown Baltimore when Hammett began with the agency—undoubtedly the source of the name of his fictitious agency which is directly modeled on Pinkerton. But of his new sleuth Hammett wrote:

> Spade had no original. He is a dream man in the sense that he is what most of the private detectives I worked with would like to have been and what quite a few of them in their cockier moments thought they approached. For your private detective does not—or did not ten years ago when he was my colleague— want to be an erudite solver of riddles in the Sherlock Holmes manner; he wants to be a hard and shifty fellow, able to take care of himself in any situation, able to get the best of anybody he comes in contact with, whether criminal, innocent bystander or client.

The novel which Hammett had in first draft was *The Maltese Falcon*, now his most famous book.

The modern San Francisco mystery writer Joe Gores in his essay "A Foggy Night" (*City of San Francisco*, Nov. 4, 1975) determined that 891 Post has greater significance than simply being the place Hammett created Sam Spade—this is the building where Spade *lives* in *The Maltese Falcon*. At one point Spade rides the Geary streetcar from downtown (there used to be streetcars heading both ways up and down Geary), debarks at Hyde, and goes "up" to his apartment: up the short hill you just climbed between Geary and Post. At another point Spade goes out to see if Wilmer Cook, the boy gunman, is still watching his rooms. The line reads: "Post Street was empty when Spade issued into it." You might quibble that Spade could have lived in any of the residential buildings near this intersection, yet since Hammett himself was living here at the time he created the novel, who but a sap would argue against Hammett placing Spade's apartment in 891 Post Street?

It is in this building that Sam Spade, at the end of *The Maltese Falcon*, sets the edges of his teeth together and says to Brigid O'Shaughnessy: "I won't play the sap for you."

Head east on Post to Leavenworth, then take a right and go one block down to Geary. At this intersection was located:

2 FLOYD THURSBY'S APARTMENT Thursby was Brigid's partner, but a partner she feels she can do without. She kills Spade's partner, Miles Archer, with one of Thursby's guns to frame him for the crime, but when she learns that Thursby himself has been gunned down (by Wilmer Cook), she goes back to Spade. She will need help against the fat man.

Thursby never appears "onstage" in *The Maltese Falcon.* He is always referred to by others, never seen. Even his death, in front of his apartment on "Geary near Leavenworth," occurs offstage. You may take your pick of the buildings at this intersection as the original of Thursby's — Hammett gives no clues, leaving the place where Thursby lives and dies as shadowy as the character himself.

Go east on Geary toward downtown. Fritz Leiber noted in the first walking tour article based on The Maltese Falcon, *"Stalking Sam Spade" (California Living, Jan. 13, 1974) that "Geary Street between Hyde and Market is the spine of* The Maltese Falcon—*most of the action was on or near it, though once Spade uses the streetcar on Sutter"—and once he goes by taxi on a wildgoose chase down to Burlingame. Only two blocks from Thursby's place, on the southwest corner of Geary and Taylor, you will find the:*

3 BELLEVUE HOTEL Because of its location and similar name, the Bellevue is accepted as the model for the Belvedere, the hotel in which Joel Cairo stays in the *Falcon.*

Still at the intersection of Geary and Taylor, the building on the southeast corner is the:

4 CLIFT HOTEL This building is one of the major choices as the original for the Alexandria, Gutman's hotel. Others are the Sir Francis Drake, the old Plaza Hotel which stood where the Hyatt Union Square is today, and possibly the St. Francis. None of these hotels match the contradictory descriptions Hammett gives — his Alexandria is at least twelve stories high, with windows overlooking Geary, but also a short walk up Sutter Street from Spade's office at Sutter and Montgomery.

In the same block as the Clift you will find at 415 Geary the:

5 GEARY THEATRE — where Joel Cairo had tickets to see George Arliss as Shylock in "The Merchant of Venice," with its appropriate "pound of flesh" scene (Spade handed more than a pound over to the law at the end of the novel). Hammett researcher William Godshalk determined from the fact that Cairo is seeing this play, and from other clues in the novel, that all the action occurs in a five-day period in December 1928, when Arliss was onstage as Shylock at the Geary Theatre.

Another block down Geary to Powell will put you at Union Square. Directly across Powell from the park looms the twelve-story stone structure of the:

6 ST. FRANCIS HOTEL From the lobby of the St. Mark Hotel, Miles Archer shadows Brigid O'Shaughnessy and Floyd Thursby to his death. The *original* of the St. Mark would be either the St. Francis or the Mark Hopkins on Nob Hill, and most Hammett fans go for the St. Francis. When you enter the red-carpeted lobby through the Powell Street doors (in the 1920s a circular registration desk ushered in the guests, but check-in services today are in the St. Francis Tower addition, past the original lobby), you're in the vast room where Miles Archer began work on his last case.

The most famous case Hammett said *he* worked on as a Pinkerton operative in San Francisco originated here in the St. Francis, when the famous Hollywood silent comedian Roscoe "Fatty" Arbuckle had a party on Monday, September 5, 1921, in a suite of three rooms — 1219, 1220, and 1221 — overlooking the corner of Geary and Powell. Arbuckle later was accused of raping the young actress Virginia Rappe, who died four days after the party. Arbuckle found himself on trial for murder in one of the most sensational cases ever to rock Hollywood and America. Hammett said he worked for Arbuckle's lawyers gathering evidence; it was his opinion that Arbuckle had been framed "by some of the corrupt local newspaper boys."

Cross Union Square to Stockton Street on the east side, then turn north. Pause on the northeast corner of Stockton and Sutter. Look down Sutter. You will see a tall but old, ornate skyscraper with a brown roof and green railing on top. More modern skyscrapers tower over it now, but this is the building to interest mystery fans:

7 111 SUTTER The Hunter-Dulin Building is the place Joe Gores in "A Foggy Night" pinpoints as the office building of Spade and Archer. It is larger, more grand than one would expect, yet Gores' argument in its favor is painstaking and it matches the street directions in *The Maltese Falcon* perfectly. Others have argued that Spade worked out of the old Hallidie Building at 130 Sutter, just up the block.

You may decide to go the three blocks down Sutter for a closer look at the Hunter-Dulin Building on the southwest corner of Sutter and Montgomery—or press on to the next site, continuing north on Stockton on the west side of the street. Climb the first stairs to the Bush Street overpass, atop the:

8 STOCKTON TUNNEL   At 2 a.m. the telephone awakened Sam Spade in his apartment at 891 Post. He said "Hello . . . Yes, speaking. . . . Dead? . . . Yes. . . . Fifteen minutes. Thanks." He dressed, phoned for a cab, and had it drop him "where Bush roofed Stockton before slipping downhill to Chinatown." Then, "Spade crossed the sidewalk between iron-railed hatchways that opened above bare ugly stairs, went to the parapet and, resting his hands on the damp coping, looked down into Stockton Street."

He looked down toward a vacant lot on the righthand side of Stockton, where the north wing of the tall white McAlpin apartment building stands today. A billboard fenced the lot from the sidewalk. Flashlight beams flickered up and down the hill.

Spade left the parapet and walked through the night-fog a short distance west on Bush to where a small group of men stood looking into:

ON APPROXIMATELY THIS SPOT
MILES ARCHER,
PARTNER OF SAM SPADE,
WAS DONE IN BY
BRIGID O'SHAUGHNESSY.

9 BURRITT STREET   Beneath the street sign a bronze plaque tells all, summing up in one sentence why this alley is the most popular Hammett site in San Francisco: "On approximately this spot, Miles Archer, partner of Sam Spade, was done in by Brigid O'Shaughnessy." The *first* murder in *The Maltese Falcon*, this was the crime that led to other deaths, and put Spade on the trail of the Black Bird.

The plaque was worded by Warren Hinckle and masterminded by San Francisco advertising man Howard Gossage in the late 1960s, but was not installed until February 12, 1974. In the novel, Spade walks up to "a uniformed policeman chewing gum under an enameled sign that said *Burritt St.* in white against dark blue." Today city street signs feature black letters on white, and if you follow Spade's steps halfway down the alley you will see the original brickwork McAlpin building on the left, running down the bottom half of Burritt. The poured concrete section of its newer north wing was not there in 1928. Instead a board fence ran along that part of the alley. Past it "dark ground fell away steeply to the billboard on Stockton Street below."

Fifteen feet down the hill Miles Archer's corpse lay, lodged between a boulder and the slope of fog-damp earth, a bullet right through his pump.

When you leave Burritt Alley turn left and go back to Powell; turn left again and head south on Powell to Sutter. You'll notice the Sir Francis Drake, a possible model for the fat man's hotel, on the southeast corner at Sutter. Continue down Powell, past Union Square two blocks to the inter- section of Powell and Ellis streets. On the northeast corner stands:

Dashiell Hammett, late 1920s

10   114 POWELL   Now the Hotel Union Square, in 1921 it was named the Golden West Hotel. Josephine Dolan stayed here be- fore her marriage to Hammett July 7, 1921, in the old St. Mary's Cathe- dral at 1115 Van Ness (now gone). The Union Square is recognizing Hammett's part in its history — they have a penthouse "Dashiell Hammett Suite" and (for some reason) a "Lillian Hellman Suite" as well, and a bar named "Dashiell's" recently opened off the hotel's ornate art deco lobby.

Directly across Powell on the northest corner you'll see:

11   120 ELLIS   This place, the old Woodstock Rooms, is where Hammett stayed before the marriage.

Continue down the remaining block of Powell to Market and the cablecar turntable; turn to your left around Woolworth's. At 856 Market you will find:

12   SAMUELS JEWELERS   After quitting Pinkerton, Hammett be- gan writing ad copy for Albert Samuels, Sr., and worked for the jeweler until July, 1926. In the 1920s Samuels was located at 895 Mar- ket on the corner of 5th Street — half a block away and across the street from its present location. Samuels moved here in 1943. Hammett dedi- cated his last Op novel, *The Dain Curse*, to Samuels, and based the character of Brigid O'Shaughnessy in part on his secretary in the adver- tising department.

Next door to Samuels you will find the cavernous front entrance to:

13   870 MARKET   The James Flood Building is where Hammett worked for Pinkerton, out of suite 314. He had been about twenty-two years old when he started with the agency in Baltimore. He was twenty-seven when he signed in with the San Francisco office in 1921, and would resign permanently before his next birthday on May 27, 1922. Over a five-year period he was on active assignment for slight- ly less than three years.

From clues in the first Op novel *The Big Knockover* it is apparent that the fictitious Continental Detective Agency had *its* offices in this building as well. If you walk from the front entrance on Market to the rear doors on Ellis, you're treading the same marble halls that Hammett *and* the Continental Op gumshoed over half a century ago.

A right turn from the Flood Building's rear entrance at 71 Ellis will put you in front of the last stop on this walk:

14 JOHN'S GRILL Immediately before going by cab down to Burlingame, Sam Spade "went to John's Grill, asked the waiter to hurry his order of chops, baked potato, and sliced tomatoes, ate hurriedly, and was smoking a cigarette with his coffee" when the driver came in.

John's Grill has been doing business at 63 Ellis Street since 1908, and is one of only two restaurants where characters eat in *The Maltese Falcon* that survive today (the other is the Garden Court of the Palace Hotel at Market and New Montgomery). On January 16, 1976, owners Gus and Sydna Konstin officially converted the second floor into the Maltese Falcon Dining Room (this upstairs room, by the way, was added to John's in 1921, the year Hammett came to the city). The walls feature photos of Hammett, Lillian Hellman, authors such as Fritz Leiber, Joe Gores, and William F. Nolan who have written about Hammett; as well as photos of detectives such as David Fechheimer, who did much pioneering research into Hammett's life, and Hal Lipset, now San Francisco's best-known private eye. Also featured are still photos and dialogue captions from the John Huston-Humphrey Bogart film of "The Maltese Falcon," and a glass case contains a selection of books by and about Hammett, even a facsimile of the fabled Black Bird itself.

A third-floor Hammett Den was opened May 12, 1982, to meet the growing ranks of hungry Hammett fans. John's is a major Hammett attraction, the second most important place to go after a trip to Burritt Alley. John's Grill offers souvenir menu covers, "Sam Spade Chops," and even a drink named the "Bloody Brigid" which comes in a souvenir glass with a falcon emblazoned on it.

John's is a good place to have a drink and ponder the literary world Hammett created in The Maltese Falcon *and in his hard-boiled narratives of the Continental Op, a mysterious and dangerous San Francisco created in the pulp magazines of the 1920s that has not lost its fascination nor its hold on our imaginations.*

UNION SQUARE

George Sterling, 1926

   Named in 1860 for the demonstrations held here in support of the Union of northern States, this square has always been a center for San Francisco—first deeded for public use early in 1850 under John White Geary, the city's first mayor and post-master, now centerpiece of San Francisco's largest hotel and shopping district. A walk around the square and on the lower shoulder of nearby Nob Hill gives one of the best looks into our literary history.

*Begin at Powell and O'Farrell.
The 38 Geary eastbound will
drop you here; this intersection is only two blocks up
from Powell and Market, where
over a dozen Muni lines as
well as BART stop. (Large
The building on the northeast
corner with the green art deco
ornamentation used to house:*

William Saroyan

1 OMAR KHAYYAM'S Closed after a fire in the 1970s, this famous Armenian restaurant, operated by George Mardikian, was here for decades. It was a favored hangout for the even more famous Armenian writer William Saroyan during the years he lived, off and on, in the city *after* he became famous.

In the basement of this building in the 1920s yet another legendary San Francisco hangout was located — the speakeasy Coffee Dan's. You could walk down the stairs or slide down a chute to rub shoulders with the bootleggers, gangsters, newspapermen, and other drinkers who populated the joint. Joe Gores sets a scene here early in the pages of his novel *Hammett* (1975), a hard-boiled mystery in which Dashiell Hammett himself is featured as the detective-hero. It seems safe to suppose that the hard-drinking Hammett would have come into this speak on occasion — and, for that matter, George Sterling and many another literary son of Bacchus in that decade.

*A few steps east will put you
before:*

2 MACY'S If it is open when you do this walk, take a shortcut through it. (If it's closed, go to Stockton and turn left.) Robert Stone sets a chase scene on Macy's escalators in the National Book Award-winning novel *Dog Soldiers* (1974), where thugs pursue one of his heroin-smuggling heroes. According to his publisher's jacket-copy, Stone lived "in San Francisco as an involved member of the counter-culture." Translation: Stone was part of the Ken Kesey-Merry Prankster scene in Palo Alto and La Honda in the early 1960s when the Pranksters were adventuring with LSD. As a journalist he traveled through Mexico with Kesey when that writer fled the country on drug charges (those months when Kesey was "salt in J. Edgar Hoover's wounds"), and Stone also worked as a foreign correspondent in South Vietnam. *Dog Soldiers* makes excellent use of this background, as a heroin shipment comes from Vietnam into San Francisco and the drug-runners go to war among themselves in the Tenderloin, Oakland, and the mountains of Mexico.

(Also, in Macy's basement Lawrence Ferlinghetti conceived and wrote the poem "Director of Alienation," proving that literary inspiration can strike *anywhere*.)

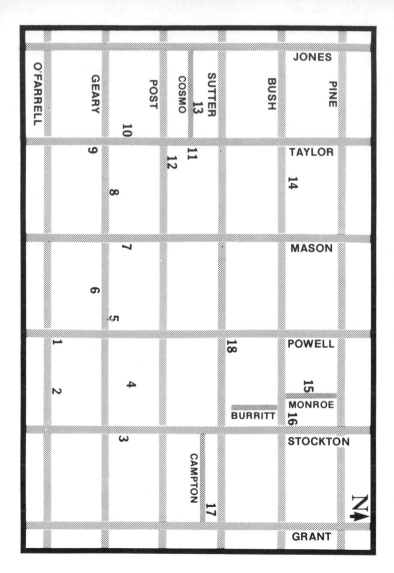

O'FARRELL

GEARY

POST

COSMO

SUTTER

BUSH

PINE

JONES

TAYLOR

MASON

POWELL

MONROE

BURRITT

STOCKTON

CAMPTON

GRANT

10

9

8

7

6

5

13

11

12

14

1

2

4

3

18

15

16

17

N

Go to the corner of Geary and Stockton. On the east side of the street opposite Union Square is a brick building, now offices for Pan Am Airlines, but once the doorway to 222 Stockton led to the bookstore and publication offices of:

3 A. M. ROBERTSON Robertson was the dean of San Francisco's booksellers. He worked in his first shop at 126 Post from 1888 until the fire of 1906 destroyed it, then set up temporary shelves at 1539 Van Ness on the edge of the burned zone before establishing his last shop here in 1909, where he sold books, printed stationery, and also published a large number of volumes until his death in 1933. He issued Stoddard's *In the Footprints of the Padres*, Markham's *The Man With the Hoe*, a travel book by James D. Phelan, ten volumes of poetry by

George Sterling, Clark Ashton Smith's first book *The Star-Treader and Other Poems*, and many other titles.

Walk across Stockton to:

4 UNION SQUARE This park undoubtedly has been crossed by every writer who has lived more than a week in the city. But Union Square best lends itself to crowds and spectacle, as in the early days of the pro-Union rallies, rather than the solitary walking writer. The day before the hippie-historic Trips Festival began in Longshoreman's Hall in 1966, Ken Kesey and the Merry Pranksters staged a happening here at noon. Music critic Ralph J. Gleason said that Kesey wore jeans with "Hot" on the left hip, "Cold" on the right, and "Tibet" across the butt: "He and the Pranksters arrived in Union Square in the Prankster bus (the first of the psychedelically painted vehicles that were to become such a mark of the hippie scene) and ballyhooed the Festival. A dark-haired girl chanted 'Trips, Trips, Trips Festival' and 'electric frugging' as three big black weather balloons were blown up with helium and, attached to a banner reading 'NOW,' rose into the sky."

Gordon de Marco featured another massive scene in the Square as Upton Sinclair gave a speech here in his run for governor during 1934 in the novel *October Heat*. And for a great *visual* look at Union Square in the days before the fine old City of Paris building was torn down and re-placed by Neiman-Marcus, before Saks Fifth Avenue took over another corner, check out Francis Coppola's film *The Conversation* (1972) — much of it was shot in this park.

Across Powell Street from Union Square you'll find the:

5 ST. FRANCIS HOTEL The Soviet poet Yevgeny Yevtushenko stopped here in 1972 — one of countless visiting writers who have used this hotel. Carolyn Cassady mentions in *Heart Beat* (1976) that she applied for a job here in 1952 when Jack Kerouac was staying with her and Neal Cassady at 29 Russell. She was not hired.

The literary associations seem endless. In mystery fiction alone, the presence of the St. Francis could fill a chapter. It is the original of the St. Mark in *The Maltese Falcon*, where Sam Spade's partner Miles Archer begins his last case, and where Hammett himself as a Pinkerton opera-tive worked on the notorious Fatty Arbuckle rape-murder case. In Ross Thomas's *The Backup Men* (1971) the espionage team of Padillo and Maccorkle rent a room overlooking the square. "I used to come up here from L.A. on weekends sometimes," Padillo says. "I knew a girl who lived on Russian Hill. She got mad when I called it Frisco."

"The natives here have a lot of civic pride," Maccorkle replies. "She was from New Orleans."

David Siefkin's *Meet Me at the St. Francis* (1979) numbers Edna St. Vincent Millay, James Hilton, Mary McCarthy, Tennessee Williams, and Louis L'Amour among the writer-guests to stay in the St. Francis since the hotel opened in 1904. In 1920 Damon Runyon, Ring Lardner, H. L. Mencken, and Irvin Cobb all stopped here while reporting on the Democratic National Convention, and Cobb developed a dread of being killed in — or under — one of the taxis ranked in front of the hotel, observing that "the youth who has been driving me about is a lineal descendant of Ben Hur." Over lunch in the Mural Room in 1943 Ernest Hemingway persuaded Ingrid Bergman to star in the film of his novel *For Whom the Bell Tolls*. Helen Gurley Brown stayed here during a promotional tour for *Sex and the Single Girl*; Mickey Spillane, whose scenes of mayhem and heavy breathing made him the bestselling writer of the 1950s, checked in during a publicity sweep for *Bloody Sunrise* in 1965. The St. Francis even rates a passage in Sinclair Lewis' American classic *Babbitt* (1922), as three traveling salesmen declare that it is "a swell place, absolutely A-1."

In the next block north on Powell you'll find the Sir Francis Drake Hotel, in whose towering shape the poet Allen Ginsberg discerned the leering face of Moloch, Phoenician god to whom children were sacrificed, and was inspired to create part of "Howl," with its dark invocation of "Moloch whose eyes are a thousand blind windows! Moloch whose skyscrapers stand in the long streets like endless Jehovahs!"

From the St. Francis drop down to Geary Street and head west. At 351 Geary stands the:

6 STEWART HOTEL — where the world-famous sleuth Charlie Chan stays before relocating to the "Kirk Building" to investigate a murder in Earl Derr Biggers' *Behind That Curtain* (1928), a mystery completely set in San Francisco.

Go to Mason, turn right. In the early 1970s, 420 Mason in the Native Sons Building housed:

7 THE CITY LIGHTS POETS THEATRE This enterprise provided a downtown forum for public readings of poetry. Founded by Lawrence Ferlinghetti, its programs also roved over the city. On September 4, 1973, the great L.A. writer Charles Bukowski gave his first poetry reading under the banner of the City Lights Poets Theatre, but the hall used was the Telegraph Hill Neighborhood Center over in North Beach. *Literary San Francisco* notes that the Buk "drank all the beer in the refrigerator onstage, read pugilistically from his works, and roused the huge audience to cheers, sneers, and insults. . . ."

Near the southwest corner of Mason and Post, just up the block, was once located 521 Post. In this house on May 19, 1880, its owner, the Reverend Doctor William Anderson Scott, performed the marriage ceremony for Robert Louis Stevenson and the former Mrs. Fanny Osbourne.

*Go back onto Geary, continue
west. In this block you'll come
to 440 Geary, the:*

8 HOTEL SOMERTON   The South African Alan Paton stayed here
about a month at the end of 1946 into 1947. He was touring the
world's penal institutions, and had visited the Nazi concentration camps
and other prisons; he toured Alcatraz on January 8th, 1947.

At a party Paton met Aubrey and Marigold Burns of Fairfax and was
invited to their home. Paton noted in his autobiography *Towards the
Mountain* (1980) that Aubrey was a poet and showed his guest some of
his work. "It then could hardly help emerging that I was a writer too, and
that I had in the Hotel Somerton a novel almost finished." Paton was
afraid his creative energies might fade, but all he had to do was reread a
few pages for his inspiration to return with full force—and since "San
Francisco was in the grip of the Christmas spirit . . . I had a great deal of
time for my own affairs." He let the Burnses read the manuscript while
he spent his last days in the Bay Area in their house. They exclaimed:
"This book will go on living long after you are dead."

The novel was *Cry, the Beloved Country*—an international success
when it appeared in 1948. The dramatic adaptation by Maxwell Anderson was hugely popular, and Felicia Komai even adapted it as a verse
drama. One of those rare, instant classics of literature, *Cry, the Beloved
Country* was completed in this hotel.

*Across the street on the
southeast corner of Geary and
Taylor is:*

9 THE CLIFT HOTEL   As is the case with other major hotels, the list
of writer-guests in the Clift might fill a book. In *The City at the End of
the Rainbow: San Francisco and Its Grand Hotels* (1976), David Siefkin
describes the activity in the city during the 1939 World's Fair on Treasure
Island, noting that, "A stroll through the lobby of the Clift Hotel could
bring one close enough to overhear Bertrand Russell talking to a reporter. . . . 'When I consider what clever men do'; he said, 'I think it's well
to be stupid.' "

The great fictioneer Sir Arthur Conan Doyle and his family stayed
here for a week during his second and final lecture tour of America, the
only visit he made to San Francisco. Doyle arrived on the Lark from Los
Angeles the night of May 30th, 1923. He gave his first of five lectures on
June 2nd, but it did not concern his most popular creation, Sherlock
Holmes. Doyle's talks were on spiritualism, the major interest of his later
years, after the sudden death of one of his sons. He gave a single presentation in Oakland on June 5th, and left by train for Portland after his
talk in the city on the 6th. (In a Holmesian play Doyle wrote—which was
never published as part of the official series about Sherlock—Doctor
Watson mentions that he once was married and practiced medicine in
San Francisco.)

*Turn north up Taylor. On the
west side of the street,
mounted next to the entranceway at 501 Taylor, you'll find the:*

10 **ISADORA DUNCAN PLAQUE**   Dedicated May 27, 1973, this
plaque marks where the legendary dancer was born in a small
house May 27, 1877. Irma Duncan spoke at the ceremony, which she
described as "a real 'Isadora Happening,' " featuring "Speeches, cheers,
tears . . . with some young girls in tunics and bare feet dancing on the
sidewalk to music by Schubert, in the roaring traffic, to and in her honor."

Isadora of course has many literary connections. Raised here and in
Oakland, she was guided in her early reading—as was Jack London—by
Oakland librarian and poet Ina Donna Coolbrith. She was married to
the Russian poet Sergei Essenin from 1922 until 1925; he committed
suicide after their separation. And Isadora became a writer herself with
My Life (1927). Her death, September 14, 1927, when one of her typical
long scarves wrapped around the axle of her open-topped Amilcar and
strangled her, created a sensation and added to the already large Isadora legend.

*Go north half a block. The
brick vine-covered building on
the northeast corner of Taylor
and Post is:*

11 **THE BOHEMIAN CLUB**   The plaque on the corner of this building on Taylor features the Bohemian Club owl (a motif repeated
in the lintels of the top floor windows), with the motto "Weaving spiders
come not here" and the dates 1872, 1909, and 1933. In 1872 the club
was established in the old Astor Building on Sacramento Street; it
evolved from breakfasts the *Chronicle* writer James Bowan hosted for
fellow newsmen. They soon allowed others interested in the arts to join,
and the membership swelled with lawyers and businessmen. The club
leased new quarters in 130 Post on the northeast corner of Grant in
1877 (A. M. Robertson shrewdly opened his first bookshop next door at
126 Post in 1888), and during this period bought land on Russian River
near Monte Rio—the Bohemian Grove. Three years after the 1906 fire,
they built here on Post, but had the original structure torn down and a
practically identical one, this current building, erected in 1933.

The Bohemian Club motto is taken from Shakespeare's *A Midsummer Night's Dream*, from the song of protection the fairies conjure
about Queen Titania so no one will disturb her rest. In their Grove, un-
disturbed by the world, the Bohemian Club members began annual
Midsummer Jinks—both Low Jinks, comedy and recitations *à la* Bottom
the Weaver and the infamous Puck (who manage to disturb Titania
most soundly), and High Jinks—a lofty, elaborate pageant in the style of

the great wedding feast with which Shakespeare ends his play. The club's literary members began writing plays for the occasion: Porter Garnett's was *The Green Knight*, Jack London wrote *Gold* with Herbert Heron—a play never performed for the club, and George Sterling composed that Grove classic *The Triumph of Bohemia*, in which the Spirit of Bohemia slays Mammon.

Yet, as Nancy Peters observes in *Literary San Francisco:* "Mammon triumphed after all. . . . Gradually, the Bohemian Club evolved from a group of men with talent and no money to a group of men with money and talent for ruling the world." The modern midsummer encampments see the likes of David Rockefeller, Richard Nixon, and Henry Kissinger in attendance—many feel that national and international policy is decided among these representatives of the super-rich and top levels of government as they cavort between Low and High Jinks.

Henry George, Ambrose Bierce, Joaquin Miller, J. Ross Browne, Prentice Mulford, John Muir, Charles Warren Stoddard, and Edward Rowland Sill were among the writers associated with the club. Kevin Starr writes that Frank Norris, during his years editing *The Wave*, ". . . preferred to pal around with young men of his own class, many of them fellow members of the Bohemian Club at the corner of Post Street and Grant, in whose sunny bay windows Norris would laze of an idle afternoon, making comments on the comparative merits of passing women to companions playing cards within." Ina Coolbrith, as the club's librarian, was one of only four women granted an honorary membership in this society.

Despite the presence of Jack London, Norris, and Bierce, the poet George Sterling is the writer now most associated with the Bohemian Club—the King of Bohemia, the Last Bohemian. Born December 1, 1869, in Sag Harbor, New York, Sterling came to Oakland in 1890 to work for his uncle Frank C. Havens. He met Joaquin Miller in 1891 and Ambrose Bierce in 1892, and began writing poetry in the elevated romantic style preferred by Bierce and assumed a flamboyant public style in the grand manner of Miller. Sterling was one of the most famous San Franciscans of his day—a founder of the artist colony in Carmel, best friend to Jack London, unofficial yet unquestioned laureate of his "cool, gray city of love."

On February 11, 1904, Sterling was given membership in the Bohemian Club, and in the 1920s he lived in quarters on the third floor of the club, after returning from an unsuccessful attempt at a literary career in New York in 1914, where they were not appreciative of his traditional romanticism. The esteem given to Sterling locally, however, is exemplified by the Court of the Four Seasons pavilion erected for the Panama Pacific Exposition of 1915, on which was carved quotes from the Immortals—Shakespeare, Goethe, Socrates, Dante, and George Sterling.

In late 1926 the literary lion of Baltimore and the nation, *American Mercury* editor H. L. Mencken, was scheduled to appear at the Bohemian Club with due pomp and ceremony. Sterling, who had guided Mencken through the speaks and night-life when the journalist had come to cover the Democratic National Convention in July 1920, began to gather liquor for the affair. Mencken, however, stopped over in Los Angeles longer than expected—his anticipated arrival was first set back for days, then weeks. It is said that the bored poet began drinking the liquor stacked in his room "like the storeroom of a speakeasy." It's said he drank it *all*, and when Mencken did arrive was too inebriated to welcome him. Sterling, unable to serve as master of ceremonies, was nonetheless hurt when another was assigned the post. In his room the night of November 16th Sterling took cyanide.

Idwal Jones said, "It was like a unicorn dying . . . , or one of those sinewy and eternal children of Pan." Over one hundred women of all ages and stations in life came to Sterling's funeral, each claiming that she alone was the inspiration for his many love poems. Thomas Benediktsson in *George Sterling* (1980) notes: "And at Newbegin's Bologna Cafe that night, all the patrons stood while the orchestra played Debussy's *L'Après midi d'un Faun*."

Step around the corner from the Bohemian Club plaque, where you'll discover, mounted on the Post Street side of this building, a plaque designed by Jo Mora:

12 BRET HARTE PLAQUE Complete with *bas relief* figures from Harte's large cast of pioneer California characters, this plaque was dedicated December 20, 1919, in honor of the most popular western writer of his day — a man the *Atlantic Monthly* signed to a $10,000-a-year contract in *1870* for contributing just one story or poem each issue. Harte's success was a major incentive for the development of "local color" or regional fiction.

At the ceremony George Sterling read the poem "Art and Life," composed for the occasion; it was published in the dedication folio *In Memoriam Bret Harte* issued by A. M. Robertson in 1920.

Across Taylor Street from the Bohemian Club you'll see Cosmo Alley, home of:

13 TRADER VIC'S A leading San Francisco restaurant for many years, Trader Vic's is headquarters for a literary group that has met monthly around the Captain's Table. Begun by the late Jack Vietor, a publisher, this group includes Jerome Weidman, Paul Erdman, Herb Gold, Curt Gentry, Arthur Hailey, and Niven Busch. When a writer-knight of this literary round table regularly fails to attend, his champagne glass is ceremoniously smashed and mailed to him — an apt modern equivalent for the broken swords of old.

The Trader's also was the scene for a huge party in January, 1979, on the occasion of Erskine (*Tobacco Road*) Caldwell's seventy-fifth birthday, and for another party on April 4, 1981, when Gus and Sydna Konstin, owners of the Hammett hangout John's Grill, celebrated their twenty-fifth wedding anniversary.

Go back onto Taylor and head north, with a last look at the Bohemian Club.

An intriguing question arises as to why the first clubhouse on this site was torn down, since it was constructed after the 1906 quake and surely was built up to code, and replaced by this virtually identical building. A supernatural answer is suggested by Sterling's protege Clark Ashton Smith, writing in 1934: "About 1918 I was in ill health and, during a short visit to San Francisco, was sitting one day in the Bohemian Club, to which I had been given a guest's card of admission. Happening to look up, I saw a frightful demonian face with twisted rootlike eyebrows and oblique fiery-slitted eyes, which seemed to emerge momentarily from the air about nine feet above me and lean toward my seat. The thing disappeared as it approached me, but left an ineffaceable impression of malignity, horror, and loathesomeness. If an hallucination, it was certainly seen amid appropriate surroundings; if an actual entity, it was no doubt the kind that would be likely to haunt a club in one of our modern Gomorrahs."

Who knows what weird forces have been unleashed by the secret Bacchic revels in the Bohemian Grove? How many times may the name of Pan be evoked in mock ceremony before Pan takes notice? At what point might the mystic Illuminati have introduced their agents into this society, turning it from its innocuous origins into the locus for the world-power elite it is today? Prentice Mulford, a writer for the Golden Era *and a serious occultist, later founder of the* White Cross Library, *was an early figure in this club — one of many people in nineteenth century San Francisco interested in spiritualism. Before swallowing the cyanide, George Sterling burned some of his poems and personal effects in his third-floor room. Strangely, two fragments of scorched paper bore recognizable lines from Sterling's* Lilith — *"Deeper into the darkness can I peer than most, yet find the darkness still beyond" — "I walk with phantoms that ye know not."*

Go north to Bush, turn right. On the north side of the street at 870 Bush you'll see the headquarters of the San Francisco Fire Chief. Mounted on the wall is the:

14 DENNIS T. SULLIVAN MEMORIAL PLAQUE Sullivan was fire chief from April 1893 until 1906, when a chimney fell in his home in the Presidio during the quake of April 18th, killing him and his wife. Sullivan had tried to persuade the other city officials to invest in fire-fighting equipment which could utilize salt water pumped from the Bay, but the cost was deemed exorbitant. When the quake broke the major water mains, his firemen found themselves without an effective means of combating the flames. San Francisco burned.

Sullivan and his wife were among the relatively few casualties of that great disaster. This building was erected in his honor in 1922 as an official home for the city's fire chiefs. It is of literary interest for the memorial verse on the plaque, written for the dedication of this building by George Sterling.

*Continue on Bush to the east,
past Mason and Powell to
where a one-block street joints
Bush from the north:*

15 **MONROE STREET** On the east side of this street, halfway up, you'll find No. 20, where Dashiell Hammett had a room in 1926, during a period when his tuberculosis was active. He sent his wife and two daughters to live on a farm near San Anselmo, a vacation from city life, and so he would not expose them to TB. Hammett was working his last few months at Samuel's Jewelers as director of the advertising department at this time, as well as putting the Continental Op through the meatgrinder in story after story.

The peripatetic Bret Harte also lived on this street in 1869 at 13 Monroe— one of many addresses for Harte in the Bay Area. Yet as Idwal Jones noted in 1936: "Such have been the changes in the town that no roof may be pointed out under which he lived."

*Return to Bush and continue
east a few steps to 608 Bush,
where you'll find mounted on
the doorway a:*

> ## ROBERT LOUIS STEVENSON
> ### LODGED AT 608 BUSH STREET,
> ### DECEMBER 1879 TO MARCH 1880,
> ### AND THERE WROTE ESSAYS, POEMS
> ### AUTOBIOGRAPHY AND FICTION.
> **PLAQUE PLACED BY ADMIRERS OF THE
> AUTHOR IN COOPERATION WITH THE
> CALIFORNIA HISTORICAL SOCIETY**
> ## JULY 26, 1972

16 **ROBERT LOUIS STEVENSON PLAQUE** Stevenson first came through San Francisco in late August, 1879, but quickly took train to Monterey, where Mrs. Fanny Osbourne was living with her two children during a separation from her husband. When Fanny returned to her Oakland home, R.L.S. also came north. He kept a discreet distance while Fanny's divorce proceedings went through the courts, renting a room across the Bay from his still-married fiancée shortly before Christmas 1879.

During Stevenson's stay, 608 Bush was a narrow three-story wooden building with rooms to let, operated by Mary Carson. A waist-high iron grill ran completely across the front of the building on the second and third floors before French windows, reminding the twenty-nine-year-old Scot of his family home in Edinburgh built in the same architectural style.

In this building Stevenson worked on *From Jest to Earnest*, the essays "The Art of Virtue" about Benjamin Franklin and "The Fruits of Solitude" about William Penn, and a novel (which he eventually abandoned) modeled on the paperback Dime Novels that were so popular in that time: *A Chapter in the Experiences of Arizona Breckenridge; or, A Vendetta in the West.* (Dime Novels all had weighty titles, as in *The King Pin Tramp; or, Hustling Frisco Hoodlums; Prince John, Detective Special; or, Unmasking the Frisco Firefiends, Father Ferrett, the Frisco Shadow;*

or, the Queen of Bowie Notch, Cool Conrad, the Dakota Detective; or, From Lair to Lair, a Tale of Frisco and the Gold Camps, to name only a few with a San Francisco scene.)

Stevenson also helped nurse Mary's four-year-old son Robbie over a serious bout with pneumonia—but the exposure to illness, his lack of money for food, his work writing, and the nervous strain of waiting for his union with Fanny, all contributed to the failure of his own health. Mrs. Carson returned his kindness by tending him, but when the tubercular Scot's condition worsened and he began hemorrhaging, Fanny had him moved from 608 Bush to the Tubbs Hotel near her Oakland home, in March, 1880.

Across the street from this plaque is Burritt Alley, a highlight of the Hammett tour. Go across Bush to the stairs leading down to Stockton, follow Stockton south one block to Sutter. On the east side of the next block of Stockton is Campton Place, an alley running next to the Campton Hotel. At the other end of this alley you'll find, dating from 1906:

17　THE TEMPLE BAR　One of the oldest establishments in the city, the Temple Bar is said to have been a haunt for Ambrose Bierce and many other writers. It's possible, though at this point it would be hard to say what drink Bitter Bierce favored.

One block west of Stockton on the northeast corner of Sutter and Powell stands a Holiday Inn, and on the top floor you'll find:

18　THE S. HOLMES ESQ. PUB　With an excellent rooftop view looking west to the Pacific and up the rolling shoulders of Nob Hill and Telegraph Hill, this plush bar is another good place to come for a drink. In the hallway off the bar our local Sherlock Holmes *aficionados*, the San Francisco branch of the international club the Baker Street Irregulars, have re-created with authentic detail 221B Baker Street, home and headquarters of the great investigator and his boon companion Dr. John H. Watson. There is a similar pub in London. A tape plays the sounds you might have heard on a day when fog covered that great city: the tolling of Big Ben, the clatter of horses' hooves and the wheels of a hansom cab on the cobblestones—a literary universe where it is always 1895. You'll see the "V R" Holmes shot idly into the wall, Holmes' notorious violin, the Persian slipper, even ("Quick, Watson!") the *needle*. Well worth the elevator ride.

NOB HILL

Refugee tents in the ruins of the Flood mansion and the Fairmont, 1906

In San Francisco's early years this summit was known as the California Street Hill, but when the big Four of the Central Pacific Railroad—Governor Leland Stanford, Charles Crocker, Mark Hopkins, and Collis Huntington—and the Comstock Silver Kings—James Food and "Bonanza Jim" Fair—built their enormous, ornate mansions in square-block lots on the crest, the hill was dubbed Nob. The name is a shortened form of Knob, Snob or Nabob—take your pick. Robert Louis Stevenson called it "The Hill of Palaces" which "must certainly be counted the best part of San Francisco. It is there that the millionaires are gathered together vying with each other in display." The summit, today built up with grand hotels and apartment houses, retains its aura of wealth, luxury, exclusivity—tempting some, looking up from below, to sarcastically call it "Tenderloin Heights."

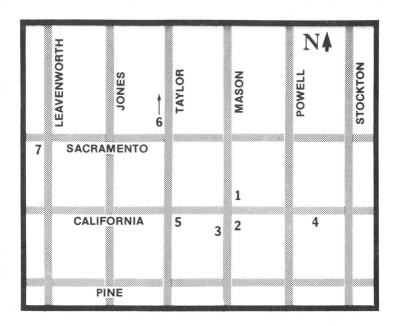

LEAVENWORTH

JONES

TAYLOR

MASON

POWELL

STOCKTON

N↑

6

7 SACRAMENTO

1

CALIFORNIA 5 3 2 4

PINE

*Begin at California and Mason.
The California Street cable car
will drop you at this corner, the
Powell Street cable car stops a
block east, the 1 California
trolley westbound stops a
block north.*

*The brownstone mansion on the northwest corner belonged to James
Flood—it was the only mansion that survived the 1906 fire (the others
were built of wood) and will give you an idea of the scale of nineteenth-
century Nob Hill homes. The ubiquitous architect Willis Polk, who was
affiliated with the writers of the* Lark *renaissance, did add to this building
in 1912, and George Kelham in 1934, so it is not exactly as it was before
the fire.*

*Across Mason from the Flood
mansion, bedecked with flags,
stands:*

1 THE FAIRMONT HOTEL Built in 1906 on the block owned by
Comstock king James G. "Bonanza Jim" Fair, this hotel was gutted
by the fire of April 18th before its grand opening, but was quickly rebuilt
and opened a.year later.

The first "Author's Reading" ever held in San Francisco was given in
the ballroom of the new hotel November 27, 1907. A benefit for poet-
librarian Ina Donna Coolbrith, who had lost her home in the fire, it was
organized by Gertrude Atherton, with help from former Mayor James
D. Phelan, then president of the Bohemian Club and host for the affair.

Edward Robeson Taylor, later a member of the U.S. Supreme Court
and a poet, whose *To Arms* (1920) won for him the cross of the Legion
of Honor, spoke. He was San Francisco's new reform mayor, filling the
office vacated in disgrace by Union Labor Mayor Eugene Schmitz, a
flunky of "Boss" Ruef. Atherton biographer Emily Leider, writing about
this event (*California Living*, June 21, 1981), said: "However apolitical,

festive and escapist it might appear, the Author's Reading had a political cast. It was pro-prosecution, pro-reform. . . . The friends of Ina Coolbrith, the friends of clean government and the partisans of High Culture, this night were one and the same."

The poet George Sterling, visiting from Carmel, brought his melancholy romantic perspective to bear on the fire, which had made of San Francisco the world's finest ruins and created in three days a lost land as fabulous as Atlantis or Avalon—a well-remembered City That Was, gone forever in the devouring flames. Charles Warren Stoddard, Charles K. Field, Herman Scheffauer, Jimmy Hopper, and Gertrude Atherton all read from their work. Botanist Luther Burbank, internationally famous, came down from Santa Rosa to read a paper and lend his name to the cause, though he fell asleep in a back row between rounds of applause.

The last reader on the program was Joaquin Miller, still the most flamboyant poet in the West. He brought the crowd cheering to its feet with his famous poem "Columbus," with its epic sweep and rousing finale: "What shall we do when hope is gone," he shouted. "Sail on! Sail On! SAIL ON! AND ON!"

The reading brought in one thousand dollars, which Coolbrith used to make a downpayment on her lot at 1027 Broadway on Russian Hill. She did not attend the benefit—either from embarrassment or perhaps because of her painful arthritis. Other donations came in, and Phelan as a senator in 1918 made her California's Poet Laureate with a $1500 per year honorarium, so that Coolbrith—whom Atherton described as "the first California woman to distinguish herself"—could live her last years in comfort.

A similar reading had been proposed to benefit the popular young poet Nora May French, but she committed suicide by swallowing cyanide on November 14th, 1907, two weeks before the Coolbrith gala, in George Sterling's home in Carmel. French launched a suicide march among the California Romantics that would include London, Carrie Sterling, Herman Scheffauer, Una Waldrop, and Sterling himself, who also swallowed cyanide the night of November 16, 1926—perhaps in morbid recollection of the nineteenth anniversary of French's death two days before.

The Fairmont is also a place Dashiell Hammett lived for about a week in the early 1930s. He had borrowed a couple of thousand dollars from his ex-employer Albert Samuels with which to make an assault on New York and Hollywood. Hammett knocked over both places—for a season or two he was the hottest writer on the East and West coasts. With bundles of money in his pockets he had his black chauffeur, dressed in a fancy outfit wi th epaulettes and white gloves like one of the doormen at these Nob Hill hotels, drive him up from Hollywood to repay the loan in style. Hammett rented a suite in which to entertain his old friends and renewed a blazing love affair with his former secretary at Samuels—who was then engaged to the manager of another jewelry store. (Her husband still won't let Hammett researchers talk with her.) At the end of the week the prolifically-spending Hammett had to borrow *another* thousand from Samuels to finance his return to Hollywood.

On December 17, 1936, Eugene O'Neill and his wife checked into the Fairmont. The previous month O'Neill had become the first American playwright to win the Nobel Prize. They toured about the area, taking a ferry to Marin County—the Golden Gate Bridge, under construction, did not yet span the Bay. O'Neill kept complaining of pain; he was admitted into Merritt Hospital in Oakland to have his appendix removed.

In an interview in the *Examiner* January 12, 1937, O'Neill announced his intention to settle in northern California—"not Los Angeles . . . , not south of San Jose." With O'Neill still in the hospital, his wife packed their belongings and left the Fairmont January 14th to stay with her mother in Oakland, but they moved back into the hotel for a few weeks beginning March 13th, then rented in the East Bay while their place near Danville, Tao House, was being built. The O'Neills came back to the Fairmont February 25, 1944, when they decided to sell their home. They stayed until April.

Doubtless many other writers have stopped here: it is reported to be Woody Allen's favorite hotel in the city, though Allen is far more famous for his films than for his humor writing in the tradition of Robert Benchley and S. J. Perelman which is partly collected in the books *Getting Even* and *Without Feathers.*

.

*From the Fairmont cross
California at Mason to the:*

Woody Allen

2 MARK HOPKINS This magnificent twenty-story hotel stands on the lot of Mark Hopkins of the Big Four, whose incredible redwood palace became a pyre on the skyline in 1906. The present building was designed by Weeks and Day in 1925, completed and opened in December 1926. The Top of the Mark bar and lounge, designed by Timothy Pfleuger, opened a decade later.

When Gertrude Stein and Alice B. Toklas came through on their American tour in 1935 they stayed here. Gertrude Atherton acted as their sponsor in San Francisco and as their guide through local society. Stein met with William Saroyan during this stop in the Mark.

Mystery writers, always quick to use such well-known places, have made heavy use of the hotel. The local husband-and-wife team of Darwin and Hildegarde Teilhet wrote a series of books featuring the pompous Baron Franz Maximilian Karagoz und von Kaz, formerly of Vienna, who carries a sword inside his green umbrella. When the Baron marries in *The Broken Face Murders* (1937): "One hundred and three guests came to the reception at the Mark Hopkins in San Francisco. . . ." Leslie Ford (a pen name for Zenith Jones Brown) traveled about the world setting her murders in exotic locales. She spent six weeks in the city, taking notes, talking to San Franciscans, and drawing maps, though she set the action for *Siren in the Night* (1943) in a mythical "San Joaquin Terrace." But to prove she'd *really* been to the scene of the crime, her sleuths Grace Latham and Colonel Primrose have a drink at the Top of the Mark.

In a special Herb Caen issue of *City* magazine (May 14, 1975) Burton H. Wolfe answers the twenty questions most often asked about San Francisco's leading columnist, such as HAS HE BEEN THREATENED OR BEATEN UP?: ". . . few know Caen was beaten up twice circa 1940, both times in the Mark Hopkins Hotel. The first assailant was a Nob Hill playboy; Caen wrote about his secret love affair with a rich lady from a famous family of racehorse breeders, and the playboy knocked him down with a sock on the jaw. The second attacker was the wealthy scion of an old San Francisco family. Caen wrote that the man and his wife were experiencing marital difficulties. Caen: 'He let me have it the minute I walked into the lobby of the Mark. Pow! Just like that.' "

Not all writers are impressed with the Nob Hill hotels. In a letter to Carl Brandt November 12, 1948, the outspoken Raymond Chandler stated: "San Francisco I liked, but its hotels stink. The Fairmont has a magnificent lobby and that's all. The Mark has a beautiful grill room (and the sky lounge, of course) but its food is exorbitant, its lobby has no trace of style, and the place is full of chisel-eyed characters who look as if they were afraid they might not smile at a producer." But of the cabs which you see swarming around the hotels Chandler said: "The taxi drivers are wonderful. . . . They obey no laws but those of gravity and we even had one who passes street cars on the left, an offense for which you would probably get ninety days in Los Angeles." (One of the cabs you see today may be driven by a writer—perhaps by Ken Wainio, George Benet, or David Frankel who bills himself San Francisco's "cab-driver poet."

Herb Caen

Just across Mason from the Mark is a row of townhouses designed by Willis Polk that runs up this steep block from 831-849 Mason. The lowest is at:

3 831 MASON is where Erskine Caldwell stayed circa 1961. Caldwell also had a house on Twin Peaks from 1956, when he came to the city, until he left in the late 1960s. He wrote the novel *Certain Women* (1957) in the city; local critics savaged it. *Literary San Francisco* notes that "Caldwell staged 'a one-man revolution against critics in general and literary critics in particular' at the Mark Hopkins Hotel" in retaliation.

From this temporary residence of the bestselling author of **Tobacco Road** *and* **God's Little Acre** *you may climb back up to California and go east a block and a half to:*

4 845 CALIFORNIA In 1961 Marc H. Spinelli, beauty specialist, lived here in apartment 406. As "Count Marco" Spinelli began a grossly comic column in the *Chronicle* in 1959 to help women land—and keep—their mates. He wrote the successful column for fifteen years, with such outlandish observations as: "When you unsnap your brassiere, do you let out a loud 'Whoosh' of relief and stand there grunting and scratching like a happy sow or do you have your husband help with the snaps, then gracefully cross your arms as you let it slip down?" The first collection from Count Marco's column was published as *Beauty and the Beast* in 1960.

Return west on California past Powell and Mason to 1075 California, the

5 HUNTINGTON HOTEL   Another Weeks and Day design, from 1924, this is also another Nob Hill address for dramatist Eugene O'Neill. After selling Tao House near Danville, O'Neill and his wife came back to the Fairmont in February 1944; in April they moved to a larger suite of rooms in the Huntington. Only their closest friends knew they were still in San Francisco. After World War II ended they left the city forever, renting a suite in late 1944 in the Barclay Hotel, New York.

Across California Street from this hotel is Huntington Park, one of many local sites used in Alice Adams' novel Listening to Billie *(1978). And in the gothic Grace Cathedral across Taylor from the park a Totem Ceremony was held in 1971 under the auspices of Bishop James Pike—poets Gary Snyder, Allen Ginsberg, and Janine Pommy-Vega participated in this ceremony uniting the religions of the West and East with Native American spiritual traditions.*

From California and Taylor and the center of Nob Hill—the place Lt. Doug Roberts really wanted to be all the while he was stranded on the S.S. Reluctant in Thomas Heggens' Mr. Roberts—*you may walk a few blocks north on Taylor to:*

6 1441 TAYLOR   Local writer and school teacher Howard Pease lived here in 1929. Occasionally a copy of one of his books will turn up with an inscription to one of his pupils "with best wishes for a successful new school term." Pease wrote *The Long Wharves*, a history of the waterfront, and several other books, but is best known for his large series of boy's novels featuring Tod Moran: *The Jinx Ship, The Black Tanker, Captain of the Araby, Shanghai Passage, The Ship Without a Crew*, etc. which take the young hero from his home port of San Francisco to adventure around the world.

From the corner of Taylor and Sacramento it is only two blocks to Sacramento and Leavenworth, where you'll see on the southwest corner:

7 1155 LEAVENWORTH   Apartment 2 in this building was Dashiell Hammett's last address in San Francisco before he made his successful move on New York and Hollywood. He came here from 891 Post Street (Sam Spade's apartment house in *The Maltese Falcon*) in March 1929 and left that fall for the East. He was literally moving up in the world, from today's Tenderloin where he first lived with his family, onto Nob Hill. Though he had separated from his wife (too much drinking and womanizing) in 1927 he also brought her and their two daughters uphill to 1309 Hyde, just two blocks from here, and helped them settle in southern California when he went to write for the movies. In this building Hammett completed a final draft of the *Falcon* and began his next novel, *The Glass Key.* Here Hammett listed himself for the first time in the city directory as a "writer"—he knew he had made it.

RUSSIAN HILL

Gelett Burgess on Russian Hill, late 1880s

Named for the Russian sailors who died during an expedition to this area in the early 1800s and were buried on its southeast crest, Russian Hill has housed a continuous literary population since the 1850s. Ambrose Bierce, Caxton, Gelett Burgess and the turn-of-the-century Bohemians of the Lark were hill dwellers. California laureate Ina Donna Coolbrith held literary salons here until her death in 1928. Mystery writers such as Virginia Rath and Mary Collins littered the ridges with bodies in the 1940s; and Jack Kerouac spent seminal months here with Carolyn and Neal Cassady. Margo Patterson Doss, *Chronicle* queen of walking-tours, entertained the literati in her Greenwich Street home in the 1960s. Today, this elegant neighborhood is the home of Herb Gold, Charles Reich, Diane Johnson, Mel Zeigler, Dennis McNalley, and Ruth Freeman Soloman.

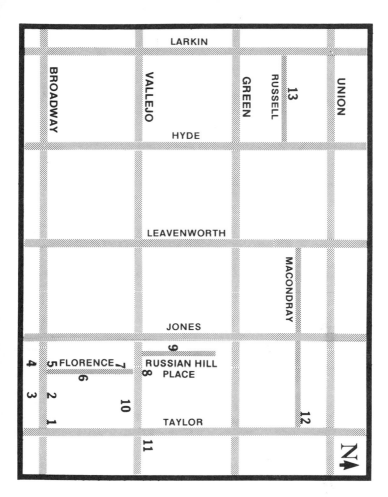

LARKIN

BROADWAY

VALLEJO

GREEN

RUSSELL

13

UNION

HYDE

LEAVENWORTH

MACONDRAY

JONES

9

4

5

FLORENCE

7

RUSSIAN HILL

8

PLACE

6

3

2

10

1

12

TAYLOR

11

N

This tour begins at the inter-section of Taylor and Broadway. The 83 Pacific will drop you at Taylor and Pacific, a block away.

On the heavily wooded shoulder of Russian Hill that rises on the northwest corner of this intersection stand:

1 **1629 TAYLOR and 1020 BROADWAY**   Adjacent on this corner, these houses are nearly invisible from this point; trees and under-growth screen them from casual inspection. You may get a better look at 1629 Taylor by hiking up that street a few steps, but 1020 Broadway remains hidden. The writer Charles Erskine Scott Wood and his wife, poet Sara Bard Field, first lived in the Taylor Street house early in the 1920s, and then moved next door to Broadway in 1922. Wood wrote satirical essays for *The Masses* which were collected as *Heavenly Dis-course* in 1927 — a book which went through dozens of printings. Field wrote many volumes of poetry, typified by *Darkling Plain* (1936). Lawrence Ferlinghetti notes in *Literary San Francisco* that "Wood was a West Pointer who fought against Chief Joseph of the Nez Perce (as well as in other campaigns to exterminate native Americans)" and that it was probably his much younger wife, a "feminist leader in San Francisco, who prompted his later liberal leanings." In the 1920s their homes were a frequent hangout for their friend George Sterling, then the major poet in the city.

Helen Hunt Jackson, whose novel Ramona *(1884) was the popular success of its decade, died August 12, 1885, in a house that stood on the northeast corner of this intersection, opposite the homes of Wood and Field. Begin climbing up Broadway — a steep hike that will impress anyone by the stamina of those early San Francisco writers who secluded themselves in cottages and rooms on this hilltop. A low concrete wall runs across the street at its crest, preventing through automobile traffic on this grade. Standing against the rampart, you might wonder if the asthmatic Ambrose Bierce ever walked this way to one of his residences four blocks further west, at 1428 Broadway (like Jackson's last residence, now gone). One would think he'd have chosen another route, but tradition has Bierce, as well as Mark Twain, Bret Harte, and (of course) Robert Louis Stevenson as visitors in the house just to the north of this spot, at:*

2 1032 BROADWAY   The home of Kate M. Atkinson was an open house for the city's writers and artists for decades, a special gathering place for members of *Les Jeunes*. Fellow Russian Hill resident Gelett Burgess called her "Cousin Kate," composed the amusing poem "Chewing-Gum Man" for her, and wrote her regularly after he moved to New York at the end of the century. When Kate Atkinson had her house renovated, *Les Jeunes* supervised: Willis Polk was overseer on its exterior, Bruce Porter on the interior. The house has a layer of stucco over the original boards today, but the basic lines of the building, and the landscaping inspired by the Japanese Tea Garden in Golden Gate Park, still recall the era when Kate Atkinson held her salons.

The lawyer William Henry Rhodes, a member of the Vigilance Committee, stayed in the Atkinson house in the years 1856-57. Under the pen-name "Caxton," Rhodes published the usual variety of essays, poetry, and fiction, including a number of amazingly successful hoaxes. His "The Case of Summerfield" appeared as a straight news feature May 13, 1871, in the *Sacramento Bee*. A man named Summerfield demands a million dollars or he will set the ocean afire chemically, the story reported — and gullible readers panicked. In a sequel, an outlaw named Black Bart steals the chemical and threatens to destroy the world. Thus, Caxton is remembered as a pioneering writer of what we now label "science fiction" (Kurt Vonnegut's *Cat's Cradle* takes off from Caxton — the crystal Ice-9, if a drop is placed in the ocean, will start a chain-reaction which will freeze the oceans of the world), and as the man who gave the poet-bandit Charles E. Bolton his immortal pseudonym.

Directly south of the spot
you're standing is:

3 1051 BROADWAY — where novelist and essayist Herbert Gold, a San Francisco resident since 1960, has kept a flat for some years.

Herbert Gold

A contemporary of Allen Ginsberg at Columbia University (they both wrote for the campus literary magazine), Gold's autobiographical novels have been compared with those of J. D. Salinger, Philip Roth, and Bernard Malamud. In *Fathers* (1967), Sam Gold comes from Cleveland, Ohio, to visit his son. Standing at this point, looking out on the spectacular view of the San Francisco roofscape toward Telegraph Hill, with the Bay beyond, Gold's father grows nostalgic for his hometown: he misses the familiar sight of smokestacks.

A couple of doors west will
put you before:

4 1067 BROADWAY   In this upper flat Ina Donna Coolbrith reigned in her last years as the matriarch of the California Literary Society, renting out the lower flat. In 1915 James D. Phelan in his first year as U.S. Senator moved to create a Poet Laureateship for California. On April 21, 1919, the laurel wreath was bestowed on Coolbrith—along with a $1,200 a year honorarium. An early California poet, editor of the *Overland Monthly* with Bret Harte and Charles Warren Stoddard (they were called the "Golden Gate Trinity"), a librarian in Oakland, one of only four women to be granted an associate membership in the Bohemian Club, Coolbrith was a respected and beloved figure in this city.

The society met every third Sunday, with a usual attendance of twenty or so members. Poets George Sterling and Edwin Markham came to speak, and Bret Harte's grandson created quite a sensation in this group, most of whom were over fifty years old, when he visited. Franklin Walker in *San Francisco's Literary Frontier* notes that the club's secretary Ella Sterling Cummins Mighels (pronounced Miles) recited their *creed*:

> Why do we have this society? We have it, my good friends, so we can pass to the next generation the memory of our writers. We have it so that the old traditions and customs of California may not die out and be forgotten. We must not forget the *pioneers*.

Mighels asked: What can we do for California authors? Members would respond: *We can buy their books.*

Across the street you'll see the
Florence Street stairs rising up
the hill. Climb until you're at the
landing just short of the top of
the steps. A small wooden gate
leads off to the garden of the
modern apartment house on
the corner of Florence and
Broadway—a gate which once
led to 1078 and 1080
Broadway, the:

5 "POP" DEMAREST COMPOUND "Pop" Demarest was a colorful San Francisco character who is said to have lived in a converted cistern on this property with a couple dozen cats, and danced by moonlight to his thousands of gramophone records among the small cottages in his compound. He rented cheaply, often to writers. Tradition insists that Bierce, Burgess, Charles Caldwell Dobie, and Frank Norris all resided here at one time or another. Certainly photographer Dorothea Lange and her husband, painter Maynard Dixon, lived in the compound, as did Helga Iverson, an editor for *Sunset* magazine, and Bill Simons, a *Chronicle* columnist. Another couple moved here after Pop's death in 1939: Jack Lord, co-author of *Where to Sin in San Francisco*, and his wife Elizabeth Field, editor of the neighborhood paper the *Russian Hill Runt*.

At the top of the stairs you can
get a good view of Coolbrith's
flat, and another vantage point
with a sweeping view—
undoubtedly the major reason
so many writers and artists
made the stiff climb to this
summit in the days before cars
made access easier, before
many of these small streets
were paved. In this block you'll
find:

Ina Coolbrith

6 40-42 FLORENCE Coming to the city in 1889, architect Willis Polk resided for a period in this house, which was built in 1860. Polk was a pioneer of the Bay Region Style along with Bernard Maybeck, Julia Morgan, and other architects—he combined classical lines with eclectic borrowings from the architectures of the world, with an especially creative use of building materials. In his decades here Polk designed and supervised construction of hundreds of houses, churches, banks, and other commercial buildings. His Hallidie Building in 1917 was the first glass curtain-walled structure built in this city—or elsewhere.

Few people made as much of a physical mark on San Francisco as Willis Polk, who somehow found time to be sportive with Gelett Burgess and the Bohemians, to contribute illustrations to *The Lark*, architectural essays to *The Wave*, and to host—here and in other San Francisco residences—*Les Jeunes*-style parties. Polk added the third floor to this house for its owner circa 1902.

Across the street you'll see:

7 **37 FLORENCE**   Annie Laurie lived here from about 1925 until 1932. She was a "Sob Sister" for the Hearst papers.

*Near the corner of Florence
and Vallejo was once
located:*

8 **THE PEANUT SHELL**   Destroyed in the 1906 fire, 1031 Vallejo was Gelett Burgess's home for several years. It's said that the sight of cattle grazing in wild mustard patches nearby occasioned his "The Purple Cow," which he first included in handmade booklets of verse given at Christmas to Bruce Porter's young nephews. The poems and drawings created for these boys, then ages five and six, later passed with minimal revision into the bamboo pages of *The Lark*, and enjoyed great success with much older "youth." President Teddy Roosevelt, for one, loved to shout out "The Purple Cow." It became so distressingly popular that Burgess the literary anarchist felt the call to deflate it with a sequel:

> Ah, yes, I wrote the "Purple Cow" —
> I'm Sorry, now, I wrote it:
> But I can tell you Anyhow
> I'll Kill you if you Quote it!

The outrageous Burgess, only five feet, four inches tall, sported a shiny tophat and circular wire-rimmed glasses which gave him an uncanny resemblance to the Planters' trademark Mr. Peanut. His neighbors called him the "Little Peanut" — his house was the "Peanut Shell." He continued literary pranks long after removing to New York. His *The Master of Mysteries* (1912) was issued anonymously, but the first letters in each story spell out THE AUTHOR IS GELETT BURGESS — and the last letters read FALSE TO LIFE AND FALSE TO ART. The detective-hero of the book, Astro, wears a jeweled turban, silk robes, and keeps a white pet lizard.

Burgess used San Francisco settings in *The Heart Line* (1907), *The Reign of Queen Isyl* (1903), and *The Picarroons* (1904), the last two co-authored with Will Irwin in New York. When Irwin, who had also lived near here at 1041½ Vallejo, heard about the disastrous 1906 fire he sat down and wrote the fine memoir *The City That Was* in four hours.

*Across the street and a few
steps west is another of San
Francisco's one-block streets:*

9 **RUSSIAN HILL PLACE**   In Virginia Rath's series of mysteries set in San Francisco, her amateur sleuth Michael Dundas lives in this street — undoubtedly in one of the houses on the west side designed by Willis Polk. *The Dark Cavalier* (1938) introduced Dundas, who runs a fashionable women's clothing store called Giselle's and is acutely aware when a woman is poorly dressed — before *or* after she's murdered. Rath lived at 1843 Leavenworth off Vallejo and knew this area well. *A Dirge for Her* (1947) makes especially good use of the parks and stair-streets on this part of Russian Hill. Her friend Mary Collins used the weird old Humphrey-Giffens house on Chestnut, now gone, as the setting for her mystery *The Sister of Cain* (1943) — and Lenore Glen Offord, for years mystery critic for the *Chronicle*, set her first book here: *Murder on Russian Hill* (1938).

*Turn east again, back up
Vallejo—you're following
Dundas's route as he chases a
murderer down the tree-lined
Vallejo Street stairs. On your
right you will come to a shingle-
style home at:*

10 **1013-1017 VALLEJO**   Mrs. Virgil Thomas commissioned Willis Polk to design a house on her property; his fee was the eastern third of the building, 1013 Vallejo (which has, incidentally, the best view). Built in 1892, this innovative house was a lodestone for writers and artists in the early and middle 1890s, the years Polk lived here with his father and brother, before he married. With Burgess just up the street, and the home of Kate M. Atkinson only a block away, this area of Russian Hill clearly was a major center for *Les Jeunes.*

*At the bottom of these stairs
cross Taylor Street to:*

11 **INA COOLBRITH PARK**   One of only a handful that commemo-rate a writer, this park is a peaceful series of landscaped terraces on the steep eastern slope of Russian Hill — a pleasant place to eat a bag lunch or just sit on a bench to take in the panoramic view of San Francisco's skyscrapers, the vast expanse of Bay and Coast Range.

On a boulder at the entrance to the park, a plaque dedicated June 15, 1947, by the San Francisco Parlors, Native Daughters of the Golden West, describes Coolbrith's fascinating history. Born Josephine Donna Smith, March 10, 1841, in Nauvoo, Illinois, her father was a Mormon mystic, President of the quorum of High Priests and Brigadier General of the Nauvoo Legion, who died at age twenty-five. Her uncle was Joseph Smith, the prophet. Donna's mother renounced Mormonism and with a new husband chose to head West. The wagon train reached the Sierra Nevada range to face what could be called in football terminology a potential Donner Pass Situation: they were exhausted, unsure of the route, with winter snows only weeks away. James P. Beckwourth, the mulatto mountain man, scout, and dispatch rider, who came by his passion for taking scalps when he was a chief among the Crow Indians (he once clubbed one of his squaws to death for being disobedient), hap-pened across the caravan.

This primordial figure led them to safety across a pass in the moun-tains, placing the ten-year-old girl before him on the saddle as he guided the wagons west, saying to her: "There is California; there is your king-dom." (Today Mount Ina Coolbrith in Lassen County overlooks Beck-wourth Pass, in honor of this moment.)

The family settled in Los Angeles, where Donna published lyric poetry under the name "Ina". She married businessman and erstwhile actor Robert B. Carsley September 9, 1858 — a decided mistake. His jealousy reached insane levels, and in a rage he shot at his wife and threatened her with a carving knife. Donna went to her stepfather for protection; he wounded Carsley through the hand, which had to be amputated. She was granted a divorce December 30, 1861, on grounds of extreme cruelty, and moved to San Francisco early in 1862, adopting the name Ina Donna Coolbrith—combining her pseudonym, her own middle name, and her mother's maiden name—to begin a new life.

Hinted rumors of affairs the poet had with other writers persist. As Franklin Walker noted in *San Francisco's Literary Frontier*, she "managed to be a good friend to Bret Harte and Mark Twain, who are said to have been rivals for her smiles. One story even credits Mark Twain with calling his rival a dirty name in the heat of the contest, but the charge can hardly be taken seriously, for Harte, as a married man, was in no position to defend himself against fighting words."

Coolbrith lived near this park at 1604 Taylor before the 1906 fire destroyed her flat. (Her poem "San Francisco—April 18, 1906" evokes "Gray wind-blown ashes, broken toppling wall/ And ruined hearth.") Her collection of letters, memorabilia, and notes from which she had planned to write a definitive history of literary California were lost. Friends urged her to attempt the history from memory—it *still* would be the best work on the subject—but the aging Coolbrith declined with the comment, "Were I to write what I know, the book would be too sensational to print; but were I to write what I think proper it would be too dull to read."

From the park head north on Taylor, down the hill past Green Street. On the lefthand side of the street you'll see wooden steps rising to:

12 MACONDRAY LANE This little street is one of several scattered about the city—Pemberton, Vulcan, Fallon, Iron, the Filbert Street stairs—that are only passable by foot. No car can fit into the narrow path, no bicycle cope with the stairs. This lane is said to have been a favored walk for Ina Coolbrith. Also, it is the major contender as the original model for "Barbary Lane," the centerpiece for events in Armistead Maupin's popular series *Tales of the City*. Maupin mentions the "precipitous wooden stairway leading up to Barbary Lane," just climbed, in *More Tales of the City*.

Continue through the next and final block of Macondray, then left on Leavenworth, right on Green one block, right on Hyde. Half a block up on the west side Russell Street joins Hyde, and half a block down that short street is found:

13 29 RUSSELL Compared to the mansions, highrises, and Polk-designed houses already seen on Russian Hill, this two-story wood frame house certainly falls under the description "unassuming." Yet it is one of the most important literary sites in post-World War II America. In 1952 Jack Kerouac came West again, staying here for six months with Neal and Carolyn Cassady and their children while he worked on *Visions of Cody*, *On the Road*, and *Doctor Sax*.

Kerouac stayed in Neal's attic study. They had told each other that Kerouac would help Cassady with his writing, getting his incredible dialogues into prose form, but Kerouac benefited more as a writer from the discussions than Cassady. He revised an early version of *On the Road*, and he and Cassady spent hours talking into tape recorders, hoping to achieve an even more natural and spontaneous means of expression, beginning "not from preconceived idea of what to say about image but from jewel center of interest in subject of image at *moment of* writing and write outwards swimming in sea of language." Kerouac incorporated transcripts of some of these tapes into *Visions of Cody*, whose immediate and surreal style—like that of *Doctor Sax*—owes great debts to Cassady's running monologues, coming at and for the moment, and to their hours drinking and smoking pot. (They drove over to Berkeley during this period to try peyote with Philip Lamantia, who had participated in Washoe Indian ceremonials.)

In her excellent memoir *Heart Beat* (1976) Carolyn Cassady describes these months when Kerouac came more into his own style of writing, drafting three of his major works—and she gives the best descriptions of their day-to-day lives: the nighttime walks in North Beach and Chinatown, Neal's job as a brakeman for Southern Pacific, and her love affair with Kerouac—begun at Neal's suggestion—that continued off and on for years.

Jack Kerouac and Neal Cassady

Walking north on Hyde, you'll see just across Union Street to the right, Hastings alley, used as the major set for Francis Coppola's production of Hammett *(1982), based on Joe Gores' novel. The tall building on the southwest corner of Greenwich and Hyde two blocks up served as Agnes Moorehead's apartment house in the Bogart-Bacall film* Dark Passage *(1947), based on the David Goodis novel. Jack Kerouac came across another film crew on Russian Hill one night in 1952, shooting a scene for RKO's* Sudden Fear *starring Joan Crawford, and used his sketch of it—immediate experience—as "Joan Rawshanks in the Fog" in* Visions of Cody, *which Dennis McNally in his Kerouac biography* Desolate Angel *(1979) calls ". . . remarkable, possibly the best thing he ever wrote, re-creating a panoramic consciousness of the fog swirling through the floodlight beams, Joan and her mink coat, the director, the*

*crew, the wealthy tenants of the overlooking exclusive apartment build-
ing . . . the description became a separate but equal reality, as close to
an experience on paper as humanly possible. . . ."*

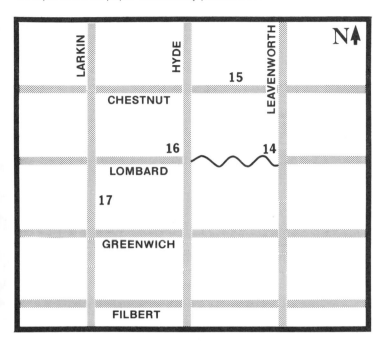

*Turn right on Filbert, down the
steep grade, then left on
Leavenworth. Two blocks north
will put you at the bottom of
the world-famous "Crooked
Street," where you'll find on
the northwest corner:*

14 **1000 LOMBARD** In her book *The Intruders* (1975) one-time
TV personality and *Examiner* columnist Pat Montandon details a
chain of unusual, possibly supernatural, events that transpired in the
late 1960s when she lived in the second floor, six-bedroom apartment of
this building — events leading to a suicide and other deaths. Montandon's
friend and personal secretary died in a mysterious fire in this apartment
June 21, 1969 — burned beyond recognition. Reports of ghosts in the
tower of the nearby San Francisco Art Institute, or in the Atherton mansion at California and Octavia, are among several traditions of spectral
phenomena in the city — with Montandon's one of the most recent.

*Another block north and west
on Chestnut will place you at:*

15 **930 and 944 CHESTNUT** *Les Jeunes* founder Bruce Porter
owned these houses in the 1920s in the city he and his fellows
termed a Pleasure Dome. Porter, who married a daughter of pragmatist
philosopher William James, is more renowned for his stained glass,

murals, and design work than for the small amount of writing contributed to *The Lark*. He was chairman of the committee that erected the Sevenson monument in Portsmouth Square and was a secretary of the San Francisco Guild of Arts and Crafts (his good friend Gelett Burgess also worked in the crafts as a furniture maker—"Old Furniture Made New, New Furniture Made Old"). Porter lived in No. 944, built in 1863, and leased No. 930, built in 1861.

Continue on Chestnut to Hyde, then up the famous Hyde Street hill that falls down to Fisherman's Wharf. Gelett Burgess's long poem, "The Ballad of the Hyde Street Grip," celebrates the cable car operators who work this grade. On the northwest corner of Hyde and Lombard you'll find the:

16 MRS. ROBERT LOUIS STEVENSON HOUSE After Stevenson's death in Samoa, December 3, 1894, his wife returned to the states and commissioned Willis Polk to design this home for her. It was completed in 1900. Many accounts insist Stevenson himself lived here, though of course he never did. In 1915 his wife's ashes were placed in Stevenson's tomb on Mount Vaea in Samoa, and the romantic saga of Robert Louis Stevenson and Fanny Osbourne—begun in France, continued in Monterey, San Francisco, Silverado, Scotland, and the South Seas—was complete.

Another block south will put you on the corner of Hyde and Greenwich, where author Idwal Jones—The Vineyard, Ark of Empire—hosted literary parties in his "eyrie" in the 1930s. Turn west into Greenwich. Walk past the Alice Marble Tennis Courts, and turn to your right down the path into:

17 GEORGE STERLING GLADE This living memorial to George Sterling, King of Bohemian San Francisco, was landscaped in 1928 on land owned by the Spring Valley Water Company. S. P. Eastman, president of the utility, was a friend of the poet and a fellow member of the Bohemian Club; he also had erected a tiled bench, bearing a memorial plaque with the verse:

> Oh Singer, fled afar!
> The erected darkness shall but isle the star
> That was your voice to men,
> Till morning come again
> And of the night that song alone remain.

Eastman, Haig Patigian, and Edward F. O'Day spoke at the dedication, and Charles Bulotti sang "Song of Friendship" accompanied by Uda

Waldrop on a grand piano. Sterling and Waldrop composed this song; a bar of the words and music were featured on the plaque. Then Waldrop's wife sang a favorite with Sterling, "The Soft Caress of Night," and the ceremonies—attended by A. M. Robertson, architect Gardner Dailey, Maynard Dixon, Dorothea Lange, Charles Caldwell Dobie, Sara Bard Field, Porter Garnett, Mrs. Frank C. Havens, Annie Laurie, Charmian London, Xavier Martinez, Gabriel Moulin, John McLaren, John Henry Nash, and many more—were over. In the 1960s the bench cracked when the earth shifted under it—the plaque was stolen in the 1970s by vandals, or by an over-avid Sterling collector.

On July 10, 1982, a committee formed by this writer, Bill Kostura, and John Law installed the present plaque on a concrete column in the glade. The two remaining sections of the original tiled bench are a few steps beyond the new memorial. Speakers for the dedication were Lawrence Dickey, a Sterling·scholar and member of the Bohemian Club, Ray Faraday Nelson of the California Writers Club, and Becky London Fleming, daughter of Sterling's great comrade Jack London. Donald Sidney-Fryer read from Sterling's verse. About one hundred people attended the ceremonies and picnic—among them members of the George Sterling Circle, the Jack London Club, the Upton Sinclair Society, and such individuals as the poets Lawrence Ferlinghetti, Philip Lamantia, Nancy Peters, G. Sutton Breiding, Suicide Club founder Gary Warne, and the columnist Herb Caen. The plaque bears lines from Sterling's famous hymn to San Francisco "The Cool, Gray City of Love" —a title often invoked in Caen's columns:

> Tho the dark be cold and blind,
> Yet her sea-fog's touch is kind,
> And her mightier caress,
>   Is joy and the pain thereof:
> And great is thy tenderness,
>   O cool, gray city of love!

Soon after the dedication the Public Utilities Commission officially named this area which is now land managed by the Water Department, the George Sterling Glade—it had been known unofficially for decades as "George Sterling Park." Sterling's other great tribute to his city would have served equally well on the plaque to commemorate the poet's lasting identification with "The City by the Sea—San Francisco".

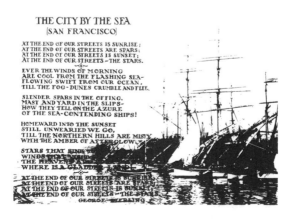

POLK GULCH

Michael and Joanna McClure, Fosters Cafeteria, 1956

The Polk Gulch area between Nob Hill and Pacific Heights provides a quick walk of six blocks that covers some of the most controversial and influential writing done in San Francisco.

			N↑
3	VAN NESS		
4 SACRAMENTO		POLK	
CALIFORNIA		**2**	
PINE			
BUSH			
		1	
SUTTER			

Begin at the intersection of Polk and Sutter. The 2 Clement 3 Jackson, 4 Sutter, and 19 Polk lines all cross this intersection. Several other Muni lines come within a couple of blocks.

The building on the northeast corner of Polk and Sutter was once named:

THE
HOTEL WENTLEY POEMS

1 THE HOTEL WENTLEY Through its doors at 1214 Polk passed many of the writers of the San Francisco Renaissance and the Beats. Several moved into the Wentley apartments when the old Montgomery Block was demolished in 1959, such as John Wieners, whose *The Hotel Wentley Poems*, written here, was published in 1958.

Fosters Cafeteria downstairs naturally became a hangout for the resident writers and artists and their friends. Ginsberg met painter Robert La Vigne here in December 1954. Telling him about the artistic scene in New York, centering on the San Remo Bar at the corner of Bleecker and MacDougal Streets, Ginsberg went with the artist to his apartment. On the wall he saw an enormous painting of a naked boy "with his legs spread" and was transfixed with desire. In a moment the model, Peter Orlovsky, an ex-lover of the painter, came into the room.

Soon enough Ginsberg and Orlovsky were companions, sitting in Fosters, exchanging vows of love. Ginsberg has said "there was a kind of celestial cold fire that crept over us and blazed up and illuminated the entire cafeteria and made it an eternal place."

Ginsberg arrived in San Francisco in 1954. His first residence in the Bay Area was the Marconi Hotel in North Beach. He spent time with Neal Cassady, visited Robert Duncan, and read Kerouac's *Essentials of Modern Prose*, while working days as a market researcher on Montgomery Street. By October he'd moved to 755 Pine Street, #5, and was meeting with Kenneth Rexroth and Robert Duncan — and seeing much of Orlovsky, LeVigne, and Michael and Joanna McClure at Foster's Cafeteria in Polk Gulch.

After an early December visit with Cassady, LeVigne, Natalie Jackson, and Orlovsky at 1403 Gough Street, Ginsberg moved into a room just across the street from the Hotel Wentley. There he wrote seminal journals (to be published in 1985 by Harper & Row) during this period of West Coast influence and inspiration.

Polk Street has been a center (along with Castro at Market) for gay culture in San Francisco for well over a decade, but with the exception of the numerous gay bars and dance clubs the character of the street has not changed much over the years. Polk remains a street of small shops serving residents of Nob and Russian Hills, Pacific Heights, Polk Gulch, and the Tenderloin, just as it was when Frank Norris lived nearby in the 1800s. Many of the blocks still consist of the original buildings constructed after the 1906 fire and give a good view of the architectural look of the day.

Unfortunately, the intersection of Polk and California, three blocks north of the Wentley Hotel, has seen a lot of modern construction and no longer evokes the late 1800s when it housed:

2 McTEAGUE'S DENTAL PARLORS ". . . in a corner room of the second floor over the branch post-office. . . . McTeague made it do for a bedroom as well, sleeping on the big bed-lounge against the wall opposite the window. There was a washstand behind the screen in the corner where he manufactured his moulds. In the round bay window were his operating chair, his dental engine, and the movable rack on which he laid out his instruments. Three chairs, a bargain at the second-hand store, ranged themselves against the wall with military precision underneath a steel engraving of the court of Lorenzo de Medici, which he had bought because there were a great many figures in it for the money."

Frank Norris's *McTeague* (1899), sub-titled "A Story of San Francisco," preceded publication of Theodore Drieser's *Sister Carrie* by a year and fully introduced naturalism into American letters; only *The Red Badge of Courage* (1895) and *Maggie: A Girl of the Streets* (1896) by the brilliant Stephen Crane anticipated Norris's work. Here was not the polite "realism" of William Dean Howells — "For McTeague was a young giant, carrying his huge shock of blond hair six feet three inches from the ground; moving his immense limbs, heavy with ropes of muscle, slowly, ponderously. His hands were enormous, red, and covered with a fell of stiff yellow hair; they were hard as wooden mallets, strong as vises. . . . Often he dispensed with forceps and extracted a refractory tooth with his thumb and finger."

Just as Dashiell Hammett in his rooms a few blocks from here in the 1920s would toss aside the propriety of the classical mystery story and move murder violently onto the streets ("where people were good at it") or Allen Ginsberg would kick mid-twentieth century American poetry in its academic ass with "Howl," Norris moved the scene from realistic if boring portrayals of society life in Boston to genuinely realistic descriptions of street life in San Francisco, where the characters had some blood in them. Close on Norris's heels came Jack London, who carried the "red-blood" realistic school into our century and paved the way for Hammett, John Steinbeck, Jack Kerouac, and others who wrote about life as they saw it—and who got out into the real world to see it.

Frank Norris

One of San Francisco's major claims in American literature is the fact that several of the first and greatest of our realistic authors have lived and written here. The literary antics of Les Jeunes or the romantic verses of George Sterling might best represent the qualities of wild fun and stylish glamor which have made the city a tourist capital of the world, but the truly influential writing has covered the back alleys and dives that most tourists want to avoid. (When Steinbeck's Tortilla Flat *was published in 1935 hotel clerks in Monterey were instructed to tell curious visitors that no such area existed.)*

By the time Norris wrote his novels as a disciple of Zola, naturalism was on its way out as a force in French literature. The work of Norris, Dreiser, and other Americans gave naturalism a longer life and a more important place in world literature. A major tenet of naturalism is that you write about what you know, and although Norris began McTeague *as a student at Harvard he set it in the area he knew best, the Polk Gulch.*

*Go north one block to
Sacramento and a block west
to Van Ness. On the northwest
side of the intersection
once stood:*

3 **1822 SACRAMENTO** In this block was located the old Henry Scott residence—a large two-story wood frame house, the front covered with bay windows, over the doorway a small ornamental balcony supported by Corinthian columns. Frank Norris was born in Chicago in 1870 but visited here with his parents in 1884. The next year his parents returned to San Francisco and bought this house. Norris fell into the company of *Les Jeunes*, served as an editor on *The Wave* — where he wrote much under the name "Justin Sturges" — and began his serious writing career here, though in time he would travel to New York, Paris, South Africa, and Cuba. (Norris was furious when Gelett Burgess, whose work Norris considered completely superficial, went to New York on the strength of his amusing writing ahead of the more serious naturalist.)

The home of Vandover in Norris's *Vandover and the Brute* (1914) is modeled on this home where he lived in his teens. His novels *Blix* and *Moran of the Lady Letty* also feature a San Francisco scene. Before he could finish *The Wolf*, a novel which would complete his trilogy "Epic of the Wheat" begun with *The Octopus* and *The Pit*, Norris died of peritoinitus from a ruptured appendix. He was thirty-two years old.

Across the street and a few yards up on the south side you will find:

4 1871 and 1875 SACRAMENTO In these apartment houses William Chambers Morrow spent his last years in San Francisco. Born in Selma, Alabama, in 1854, W. C. Morrow came to the Bay Area in 1879, and his first stories appeared the same year. He contributed to the *Argonaut*, the *Overland Monthly*, and other magazines and newspapers of the era, and supported himself for a time by writing promotional material for Southern Pacific Railroad. His novel *Blood Money* (1882) is a mystery about buried treasure; *A Man, His Mark* (1900) is a romance; *Lentala of the South Seas* (1908), illustrated by local artist Maynard Dixon, is an adventure novel. He also completed *Bohemian Paris of Today* (1899) from the notebooks of Edouard Cucuel, and wrote *The Logic of Punctuation for All Who Have to Do with Written English* (1926).

Morrow's enduring fame, however, depends on his short stories, partly collected as *The Ape, the Idiot, and Other People* in 1897. His tales of the South and the Civil War, his gruesome horror stories, were the major influence on the fiction of Ambrose Bierce. In fact, when Morrow once disagreed in print with some Biercian *dictum*, the most feared columnist in San Francisco admitted, well, yes, that great writer Morrow *did* have a point. Bierce especially praised Morrow's extremely vivid scene in *Blood Money* where a doctor has to amputate his own leg. Very few writers have ever approached Morrow for clinically realistic scenes of cold grue: "His Unconquerable Enemy" from 1889 remains to this day one of the most horrifying tales ever printed. "Over an Absinthe Bottle" is another noteworthy story, set in *fin de siécle* San Francisco.

Morrow and his wife Lydia lived in 1875 Sacramento in 1914 and 1915, then next door at No. 1871 from 1916-1921. During this period Morrow commuted by ferry to Berkeley to teach creative writing at the Cora L. Williams Institute; his classes are said to be the first in fiction writing conducted locally — Charles Caldwell Dobie was a successful graduate from one of Morrow's earlier courses. This early master of the realistic horror story died April 23, 1923, in Ojai in Ventura County.

PACIFIC HEIGHTS

Gertrude Atherton, 1908

Pacific Heights with its rows of mansions has long had a reputation as a neighborhood for the rich and successful—doctors, lawyers, stock brokers, even an occasional writer. Today the Pulitzer Prize-winning playwright and novelist Jerome Weidman lives here. So does the bestselling romance writer Danielle Steel—in a forty-two-room mansion shared with her husband, shipping magnate John Traina. A brief walk in the area about Lafayette Park provides a glimpse into writers of the past who earned wealth and status in society with their work.

Begin at the intersection of
Octavia and Bush. The 2 Clement,
3 Jackson, and 4 Sutter lines
all stop a block south on
Sutter.
On the northeast corner of
Octavia and Bush stands:

1 1700 OCTAVIA Erle Stanley Gardner, one of the bestselling writers of all time, lived in this apartment house in 1934 and 1935. Gardner was a one-man self-proclaimed "Fiction Factory"—he set himself a quota of 1,200,000 words per year and met it. For the pulp magazines in the 1920s he turned out a 10,000-word story every three days, 365 days each year, in addition to practicing law full-time. By the time he came to stay in San Francisco in February, 1934, Gardner had put his Fiction Factory on wheels, traveling about the country in a Hupmobile-8 and trailer, dictating novels to his secretaries. His biographer Dorothy B. Hughes notes: "His name for the venture was Podunking, from the old theatrical name of Podunk for the smallest of small towns. . . . In his first eight days of Podunking, he dictated three novelettes, and almost all of a book. He started the book on Sunday, dictated eight thousand words that day, fifteen thousand on Monday. . . ."

In this fashion Gardner wrote eighty-two novels about lawyer Perry Mason (a character who made Gardner a millionaire), twenty-four mysteries about detectives Bertha Cool and Donald Lam, and several dozen other books. The Perry Mason novels alone have sold some 300,000,000 copies. From this temporary base in San Francisco Gardner made camping trips to Yosemite and the desert. He wrote many magazine stories in this period, as well as a never-published novel *The Hostile Witness*, and the Perry Mason books *The Case of the Curious Bride*, *The Case of the Counterfeit Eye*, *The Case of the Caretaker's Cat*, and *The Case of the Sleepwalker's Niece*, all published between 1934 and 1935.

*From this site go one block
north to Pine, one block west
to Laguna, and one block north
to California. The building on
the southwest corner is:*

2 **2101 CALIFORNIA**   Novelist Gertrude Atherton kept an apartment
in this building for about sixteen years. She first leased it in 1929,
when she returned to her native city from years in New York, London,
Paris, Vienna. In Vienna the sixty-six-year-old Atherton took "rejuvena-
tion" treatments; her novel on the theme of a woman regaining her
youth and beauty, *Black Oxen*, was one of the ten best-selling books in
1923. (Atherton lived to be ninety-one, and it is said she seemed amazingly youthful in her last years here in San Francisco.)

Although she continued to travel, Atherton maintained her apartment in this building until her late eighties, when she moved into her
daughter's home at 2280 Green (now gone). In these places she held
famous social and literary salons in the evenings, and served on civic
commissions in the day. Before the turn of the century her novels had
made her famous as one of the most important California writers, and
Atherton continued her work. Two years before her death the interesting
My San Francisco (1946) appeared, with a chapter by the feminist
Atherton on outstanding San Francisco women — a list in which Atherton herself earned a high position.

*Return east one block along
California to Octavia. The
ornate mansion on the northeast corner is:*

3 **1990 CALIFORNIA**   Built in 1881 for Dominga de Goni Atherton,
this place perhaps has its greatest reputation today as one of San
Francisco's haunted houses. Its literary connection comes courtesy of
Dominga's daughter-in-law, Gertrude Atherton.

George Atherton was aptly characterized in Antoinette May's *Haunted Houses and Wandering Ghosts of California* (1977) as a man "who
barely had the initiative to tie his own shoelaces." His father Faxon Dean
Atherton owned a ranch covering a square mile between Menlo Park
and Fair Oaks — now the city of Atherton, named in honor of the rancher. His mother Dominga, a native of Chile, was described by Gertrude
as "a tyrannical old lady" who "was exactly five feet in height and
weighed two hundred pounds." It was the forceful Dominga who managed the estate and its house, Valparaiso.

Gertrude came into the exclusive social circle of the Athertons when
"for once and only once in his life" George "developed a persistence
worthy of a better cause": he decided to marry the eighteen-year-old
Gertrude Franklin Horn. It is interesting to note that George had been

courting Gertrude's Mother, fourteen years his senior, when his attention strayed to the daughter — who was monumentally bored with her life on a ranch down the peninsula.

George proposed five times; she "either ignored or insulted him." The sixth proposal came as she sat reading Plato, and the distracted girl replied, "Oh, well, I don't care. One has to marry some time, I suppose. But do leave me in peace. I prefer Plato." George acted on this casual acknowledgment: the next afternoon he drove her, as was by that time usual, for her Saturday visit with her grandfather in San Jose. But first George headed for a priest's house, the marriage license in his pocket. "For a moment I was dumbfounded, then furious, and threatened to jump out of the carriage," Gertrude wrote in her *Adventures of a Novelist* (1932). "He whipped up the horse. I began to feel dazzled. Surely this was romance and drama. . . . I felt like the heroine of a novel."

Her marriage to George Atherton was colossally unsatisfying — the heroines in many of the novels *she* would write later break away from the strangling presence of their husbands in search of independence and true personal fulfillment. She noted in her biography:

> If a woman's place is the home, a man's place is anywhere else between the hours of nine and six, and it seemed to me that the worst trial I had yet been called upon to endure was having a husband continually on my hands. I couldn't talk to him, for he was interested in nothing but horses. Morever, he was jealous of the very books I read, and if I smiled to myself he wanted to know what I was thinking about, and accused me of having secrets from him. I tried my best to make him read and did succeed in adjusting him to *Peveril of the Peak*. He plodded at it faithfully every day to please me, but hadn't finished it when he died nine years later.

George's death was an unexpected *coup*. Dominga's nephew, a Chilean naval officer, came into port in San Francisco in 1887. The Athertons constantly entertained the officers of the *Pilcomayo*, and Dominga hosted a gala society ball in their honor in her new home (she had abandoned the ranch and moved to the city immediately upon Faxon Atherton's death). George talked loudly about returning with the ship to visit his ancestral land, but Gertrude "was full of matrimonial wisdom by this time, and knew that if I were complacent nothing would budge him from my side. I therefore opposed the plan violently."

George left on the *Pilcomayo* and Gertrude prepared to relish a few months without her wimpy spouse. A few days out to sea George died from a ruptured kidney. His cousin placed the body in a barrel of rum to preserve it until it could be shipped back to San Francisco. In Tahiti the barrel was transferred to another vessel. The Most Famous Anecdote about this arrangement is that the barrel was unloaded by longshoremen unaware of its contents, put on a wain and taken to the delivery entrance of 1990 California. The butler popped open the barrel and up bobbed the completely pickled George Atherton.

Alas, this story — popular then and still in use today — is only a legend. Gertrude said that they were well aware of the contents of the barrel and had it taken directly to a mortuary. The reports of ghosts in this building usually refer to feminine spectres, possibly Dominga, or Carrie Rouseau, who lived here with her fifty cats from 1923 until her death in 1974. Odd drafts rush through rooms, rapping sounds emanate from walls, temperatures shift randomly from warm to chill — such are the phenomena reported by past residents. One psychic gave the mansion a reading:

she sensed the presence of three dominant female spirits—Dominga, Gertrude, and Carrie—and one submissive male spirit, "pale and frail," doubtless the unfortunate George.

*Go up Octavia to Sacramento
and turn left. A few doors down
the street you'll find:*

4 2151 SACRAMENTO   A plaque mounted next to the entranceway notifies the unsuspecting passerby that "This house, built in 1881, was once occupied by Sir Arthur Conan Doyle." True, the creator of the immortal Sherlock Holmes and Dr. John H. Watson did "occupy" this house for a couple of hours one morning during his single trip to San Francisco in late May and early June 1923. Doyle visited Dr. Abrams in his home here, then went with his family on an excursion to Mount Tamalpais and Muir Woods before returning to the city to deliver a lecture that evening. The Doyles stayed at the Clift Hotel their week in San Francisco.

This plaque was installed by a publicist who owned the house in the 1970s, and for all its exaggerated notions of what constitutes occupancy, it is still a hell of a plaque.

*Another of San Francisco's
rare literary plaques is the last
stop on this tour. Walk at an
angle across Lafayette Park.
On the opposite side of the
park, near where Octavia
connects with Washington,
you'll find a small concrete
pedestal beside one of the
paved pathways. On this
pedestal is the:*

George Atherton

5 GERTRUDE ATHERTON PLAQUE   The dedication of this plaque on the 125th anniversary of her birth October 30, 1982, drew a crowd of about one hundred people, who went to the thirty-room Whittier mansion (now headquarters of the California Historical Society, on the northeast corner of Jackson and Laguna, two blocks away) after the dedication to hear an evening program featuring Dr. James D. Hart, director of the Bancroft Library, and Atherton biographer Emily Leider. Atherton's granddaughter Florence Dickey of Santa Rosa presented brilliant reminiscences of the novelist—the youthful-looking Atherton would not permit introductions of her "grandchildren," so Florence became for social purposes a "niece." This site in Lafayette Park is close to several major Atherton locations—2101 California, Dominga's mansion, the vanished house on Green Street. In the last years of their marriage the incompatible George and Gertrude Atherton also rented a flat further out on California Street, but close enough to George's mother for him to feel comfortable.

FISHERMAN'S WHARF

The Hyde Street Pier

On first thought Fisherman's Wharf, San Francisco's tourist mecca, might seem completely lacking in literary sites. No doubt enough writers have made the pilgrimage to Ghirardelli Square or the Cannery, and returned again with visiting friends and relatives — a ritual of the modern city — but the great Fisherman's Wharf novel has not appeared. (Would John Steinbeck have written *Cannery Row* if the Cannery Row he had known was made up of the boutiques, cafes, and antique shops of today instead of the active canneries, marine biology labs, and whorehouses of his time?) Nonetheless, a visit to the Wharf offers several literary associations.

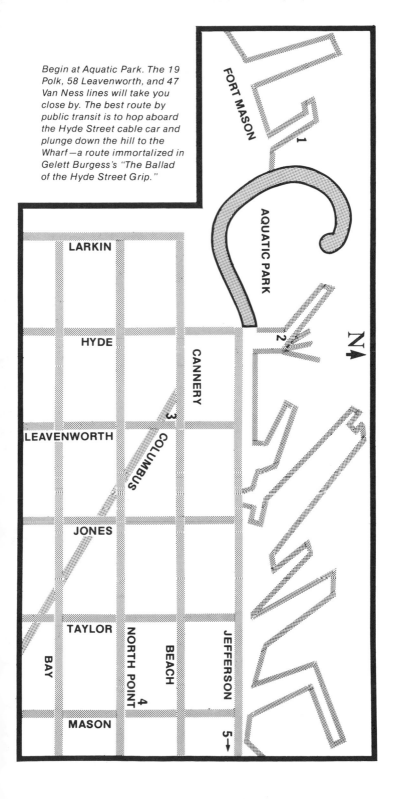

Begin at Aquatic Park. The 19 Polk, 58 Leavenworth, and 47 Van Ness lines will take you close by. The best route by public transit is to hop aboard the Hyde Street cable car and plunge down the hill to the Wharf—a route immortalized in Gelett Burgess's "The Ballad of the Hyde Street Grip."

FORT MASON

1

AQUATIC PARK

N

2

LARKIN

HYDE

CANNERY

3

COLUMBUS

LEAVENWORTH

JONES

TAYLOR

NORTH POINT

BEACH

JEFFERSON

BAY

4

MASON

5

*Walk northwest around the
loop of the park. Where the
long Municipal Pier continues
to curve out into the Bay,
angle left toward the shorter
pier a few steps to the west.
This is the old:*

1 ALCATRAZ PIER From this pier, prisoners were ferried to the
Rock before San Francisco's "super-prison for super-criminals"
was locked down in 1963. Today Alcatraz is open as part of the park
system, with tour boats leaving on a regular schedule from Pier 43 (an
excellent tour).

In a small holding cell on this dock the artist, writer, and saloon-
keeper Barnaby Conrad once had his studio. Conrad was an *aficionado*
of bullfighting, writing stories and novels about bullfighting, painting
bullfighting pictures. He opened El Matador bar on Broadway in North
Beach in the 1950s, that unlikely decade when John Steinbeck, artist
Dong Kingman, and columnist Herb Caen were frequenting many of
the same hangouts as the Beats. Conrad's most recent book is a non-
fiction account of a true crime, a not unexpected interest for a writer
who'd keep a studio on this grim pier.

*Return along the shore of
Aquatic Park to Jefferson
Street and the:*

2 HYDE STREET PIER On this pier the scholarly Humphrey Van
Weyden had thought he would dock, as usual, when returning from
Sausalito. But Van Weyden's boat met the *Ghost* on the dark bay, and
the scholar found himself shanghaied and under the command of
Wolf Larsen, in Jack London's classic of high adventure, *The Sea Wolf*
(1904).

A number of old ships are berthed at Hyde Street pier today and for a
small fee you can tour this innovative museum. A walk on the decks of
the ferry boat *Eureka* especially recalls the days when George Sterling
wrote his romantic poems en route from Oakland, and the foggy night
when the Hammett's Continental Op was sapped and tossed overboard
in the typically dangerous course of another case.

From this vantage point you can look across the bay to Angel Island,
now a State Park, where Richard Henry Dana collected a year's supply
of wood for his ship *Alert* when it stopped here the winter of 1835-36.

*Walk across Jefferson to the
Cannery and through the
arcade to Bay Street. Across
Bay from the Cannery Cinema
you'll see a triangular park
bordered by Beach, Leavenworth, and Columbus, which
was once proposed as a:*

3 JOSEPH CONRAD MEMORIAL In the late 1970s a number of
fans of that great writer of the sea worked to have this land dedicated
as a memorial park to Joseph Conrad — the only such memorial in

America. The city set aside this parcel. The Maritime Museum, located on Bay just beyond Ghirardelli Square, secured the transom and rudder of the bark *Otago*, a vessel Conrad commanded in 1888 and 1889. A bronze bust of the author by English sculptor Sir Jacob Epstein was donated to the museum, and a bronze plaque with a paragraph from Conrad's *The Shadow Line* (". . . Amongst her companions moored to the bank, and all bigger than herself, she looked like a creature of high breed — an Arab steed in a string of cart horses . . . I knew that, like some rare woman, she was one of those creatures whose mere existence is enough to awaken an unselfish delight.") was readied for placement in the park. Then the infamous Proposition 13 cut back the city's funds. Director Francis Coppola, living in San Francisco at the time, donated proceeds from the local premiere of his film *Apocalypse Now* (based on Conrad's *Heart of Darkness*) to the project; but they were not enough to see the memorial to full completion.

The park today is neatly kept, a pleasant spot to rest, but there is no bust or plaque to mark it as a memorial to the Polish native who became one of the finest stylists in English.

Angle up Columbus to North Point, and walk three blocks east to Mason. At 400 North Point on the northwest corner you'll see:

4 **LONGSHOREMAN'S HALL** "Today I went down to the new hall, near Fisherman's Wharf, but was not dispatched," wrote longshoreman-philosopher Eric Hoffer in his journal. "How disturbing the change in routine due to the removal of the hall! Of course, in a few weeks the new routine will be firmly established and seem eternal."

This present hall, opened in 1959, quickly became a major literary landmark in San Francisco — even as more and more of the dock work for the longshoremen moved from the city to Oakland. Hoffer's journal, kept between June 1958 and May 1959, and published as *Working and Thinking on the Waterfront* (1969), records his assignments on the *Dortheim, Lurline, Hawaiian Pilot, Hawaiian Packer*, the Norwegian *Hoegh Silverstream* and *Evangen* and *Tancred, Samadinda, Dowa Maru, Mikagesan Maru, Java Mail, Loch Loyal*, the Dutch *Batjan* and *Banggai* and *Duvendyk*, the German *Henriette Wilhelmine Schulte* and *Ditmar Koel* and *Thorstein, Tar Heel Mariner, Steel Scientist, Old Col-*

ony, Korean Bear, Keito Maru, Ocean Joyce, Pacific Stronghold, Pope
and Talbot *Voyager,* "the beautiful French ship *Maryland"* . . . a poetic
roster of a bygone era, when longshoremen loaded and unloaded
ships on piers 7, 9, 15, 17, 19, 22, 23, 24, 26, 31, 32, 34, 35, 37, 38, 39,
40, 41, 45A, 46B, 48B, 14th Street, Howard Street. . . . Many of these
piers are inactive today, and Hoffer's infrequent assignments to Encinal
and Oakland presage the shift of maritime trade to the East Bay.

In 1942 at age forty Hoffer began working on the waterfront, when
he was kept out of WWII by a medical disability. His first book, *The True
Believer, Thoughts on the Nature of Mass Movements* (1951) made his
fame—it was a favorite of President Dwight Eisenhower and became a
bestseller. (Hoffer had solidified the manuscript of the book during a
strike in 1946.) An interview with Eric Sevareid on CBS TV September
19, 1967, made Hoffer a celebrity and he was invited to the White House
to talk with President Lyndon Johnson.

The critic Grover Sales has written that "Eric Hoffer is to philosophy
what Rod McKuen is to poetry"—Hoffer certainly has his share of de-
tractors. But when he writes about his dock work or the many years he
spent as a hobo and migrant farm worker in the Depression, he speaks
with authority. He ignored money his entire life, working just enough to
pay expenses to allow him time to read and think. He said working as a
longshoreman "was like being on the bum in one place," but when he
felt he was going soft and fitting too well into the routine, Hoffer (in his
50s and 60s) would take $5 and an extra pair of underwear, get on a bus
heading south, and get off at a random town en route. "The idea was,"
he said, "you have five dollars, you get a room there, and then you have
to cut the mustard. I used to come back with a hundred and fifty bucks. I
did it time and again. . . . I always said you could drop me anywhere in
California and within fifteen minutes I was going to have a job."

Gary Snyder, Philip Whalen, Lew Welch after the reading, 1964

The Beat poet Lew Welch also worked out of this building as a longshoreman, and participated in a poetry reading here the night of June
12, 1964, with Gary Snyder and Philip Whalen. Don Carpenter organized this reading after Snyder returned from several years in Japan. In
an article about the event (*California Living* March 29, 1981), Carpenter
describes the longshoreman-poet:

Tall, thin, handsome, always wearing a crooked smile, Welch liked to think of himself as a hip con-man. He liked to drink and sit in the Jazz Workshop and listen to good music. He loved Sausalito and the No Name Bar and he loved to play pool and skulk about the Tenderloin. He had just come down from the Trinity Mountains where he had been living in a little cabin for two years, writing, and, incidentally, winning a turkey in a turkey shoot. He was a complex and interesting guy, who had worked in Chicago as an advertising writer, had traveled cross country with Jack Kerouac, and I don't know what else.

Welch saw a copy of the City Lights edition of Gregory Corso's *Gasoline* in the San Francisco airport on the way through on his commercial job and decided then and there to quit and move to San Francisco. He became a legendary figure in the Beat mythology as Kerouac's drinking companion during his last trips to San Francisco (he was "David Wain" in *Big Sur*). When visiting Gary Snyder on his place near Nevada City in 1971 he walked off into the mountains and was never seen again.

Carpenter rented Longshoreman's Hall for $75, with doubts about recovering his costs. The largest crowd at a poetry reading before this was about two hundred people who came to hear Allen Ginsberg read "Kaddish" at the old Longshoreman's Hall at 150 Golden Gate. Carpenter almost lost his money simply because he forgot to put a ticket-taker at the door. Hundreds eased in free, hundreds more paid the one-dollar fee. An estimated 800 people attended. But he paid his costs, threw a blowout at Tosca's afterward, and gave each poet one hundred dollars. "Hell," said Lew. "A hundred bucks for half hour's work? Not bad!"

The first Family Dog Rock 'n' Roll Dance and Concert, "A Tribute to Dr. Strange," was held at Longshoreman's Hall October 16, 1965, featuring Jefferson Airplane, the Marbles, the Great Society, and the Charlatans. It launched the hippie movement into full, glorious orbit. "At this dance or possibly the next one," wrote long-time *Chronicle* music critic Ralph J. Gleason in *The Jefferson Airplane and the San Francisco Sound* (1969), "poet Allen Ginsberg, long haired and shaggy bearded, led a leaping line in a snake dance for hours and ended up doing the *hora* in the center of the floor."

On January 21, 22 and 23, 1966, came the Trips Festival, conceived by Stewart Brand and managed by Bill Graham of the San Francisco Mime Troupe. The night of Saturday the 22nd was an Acid Test by Ken Kesey and the Merry Pranksters, who had given one earlier in the city in Graham's Fillmore West. The Grateful Dead, Big Brother and the Holding Company and other bands, a light show, five movie screens, and psychedelic visions provided the entertainment. Kesey wore a spacesuit and bubble helmet and held down his place on a platform high above the floor. Neal Cassady, now the Prankster "Speedlimit" and driver, always a driver, of the Prankster bus, swung out over the railing and dangled over the crowd. The Trips Festival drew an estimated 20,000 people.

Longshoreman's Hall has been a center for many other events, and many other worker-writers. Mike Vawter, Norm Young, George Benet, Ken Fox, Gene Dennis, Herb Mills, Brian Nelsen, and Max Mallia all contributed to *Waterfront Writers: The Literature of Work* (1979), edited by Bob Carson.

Walk north on Mason toward
the rigged masts of the
Balclutha *and turn right on*
Jefferson to Pier 39.

John Steinbeck also worked on the waterfront here in the late 1920s.
Ernest K. Gann's Fiddler's Green *(1950) features a good waterfront*
scene. San Francisco native Peter B. Kyne once owned a working-
man's clothing store on the Embarcadero before going on to write
many novels, many of those in his popular series about Cappy Ricks; *he*
said "the world lost a good salesman when I became a writer."

On the southwest corner of
Pier 39, on the second level
where the walkway from the
garage across the street
angles down to this large
shopping complex, you'll find:

5 THE EAGLE CAFE Of course the Eagle hasn't always been perched up here—it used to be ground-level, in a lot across the street, and this pier did once berth commercial vessels. Eric Hoffer notes in his journal for October 5, 1958: "Eight hours at Pier 39. A pleasant day. The work was steady but not strenuous, and the company good."

When plans to change this pier into a shopping center went into action, the Eagle Cafe was targeted for demolition. The developers needed its lot to put up the big parking garage. Protest was immediate: the Eagle was as much a cultural center for the waterfront as Spec's, Vesuvio's or City Lights were for North Beach, a rugged part of San Francisco's café society, a place where longshoremen (writers or not) had been going for decades. Ferlinghetti was one of the many writers working to save the Eagle (you'll find it in his "An Elegy to Dispel Gloom" of 1978). A compromise, not a bad one at that, was reached. The Eagle was raised intact in 1978 to its present site, and the garage went up on its old ground. You can imagine the Eagle going strong fifty years down the road, even if the rest of the complex sits abandoned on rotting pylons. If you get here around lunch time, it's a good inexpensive place to eat, or to have a drink to—and perhaps with—our waterfront writers.

MARK TWAIN

Mark Twain in San Francisco, 1868

"All modern American literature comes from one book by Mark Twain called *Huckleberry Finn*. . . ."

—Ernest Hemingway, *The Green Hills of Africa*, 1935

Samuel L. Clemens is one of a handful of American writers in the nineteenth century who wrote books that are still read for honest pleasure. Many critics consider Twain the greatest author this country has produced. He had an unparalleled range, encompassing the native folk fable and tall tale as in "The Celebrated Jumping Frog of Calaveras County," broad frontier humor in *Roughing It* and *The Innocents Abroad*, lyric autobiography in *Life on the Mississippi*. His classic of American childhood *Tom Sawyer* introduced characters who, in *Huckleberry Finn*, acted in a compelling adult work which many believe is the "Great American Novel," a high point in world literature. And as an old man he wrote with the bitter cynicism of *Letters from the Earth*. The vast sweep of American prose is found at its best in the work of one writer.

Clemens spent less than three years in California, yet in those years he became a fulltime writer, found his voice, and created the story that gave him national recognition and opened the doors for the many works to follow.

Born November 30, 1835, in Hannibal, Missouri, his youth is nostalgically evoked in the adventures of Tom and Huck, but by the age of thirteen Sam Clemens was laboring on the *Missouri Courier* as a printer's assistant, his own carefree youth gone with the death of his father and the necessity of eating. In his twenties he left the drudgery of common labor to apprentice himself as a riverboat pilot. For four years he studied the moods of the great Mississippi, learning the shallows and sand bars, all the backwaters and open straights between St. Paul and New Orleans.

Clemens might well have grown contentedly old in this romantic profession, a colorful, competent master pilot, but for the eruption of the War Between the States. The cliffs at Vicksburg were armed with cannon to control river traffic. Gunboats plied the Mississippi, Ohio, Tennessee, and Cumberland rivers as the North began a blockade of the Confederacy. Clemens's beloved career and the era of the majestic riverboats ended together in the sound of gunfire.

Reluctantly, Clemens served two weeks in a Confederate militia unit in Hannibal, and then fled west to the gold fields. His older brother Orion Clemens had a political appointment as secretary to the governor of Nevada territory. Traveling in his company, Twain arrived by overland stage in Carson City in 1861. He was twenty-seven years old. With the universal dream of striking it rich, he wandered the mountains and deserts of Nevada and California. He thought he could use his wealth, when he found it, to buy a slave plantation in South America, away from the great conflict raging back East, away from the dust and cutting wind of the territories, and spend the rest of his life in comfort.

His mining ventures failed. He had no taste for hard manual labor in another man's service. His brother was good for only so much credit To make some folding money, Clemens tried writing a couple of burlesques of mining life, put the name "Josh" as the by-line, and mailed them to the *Territorial Enterprise* in Virginia City, one of several papers that had appeared to inform and amuse the prospectors. Earlier, Clemens had written copy for the *Journal* in Hannibal when his brother Orion was publisher, and had sold two short travel pieces to the *Saturday Post* and another crude burlesque to the New Orleans *Picayune* during his days as a riverboat pilot. The *Enterprise* publisher, Joe Goodman, bought the new pieces and offered Clemens a job as a reporter.

From August, 1862, until May, 1864, Clemens wrote for the *Enterprise*, transcribing news out of Washoe and trying to keep pace with Goodman's star contributor, William Wright, who signed himself "Dan de Quille" — a flagrant, brilliant hoaxer, liar, and broad comic writer. De Quille's "Petrified, or the Stewed Chicken Monster" is described by Franklin Walker in *San Francisco's Literary Frontier* as "a characteristic de Quille fantasy with lurid pictures of a Washoe mine dug in a hill of chicken and gravy; of shafts cut through stuffing insecurely timbered with chicken bones; of a petrified giant discovered in a drift of cranberry sauce. No one could better Dan at that sort of orgy."

Clemens was hired to replace de Quille when he went on a short leave of absence. Inspired by the wide-open possibilities of writing whatever came to mind, and fired by de Quille's example, Clemens plunged into the job, writing voluminous "scraps of humor, delicious bits," that would be culled for his second book, *Screamers* (1871), and gathering many of the experiences and tales that he later turned into *Roughing It* (1872), a book he modeled on the work of another early western writer, J. Ross Browne, and his *Crusoe's Island . . . with Sketches of Adventures in California and Washoe* (1864). He patterned his first book, *The Innocents Abroad* (1869), on Browne's *Yusef* (1853), and borrowed his humorous style in part from Artemus Ward, who toured the area doing comic speeches. Young Clemens was learning to write, and taking what he wanted.

He stole the name "Mark Twain" and first used it in February 1863. The New Orleans *Picayune* writer Isaiah Sellers used this name; his misinformed articles on the Mississippi River had so disgusted Clemens in his piloting days that he contributed a burlesque of "Mark Twain's" pompous articles to the paper under the handle "Sergeant Fathom." In Washoe, dissatisfied with the name "Josh" and other pseudonyms Obviously preferring Seller's river-born pen name to his own crude "Sergeant Fathom," Clemens appropriated it. "Mark Twain" to the pilots signified two fathoms—twelve feet deep—the shallowest depth they could navigate without strong risk of running the steamboats aground. Eventually Clemens would have to copyright his famous pen name to protect it from other pirates.

His writing for the *Enterprise*, read throughout the Comstock Lode, the Sierras, and into San Francisco, made Twain famous in the West. When the "Washoe Giant" visited the city in 1863 he was hired to do sketches for San Francisco's literary paper the *Golden Era* before his return over the mountains. The *Era* wanted to hire him away from the *Enterprise* on the spot, but Twain was too popular—Goodman would not let him go—and Clemens himself still nurtured hopes of striking it rich by investing in mining stocks in the Comstock.

Twain remained in Virginia City and its environs until May, 1864. At that point he wrote a typical spirited frontier send-up of the local ladies' auction and fancy dress ball to raise money for Confederate wounded—he suggested the money instead would go to "a Miscegenation Society." (Late in 1865 in San Francisco he would review another ball, noting the "gentlemen wore the orthodox costume for such occasions, and the ladies were dressed the best they knew how.") The ladies were not amused. The *Daily Union*, a rival paper, took up their cries of anguish and went to war with the *Enterprise*. Denunciations swept back and forth between the *Union*'s publisher James Laird and the star reporter. All appeared in print.

Legend, in this case created by Twain's friend Steve Gillis, has it that Twain and Laird finally reached the point where mere words were inadequate to express their hatred, and so they faced off one morning in a gun duel to settle the affair on "the field of honor." The ace marksman Gillis—according to Gillis—shot the head off a passing bird to show his inexperienced friend the rudiments of pistolmanship. The amazed Laird and his seconds, coming over a rise, saw the shot but not the shootist. Gillis told them that Twain could hit such an easy mark four out of five bullets; Laird declined the honor of killing the reporter; and Twain and Gillis hightailed toward San Francisco to escape imprisonment for dueling.

Franklin Walker suggests, with less bent for sensation, that Twain simply had grown tired of the Washoe, and was ready to advance his literary career in the San Francisco press, though his feud with Laird and the pro-slavery women's group may have made leaving the *Enterprise* easier.

In the *Golden Era* for June 26, 1864, Twain gave even better reasons for his move to the city, exclaiming over the food, sunshine, breezes; calling the Occidental Hotel—one of his many lodgings—"Heaven on the half shell." For a man newly arrived from the sagebrush and alkali wastes of the Washoe, San Francisco at first appeared to be a paradise.

Much of the glamour faded when Twain and Gillis ran out of money and had to leave the Occidental for less opulent quarters. They hired on with the *Morning Call*, Twain working as a local news reporter and Gillis setting type. The *Call* would not permit the flamboyant writing style and wild invention Twain was accustomed to, and enjoyed. He found his work covering general assignments pure drudgery, rising early to check into police and court cases, chasing after the volunteer fire engine companies, covering the theatre beat after dark. Twain often worked on assignments until midnight, and then had to sit in the *Call* offices and write the articles in the uninspired, uninteresting style the publisher demanded. He lasted all of four months with this newspaper.

Writing for the *Golden Era*, and later the *Californian* and the *Chronicle*, was more to his liking, and he turned out numerous sketches, reviews, and lampoons, as well as more serious articles on corruption and brutality in the police force, the exploitation of the Chinese, and the social causes behind prostitution. In this period he met Bret Harte, favored contributor to the *Golden Era* who had moved on to the *Californian*, fast becoming the West's first major literary figure, a Pacific Coast Dickens. The somewhat younger Harte gave Twain much advice. "He trimmed and trained and schooled me patiently until he changed me from an awkward utterer of coarse grotesqueness to a writer of paragraphs and chapters that have found a certain favor," admitted Twain in his autobiography, but he also called Harte "showy, meretricious, insincere."

Twain knew Ina Donna Coolbrith, Charles Warren Stoddard, the Eastern humorist Artemus Ward—who had lectured in Virginia City in the *Enterprise* days and drank with his public and press afterwards, and other writers in the young city. In the steam baths in the basement of the Montgomery Block he met a fireman named Tom Sawyer—a name Twain liked, and remembered.

In December 1864 Twain suddenly left San Francisco. His friend Steve Gillis had nearly killed a man in a saloon brawl. Twain posted bail and the two left town to give the fellow time to heal, and to escape the jurisdiction of the police force Twain had been attacking in his articles. Gillis returned to the Washoe, figuring the duel would be old history, and Twain traveled to Angels Camp, where Gillis's brother Jim offered to put him up in his cabin on Jackass Hill. Here Twain, whose Comstock investments had collapsed, made a few feeble attempts at hitting paydirt again with pocket mining. His true treasure was found as he sat in the local tavern, listening to the yarns. He filled a notebook with accounts of the terrible victuals—"Chili beans & dishwater three times to-day, as usual"—and jotted down plots of some of the tall tales, including one about a frog-jumping contest. In February, 1865, he returned to the city, where he found waiting for him at the Occidental a letter from Artemus Ward, posted weeks before in New York. Ward was editing an anthology and wanted a humorous sketch to introduce Twain to Eastern readers.

Twain rapidly wrote "Jim Smiley and His Jumping Frog," his first true short story, though he himself told his family it was nothing but "a villainous back-woods sketch." One tradition has it that Bret Harte edited and polished the manuscript for him before he mailed it. The story arrived too late to be included in the book. But the publisher forwarded the tale to the New York *Saturday Press*, where it appeared

November 18, 1865. The story created a sensation and instantly made Twain famous on the national literary scene — it was reprinted time after time.

The reporter, however, was still grappling with the problem of supporting himself writing local articles. He contributed to the Sacramento *Union*, and got the idea that they should send him as a traveling correspondent to the Sandwich Islands — now Hawaii. He left port March 7, 1866, and returned to the city in July. Then Twain hit upon a plan that would carry him from the West to the world at large: lecturing. Recalling Artemus Ward's speeches, and the many others he had heard as a reporter, he used his first-hand experiences in the romantic islands to work up a talk, which he gave in Maguire's Opera House on October 2nd. He took the lecture on the rounds of Sacramento, the Sierras, and the Washoe; lectured again in the city in Platt's Hall on November 16th; then toured San Jose, Petaluma, Oakland. He was a popular speaker, and now without doubt famous.

The *Alta California* hired Twain to write travel articles. In Congress Hall on Bush Street December 10, 1866, he gave another talk on the Sandwich Islands. The poster for this lecture announced: "The performance to conclude with an IMPROMPTU FAREWELL ADDRESS, gotten up last week, especially for the occasion." Five days later he left San Francisco aboard a steamship for New York, en route to Europe and the Holy Land. Two years later he returned to the city for three months while he rewrote the travel articles for publication as his first book, *The Innocents Abroad*, in 1869.

In 1871 Twain settled in Hartford, Connecticut — his home there is a national historic site — writing dozens of books, among them several classics of our literature, until his death April 21, 1910, at the age of seventy-five. In the last lines of *Huckleberry Finn* (1885) he made an ironic comment on his stature as an author and gave a nod to his wild frontier days in Nevada and California, where "Mark Twain" was born:

> ". . . if I'd 'a' knowed what a trouble it was to make a book I wouldn't 'a' tackled it, and ain't a-going to no more. But I reckon I got to light out for the territory ahead of the rest, because Aunt Sally she's going to adopt me and sivilize me, and I can't stand it. I been there before."

The original Jackass Hill cabin

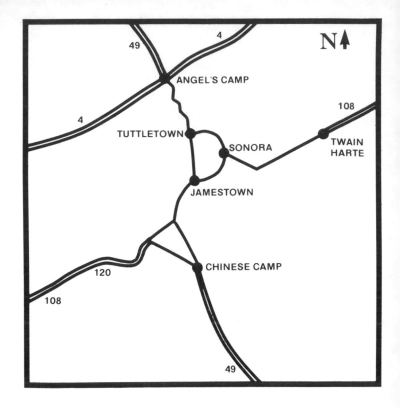

MARK TWAIN SITES

More than a century has passed since Twain's days in California. Backpacking into the Sierra, you may still visit areas little changed since prospectors roamed the hills, and in the preserved or re-created "old town" sections of Sacramento or Auburn (or Virginia City in Nevada where a restoration of Twain's *Enterprise* office can be seen), you get an idea of the architectural look of his times. In San Francisco most of the contemporary buildings are gone—the view from Cliff House today onto the Seal Rocks and the Pacific is the same Twain viewed from the bottom of a slowly emptying whiskey glass before he wrote a send-up of the traditional visit to that place, emphasizing the dismal weather and the long ride from downtown. But the "Cliff House" has burned and been rebuilt several times since Twain sat there with his inspiring shot.

In Tuolumne County in the Sierra you can find the restored:

1 MARK TWAIN CABIN One mile west of Tuttletown off Highway 49, Jim Gillis's cabin stands as a state historic site because of Twain's three-month visit. The original cabin burned, and this replica was reconstructed around the chimney and fireplace. Here Twain stayed when he heard the yarns that would inspire his tale now known as "The Celebrated Jumping Frog of Calaveras County" and made his last, half-hearted attempts at mining.

In Chinese Camp, established in the 1850s, further south on modern Highway 49, a plaque in the old town area describes the history of the settlement and notes that it is located on the "Mark Twain Bret Harte Trail"—and east from Tuttletown on Highway 108 you'll come to a town named Twain Harte, California. The most significant and entertaining look into Twain's days in the Sierras is found in:

2 ANGELS CAMP North of Tuttletown at the junction of Highways 49 and 4, across the line into Calaveras County, the town of Angels Camp is the location for the Angels Hotel, at Main and Bird Streets. In the tavern of this hotel Twain amused himself playing billiards—a life-long pastime—and listened to yarns spun by his cabin-mate Jim Gillis and a fellow ex-river pilot named Ben Coon. Here Coon told a long, monotonous tale about a frog-jumping contest with $50 at stake, and the immovable frog whose belly was filled with lead. The story, re-told in Twain's lively style, catapulted him—like a winning frog—to fame.

Angels Camp also hosts an annual Calaveras County Frog Jumping Contest—a county fair highlighted by a frog jump. You can bring your own frog or—like the fellow in Twain's story—take the frog they give you and make the best of it. Three waterfilled buckets on the edge of the stage hold fresh frogs, frogs exhausted from the rigors of the contest, and frogs that don't make it. Each contestant is given three jumps, and the frog that travels farthest from the starting point wins. The time I went to the fair one unfortunate, confused frog sprang *backward* on its third leap, erasing its gains. The grief-stricken man who had entered the amphibian fell to the stage in a Shakespearian gesture of defeat and rolled right over the frog. It went into bucket number three.

In addition to the frogs, Angels Camp at fair time has become an annual meeting grounds for the biker gangs of the West. The Stockton Chain Gang and others sit on their choppers in every open space beside the road—a dozen here, thirty there, more than you would ever want to see in one place at one time. The Hell's Angels had their colors banned from the county at fair time after they rode their machines up and down the aisles of a grocery store. I understand that the local merchants draw straws before the fair, and whoever loses has to remain open.

It's a wild experience, and really demands the re-birth of Mark Twain to do it justice in prose. If you want to give it a go, write the Chamber of Commerce, Angels Camp, CA 95222, for dates and information on local accommodations and camp sites.

In San Francisco change has been far more dramatic than in the mining towns, and you have to make some effort to scout out the very few buildings left from Twain's era.

The easiest to find, and still one of the most interesting and authentic locations dating from the city's early years, is:

3 FORT MASON   Park in the free lot of the Fort Mason Center, entrance at Buchanan and Marina Boulevard, and climb the stairs that lead uphill opposite Building D. Angle to your left on the roadway until you see another road branching off to your right towards a barracks house— now the Fort Mason Youth Hostel. Between this building and the cliff overlooking the Bay restoration work is being done on the Black Point Battery, whose cannons "were never fired in anger." When work is complete it will look much as it did when Twain investigated a murder for the *Morning Call* in his long rounds of San Francisco, work he described as "fearful drudgery, soulless drudgery . . . awful drudgery for a lazy man."

A Private Kennedy and a fellow soldier who lived in the barracks that is now the Youth Hostel (the same building, dating from the mid-1800s) were on watch at the guardhouse next to the battery. Kennedy apparently did something to annoy his companion, who stabbed him forty times with a bayonet and fled the scene.

Extracts of Twain's coverage of this gory killing were reprinted in *Clemens of the Call: Mark Twain in San Francisco*, edited by Edgar M. Branch, in 1969— one of many books that reprint the news writing he did here and in Washoe. Sunnyvale writer Lawrence Yep was inspired by Twain's coverage of murder cases such as this one, the tensions in San Francisco over the still-raging Civil War, and Twain's own great juvenile novel *Tom Sawyer* to write *The Mark Twain Murders* (1982), about a likely case Twain might have essayed with the *Call* those four months in 1864, another of the many books that have come out of the enduring interest in Twain.

A walk about Fort Mason is, architecturally, the best look you will get of a complete section of the city that dates from the 1860s. And worth noting is the fact that Twain's friend Ina Coolbrith was one of many people who sheltered in emergency tents on the lawns here after the 1906 fire destroyed their homes. Twain, writing from Hartford, observed that Providence finally had repaid the Call *for imposing its drudge work on him in the old days by gutting its new office building— but perhaps had gotten carried away in leveling the rest of the city just to even Twain's score.*

The barracks, Fort Mason

TELEGRAPH HILL

Writers party at The Old Spaghetti Factory, 1978

When the Forty-Niners rushed into port en route to the gold fields, a signal pole with movable arms was built on this barren hilltop to inform people in the shack town below that had sprung up around Portsmouth Square that another sailing ship filled with Argonauts was drifting through the Golden Gate or—less commonly—a mail-carrying sidewheeler. The first telegraph station in California was built here in September 1853, and signal hill became Telegraph Hill. Adjoining North Beach on the east, Telegraph Hill has been home for countless writers. Literary Telegraph Hill and "The Beach" can be toured on foot in a couple of hours, though most visitors like to linger in the Italian delicatessens, Chinese markets, or stop for an espresso in one of the many European-style cafés where writers gather to talk.

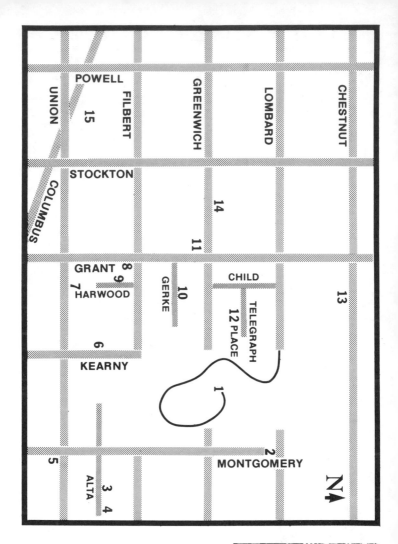

Begin on top of the hill at Coit Tower. The 39 Coit bus caught at Washington Square will drop you here. The parking lot in front of the tower has a 30-minute limit, and it can take over an hour to get to it in slow tourist traffic.

1 COIT TOWER In the poem "Redwood Highway," Philip Lamantia invokes this prominent landmark: "Climb the ocean's ceiling over the Bay Area/ my dream identical to Coit Tower . . ." The tower was erected in 1933 with $118,000 left by the 1929 Will of Lillie Hitchcock Coit—one-third of her estate to be used for "construction of a memorial for the beautification of Telegraph Hill." The city added another $7,000 to the fund. Lillie was the cigar-smoking, poker-playing mascot of the volunteer fire department's Knickerbocker Engine Company No. 5. Of the various proposals submitted for the monument, it was architect Henry Howard's nozzle-like tower that was selected by the newly formed Arts Commission as most fitting to her memory. (Howard said his drawing was not intended to represent a fire-hose nozzle, but anyone can see that it does, all intentions aside.) Novelist Gertrude Atherton served on the commission and protested the plan — she felt that none of the proposals was worthwhile, maintaining to the end of her life that Coit Tower "insults the landscape" and that Lillie Coit "deserved a better memorial." The tower was commemorated in *Gasoline* (1958) in a lengthy "Ode to Coit Tower" by Gregory Corso, which begins:

> "O anti-verdurous phallic were't not for your pouring height looming in tears like a sick tree or your ever-gaudy-comfort jabbing your city's much wrinkled sky you'd seem an absurd Babel squatting before mortal millions . . .

The interior murals painted by the Public Works Project artists in 1933-1934 in the social realism style of Diego Rivera are worth seeing. The literary panel — controversial at the time — features multiracial readers perusing grim headlines in the periodicals section of a library. Across the room, walls are lined with books by Upton Sinclair, Jack London, Floyd Dell, Langston Hughes, Bakhunin, Rexroth, and other progressive writers. In the center of the picture, a man opens a book by Karl Marx, while in the foreground the overseer of the mural project is reading a story called "The Weird Spirit."

The view from the top of Coit Tower is breathtaking — though the outlook from the parking lot itself is spectacular enough. In his rambles about the city in 1879-1880, Robert Louis Stevenson often climbed to this area and sat looking out over the Bay toward Mount Tamalpais and the Golden Gate. In Henry Mead Bland's *Stevenson's California* (1924) Charles Warren Stoddard is quoted: "I had my lodge in San Francisco on glorious Telegraph Hill when I first met him. Stevenson was out on one of his numberless strolls that took him into odd parts of the city, and came by my plover nest . . ." (Stoddard *also* wrote that he first met R.L.S. in his "eyrie" on Rincon Hill. Albert Shumate of the California Historical Society investigated the rival claims of Stoddard's birdlike apartments, which Stevenson in his San Francisco novel *The Wrecker* described as "a museum of strange objects — paddles and battle clubs and baskets, rough-hewn stone images, ornaments of threaded shell" collected by Stoddard in the South Seas. In the September 1967 issue of the society's *Quarterly* Shumate determines that now-vanished Rincon Hill was the place where this historic literary meeting occurred, setting R.L.S. on his way, ultimately, to Samoa.)

Looking out over a century later from this Stevensonian vantage point you'll get a great view of the Golden Gate Bridge — where detective Lew Archer desperately talks to a girl who is threatening to jump, in Ross MacDonald's novel *The Underground Man* (1971). "The Rock" of Alcatraz still sits starkly in the Bay, where Robert Stroud, the "Bird Man of Alcatraz" was imprisoned for many years (the papers that made him famous were actually written in other prisons). The larger, forested mass of Angel Island lies beyond. (You can still see the calligraphy on the walls of the barracks on the island, poems written by Chinese immigrants who were held here in the 1800s pending permission to enter California. They were exploited for cheap labor, and built the railroads and fortunes of men like Charles Crocker and Leland Stanford.) Further east, Yerba Buena Island rises in mid-Bay between San Francisco and Oakland, with the two reaches of the Bay Bridge leading east and west through a tunnel cut in the rock, and the man-made Treasure Island, built on landfill for the 1939 World's Fair, flattening out northeastward into the Bay. The court martial for Captain Queeg in Herman Wouk's *The Caine Mutiny* (1952) takes place here; John Mersereau set his amusing mystery *Murder Loves Company* (1940) on T.I. during the Fair; and the final scene in George R. Stewart's post-apocalyptic science fiction novel *Earth Abides* occurs on the rusted, partially collapsed roadway of the Bay Bridge, over which cars have not passed for decades.

Head down the Greenwich Street stairs.

Filbert stairs. 1880

Here Harry Lafler built his famous "compound" which was a meeting place for Bohemian writers and artists in turn-of-the-century San Francisco. It was made partially from lumber salvaged after the fire of 1906 — and from planks he pirated from the huge sign built on the summit of the hill in 1908 to honor the Great White Fleet on its world cruise. The sign, some two stories high and a block long, read WELCOME. Lafler was crowned a hero for demolishing the monstrous eyesore. George Sterling often visited the compound, and the poet Nora May French lived with Lafler here briefly in the first shack he threw together in late 1906, when San Francisco was a charred ghost of the old city, with many areas still deserted. Lafler's place is gone now, but a walk down these or, better, the Filbert Street stairs and along the narrow wood-planked streets that run from it will give you a good idea of the architectural look of that era — and the day-to-day life of hill dwellers is nicely caught in Laughter on the Hill *(1945) by Margaret Parton.*

At the bottom of this flight of steps is Montgomery Street, where you'll see to your left:

2 JULIUS CASTLE Sam Spade and his secretary Effie Perrine have lunch here in "A Man Called Spade," and Hammett's short fat Continental Op also climbs Telegraph Hill to investigate "a big frame house . . . hung dizzily on a shoulder of the hill, a shoulder that was sharp where rock had been quarried away. The house seemed about to go skiing down on the roofs far below."

The husband-and-wife sleuths, the Holidays, live on "that saucy hill they call Telegraph" in Howard Rigsby's *Murder for the Holidays* (1951). In David Dodge's *Death and Taxes* (1941), a cop "didn't like the idea of sitting up in the fog all night on Telegraph Hill" on a stakeout. Howard Pease's *The Mystery of Telegraph Hill* (1961), and Dana Lyon's *The House on Telegraph Hill* (1948), are set on San Francisco's most famous hill.

Move south on split-level
Montgomery Street

Where the condos stand on the west or upper side of the street you could once find 1443 Montgomery, where Robert Barbour Johnson lived in the basement apartment for twenty-five years. Johnson, if known at all today, is remembered for a few shockers he wrote for Weird Tales *magazine, such as "Far Below," in which hordes of sub-human cannibals derail subway trains in New York City and drag the hapless commuters off for lunch. Johnson also wrote* The Magic Park *(1940), a fine guide to Golden Gate Park, which he illustrated, and many stories about circus life for* Blue Book *— Johnson once knew every circus elephant in America by name. A 50,000-piece miniature circus, exact in every detail, that he carved was set up in the window of an Oakland department store one Christmas. The true horror stories about Johnson come from his cavalier attitude toward books. The first thing he did was to break the spine of a new hardcover book so the pages would lie perfectly flat. His friend George Haas, an avid book collector, recalled picking up a book beside Johnson's chair and was appalled to find that Johnson had marked his place* with a piece of bacon.

At the Filbert Street stairway
drop down to the lower
Montgomery roadway.

Worth noting is the art deco building with the glassed-in elevator at 1360 Montgomery — Lauren Bacall's apartment house in "Dark Passage," based on the David Goodis novel. Humphrey Bogart climbed the steps nearby and rode the elevator up to Bacall's place in this great San Francisco movie.

Turn left into Alta Street,
where you'll see at No. 60-62:

3 THE DUCK HOUSE Easily spotted by the flight of ducks painted under the eaves, this was home for Armistead Maupin, who came to San Francisco from Raleigh, North Carolina, in 1971. When his "Tales of the City" began appearing serially in the *Chronicle* May 24, 1976, Maupin became an instant success with this elaborate soap opera about newly arrived, naive Mary Ann Singleton, the Maupin-like gay Michael Tolliver, and other modern city types. Three paperback novels from this popular series have been published so far. Veteran columnist Charles McCabe is the one who persuaded *Chron* editor Richard Thieriot to give Maupin a shot. "I thought he'd end up doing a column, but he did the serial," McCabe said. "I told Armi it was vulgar as shit, and it would play."

*If you continue to the sheer
cliff at the end of Alta you'll
see a series of numbers on the
left, for the apartments built
over the edge of the precipice
that plunges down to Battery
Street.*

4 22 ALTA is where McCabe lived for many years, and where his body was found May 1, 1983, after a fatal stroke. McCabe began as a columnist for the *Chronicle* in 1959 with "The Fearless Spectator" in The Sporting Green section, and went on to become a mainstay of the morning paper. His literate columns, comparable to the prose of classic essayists Montaigne and Samuel Johnson, were written here in the early morning, usually in an hour. He would then adjourn to his favorite pub, Gino & Carlo's on Green Street. After his rise to a major position on the paper, the irascible McCabe stopped going in to the office and mailed in his pieces. In the late 1970s he said he had been to the newspaper building only "three times in twelve years." His wake was held at the Church of St. Francis at Columbus Avenue and Vallejo Street, and the mourners included many of the longtime residents, rum-pots, and writers of North Beach.

*Continue south on Montgomery
half a block to Union Street.
On the southeast corner of:*

Gregory Corso and Kaye McDonough

5 MONTGOMERY & UNION In this old wood-frame building Gregory Corso lived with his infant son Max in 1978 on one of his extended stays in San Francisco. He subsequently moved downhill, where he now lives in a large bay-windowed building on Montgomery Street between Green and Broadway. So does the poet Kaye McDonough, author of *Zelda* (1978), a poetic play that uses North Beach bohemian settings. The publisher of Greenlight Press, she handsets type and prints books in a spare room in her flat on Montgomery overlooking the Bay.

*Roll down the Union Street
hill. At Kearny turn right and
climb part of the block to:*

6 1425 KEARNY Richard Brautigan lived here in the late 1960s in the flat of anthropologist-student Valerie Estes when his first books *In Watermelon Sugar* (1968) and *Trout Fishing in America* (1967) were first capturing national attention. (During his stay, Brautigan painted pictures of trout on the toilet seat.) He'd been an active participant in the 1950s poetry scene in North Beach cafes a couple of blocks down-hill on Grant, and in the 1960s commuted between the Beach and his place in the 2500 block of Geary Boulevard, across from Sears. He was fond of the Geary bus on which he claimed to do major thinking – there and at Enrico's Sidewalk Cafe on Broadway.

The back of this building faces on Genoa, one of the hill's many Mediterranean-style alleys. Poets Philip Lamantia and Nancy J. Peters lived at 30 Genoa in the early 1970s, then moved a few doors south to their present top-floor flat.

*Return to Union Street and
continue downhill.*

7 **478 UNION**   In the 1940s and early 1950s this building housed the Pencraft Writers Studio managed by the prolific pulp writer Kenneth MacNichol and his wife Polly Lamb Goforth. Polly Lamb wrote anony-mous fiction for women's confession magazines and practiced visuali-zation magic, "seeing" checks coming to pay the rent: the checks came. The Pencraft Studio was opened for regular meetings of the San Francisco Chapter of the Fortean Society, in which followers of the un-usual books of Charles Fort (*The Book of the Damned* and *Lo!*) gath-ered to discuss UFOs, and various unexplained phenomena. George Haas came over from Berkeley and Robert Barbour Johnson walked down the Hill. Johnson maintained that Polly Lamb was a genuine sor-ceress, and that her continued delvings into the occult led to her sudden death in the mid-1950s when she unleashed some power from Outside. The seeds of interest in the occult sowed by this group in the 1940s would lead to such popular forums as the Church of Satan, begun in the early 1960s by Anton Szandor LaVey, a friend of Johnson and Haas. Interest in the occult and mystical has been consistent in San Francisco's history, with spiritualism a hot topic in the 1900s when many San Fran cisco writers essayed the supernatural – such as Gertrude Atherton In the excellent tale "The Foghorn." Even economist Henry George wrote a few ghost stories during his years in the city.

*Go on to Grant and turn right.
One block up on the southeast
corner of Grant and Filbert:*

8 **CITY LIGHTS PUBLISHING HOUSE**   In 1967 the editorial offices and backlist books were moved from the basement of the City Lights Bookstore into this place, where they stayed until 1978. At that time the offices were moved back to the store (which had expanded into the adjoining storefront on Columbus previously occupied by "James Fugazi, Bulotti and Co., Fratelli Forte, Props." – an Italian travel agency). Dozens of books were added to the City Lights list in this period – Jack Hirschman's *Lyripol*, Di Prima's *Revolutionary Letters*, Kerouac's *Scattered Poems*, Cassady's autobiographical *The First Third*, Bukow-ski's *Erections, Ejaculations, Exhibitions and General Tales of Ordinary Madness*, and Norse's *Hotel Nirvana* among them. This place was a center for the North Beach literary community and for visiting writers.

While Yevtushenko opted for the luxurious St. Francis Hotel, the Russian poet Andrei Voznesensky slept on a mattress on the floor of the upstairs apartment during his 1972 American readings. Nancy J. Peters, now co-editor and director of City Lights, came to work for Ferlinghetti here in 1970. She and her husband Philip Lamantia drove Voznesensky up to Fort Ross so he could research an epic poem about the tragic 1806 love affair of the Russian explorer Nicolai Rezanov and Doña Concepción Argüello, fifteen-year-old daughter of the Presidio commandant. In 1972 Ferlinghetti moved into the apartment over the City Lights offices, where he lived until 1978.

Glancing up the Filbert hill toward Coit Tower again, you will see at the end of this building:

9 **28 HARWOOD ALLEY** Site of innumerable literary evenings (mornings, noons, and nights), the tiny apartment belongs to Neeli Cherkovski who has cheerfully fed and entertained many an itinerant and indigent writer. Among those who have dwelt here for significant periods are Raymond Foye, Bob Kaufman, Gregory Corso, Michael Weiner, Martin Matz and Howard Hart. Of course, this is the same Harwood Alley notorious in the 1950s as "Speed Alley" — haunted by high-lifers in the fast lane.

Continue north. On the east side of the next block a small alley runs into Grant. In the late 1970s Brian Doohan lived in apartment No. 1 in:

10 **30 GERKE ALLEY** From this building Doohan continued an offbeat literary artform he had first conceived and executed in Philadelphia. The work *Greasy Fingers* was a novel one-hundred and fifty pages long, read one page at a time, using a map. Doohan pasted each page up in the toilet of a skid row bar, on the wall of a warehouse near a river, on the ceiling of a doorway of a fashionable townhouse where some gangster had lived; using a master map and guide book, the reader would travel from one page to the next to read the book, and actually going into the lowlife physical environments was an important aesthetic aspect to the work: the reader was in a real sense *living* the novel. As he moved from city to city Doohan would revise the book to meet local reference points. Here in San Francisco he made use of places like Palace Billiards on Market (open twenty-four hours a day), Tenderloin bars, Chinatown alleys, and the waterfront. *Greasy Fingers* took about a week to read, if you devoted some three hours a day to it and weren't killed in some dive along the way.

In his apartment here Doohan worked on a number of equally weird projects. He had clotheslines strung across the room with pages and notes from novels in progress hanging from them, literary laundry. He has not yet coined a name for the "Greasy Fingers" genre — "Just call it vandalism."

*On the southwest corner of
Grant and Greenwich just up
the block you could once enter
the:*

11 BREAD AND WINE MISSION Run by Pierre Delattre, a minister, the Bread and Wine Mission was one of the many hangouts for hipsters in the Beat 1950s, a place for people to meet, drink, talk, and read poetry. It no longer exists, the building having been remodeled and "gentrified," a fate which is overtaking all of North Beach and Telegraph Hill.

*Turn east up Greenwich, north
into Child Alley, and east again
into quarter-block-long:*

12 TELEGRAPH PLACE Poet Eric Barker and his wife, the dancer Madelynne Greene, lived in No. 56 in this hidden street in the late 1940s before they moved to Little Sur. Clark Ashton Smith visited them here. In 1966 Barker recalled, "In later years when we lived in San Francisco he would come and stay in our little apartment just below Telegraph Hill. But Ashton was never really at home in a city. We used to climb Telegraph Hill and look across the bay toward San Rafael and talk of the old solitary days together that the real estate promoters had killed forever. . . . Those were the days before the quiet and lovely hills above San Rafael were savaged by bulldozers in preparation for the coming real estate boom. There were sunlit glades full of giant oaks, green valleys and wooded hills where we could walk and rest all day without meeting anyone."

*Follow Child through to
Lombard, where you'll find at
404 Lombard the building in
which the writer-anthropologist
Jaime de Angulo lived from
1936 through 1939. At Grant
go north another block to
Chestnut. To the east, up the
hill, you'll find:*

Lawrence Ferlinghetti
*The Secret Meaning
of Things*

13 339 CHESTNUT This walk-up flat was rented by Lawrence Ferlinghetti soon after he moved permanently to San Francisco in 1951, and he lived here until he bought 706 Wisconsin on Potrero Hill in 1958. In this period he and Peter Martin opened City Lights Pocket Book Shop, the first all-paperback bookstore in America. And in 1955 Ferlinghetti began his City Lights publishing program with the first book in the Pocket Poets Series, his own *Pictures of the Gone World.* Many of these poems, as well as others collected in *A Coney Island of the Mind* (1958), were written here. In the following poem is reflected the architectural mood of the buildings constructed in staggered levels up the side of Telegraph Hill:

> Away above a harborful
> of caulkless houses
> Among the charley noble chimneypots

> of a rooftop rigged with clotheslines
> a woman pastes up sails
> upon the wind
> Hanging out her morning sheets

*Return to Grant, and go back
on Grant to Greenwich, then
west, downhill to:*

14 **540 GREENWICH** In the 1960s Joe Gores lived in this apartment, working as a private investigator and writing his first private eye stories. Here he created his "Daniel Kearney Agency," based on his work with the David Kikkert and Associates detective agency on Golden Gate Avenue. The first story from the fictitious "DKA File" appeared in the December 1967 issue of *Ellery Queen Mystery Magazine*; editor Queen later called this series as "authentic as a fist in your face." Gores put over 100,000 miles a year on his car doing his skip-tracing work and says he was threatened with every implement of destruction made by man. A priest once tried to run Gores over when he made an attempt to repossess the father's car! Gores uses the Bay Area as accurately as a map-maker, and his DKA stories and novels are certainly the most realistic portrayal of day-to-day detective work in the modern city. The novels *Dead Skip* (1972), *Final Notice* (1973), and *Gone, No Forwarding* (1976) are easily found in paperback, and a collection of the short stories is forthcoming.

One day during Gores' stint on this street, a trucker unfamiliar with the city wheeled his tractor-trailer rig up Greenwich, not realizing that it turns into a stair-street a block east, with a sharp turn right down a steep grade onto Kearney — the only way out for cars. The turn was impossible to negotiate with the huge rig, and the trucker couldn't back out safely because of all the cars typically parked in No Parking zones. He was stuck.

Police came, cordoning off the area, afraid the truck would lose his hold on the hill — the careening rig would cause thousands in property damage, and they didn't want any people in the way. Gores heard the commotion and walked up the hill. He saw what the problem was, identified himself to the cops as an auto repossessor, and went to get his key ring with dozens of keys that would open every make of car on the market. Gores moved the illegally parked cars, the trucker backed safely downhill and away, and then Gores and the police reparked all the cars just as they found them, illegally, with tickets locked inside.

*Continue downhill to Stockton,
then left one block to:*

15 **WASHINGTON SQUARE** On one of the benches near the Stockton Street end of this park is a small metal plaque dedicating the bench to San Francisco-born Irving Stone, famous for his biographical novels such as *Sailor on Horseback* (1938), about a fellow San Francisco native and writer, Jack London. Stone was born Irving Tannenbaum near Washington Square July 14, 1903.

In the center of the Square there's a statue of Ben Franklin, the oldest public monument in the city, presented by the teetotaling dentist Henry D. Cogswell in 1879. The base of the statue is inscribed: "Presented by

CHANGE

Richard Brautigan and Ron Loewinsohn

H. D. Cogswell to our Boys and Girls Who Will Soon Take Our Places And Pass On." A time-capsule enclosed inside was opened in a public ceremony in 1979. A few scraps of verse were found, along with other odd memorabilia, including a tooth of the French Revolutionist Robespierre. The monument once had three faucets from which ran Vichy, Cal Seltzer and Congress mineral waters. We find, ironically, Shorty the wino in Brautigan's *Trout Fishing in America* unconscious here—"He had fallen face first out of his wheelchair and just lay there without moving. Snoring loudly." The narrator thinks that Shorty should be nailed in a packing crate with a couple of cases of wine and shipped for safekeeping to Nelson Algren.

The Washington Square Bar and Grill across Columbus Avenue at 1707 Powell has become a major hangout for our more "uptown" writers in the last decade. Alice Adams, Ella Leffland, Herb Gold, Warren Hinckle, and other journalists frequent it. As a sure sign that it is a hot and widely known spot, it has already appeared as a location in a mystery novel, by former *Chronicle* reporter Julie Smith. (Smith once went undercover on a farm run by the Moonies near Boonville, California, among other assignments.) Her equally intrepid heroine Rebecca Schwartz in *Death Turns a Trick* (1982), about murder in a C.O.Y.O.T.E.-like prostitute's organization, eats a meal here between perils—she lives up Union Street on Telegraph Hill.

In his column March 19, 1982, Herb Caen (who has a condo in the new complex at the foot of the Greenwich Street stairs) reported in abbreviated Caenese: "At the Wash. Sq. Barngrill, the party of the week was for Rita Mae Brown, the lesbian activist, to launch her latest book, 'Southern Discomfort.' A pushy photogger from People mag pushed her, Armistead Maupin and Randy Shilts against the ladeez room door for a shot that only a rag like People could love . . ." Brown, who rose quickly to fame with her first book *Rubyfruit Jungle* (1973), often flies into the city from her home in North Carolina; she and Maupin once planned to host a TV talk show for the large gay community in San Francisco. Shilts, called by *Publishers Weekly* "the first openly gay establishment journalist in California"—a writer for the *Examiner, Chronicle, Village Voice*, and the gay papers the *Advocate* and *Christopher Street*—had just published his biography of assassinated gay supervisor Harvey Milk, *The Mayor of Castro Street*. And so are literary "movements" born, and literary sites established.

NORTH BEACH

City Lights Bookstore

Sprawling between the Financial District and Chinatown to the Embarcadero, up the shoulders of Telegraph Hill, North Beach has always been a center for the city's Bohemia and has housed generations of San Francisco's writers.

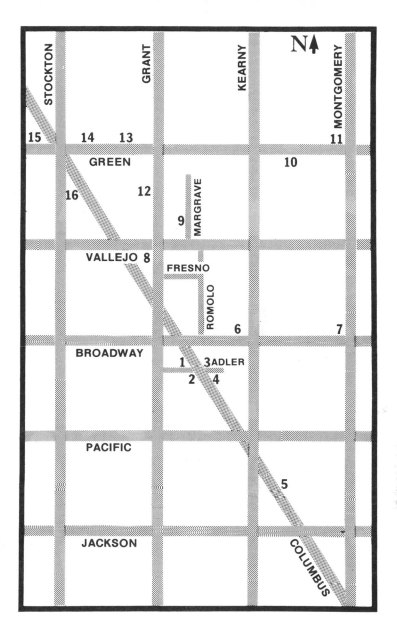

In "My San Francisco" Kathleen Norris evoked that lost literary age before the 1906 fire, when

> . . . at Coppa's, at Solari's, at the Trovatore, and at Sanguinetti's, young Bohemian San Francisco wittled free, and struggling artists arose between courses to embellish the walls with dancing Pierrettes and demons. Stevenson, Bret Harte, Mark Twain were but memories then; they had loved our city, and left their mark on her, and gone their way. But George Sterling, Gelett Burgess, Will and Wallace Irwin, and a hundred other newspaper men who were to make their names famous one day, were all a part of it, and the days of high revelry among the cabins and shanties of Telegraph Hill are wonderful to remember.

In 1922 George Sterling guided H. L. Mencken through the speak-easies that grew up more or less on the remnants of the old Barbary Coast near North Beach, and writers continued to be drawn to the area. Kenneth Rexroth said that when he came to the city in 1926 it was "still in the grip of the Jack London, Frank Norris, George Sterling tradition. Everybody we met considered George Sterling the greatest poet since Dante. We had never heard of him. . . ."

Gary Snyder in a 1976 essay in *Deep City Press* notes that Sterling's hangout, the Montgomery Block, served as home "for the artists and revolutionaries of the Thirties and Forties. Kenneth Rexroth, many others, lived there; foundations of post-war libertarianism; moves that became publicly known as 'beat' in the middle Fifties. This emphasis often neglected the deeply dug-in and committed thinkers and artists of the era who never got or needed much media-fame; who were the *culture* that nourished so much."

"In the spiritual and political loneliness of America of the fifties you'd hitch a thousand miles to meet a friend," Snyder wrote, and observed:

> Whatever lives needs a habitat, a proper culture of warmth and moisture to grow. West coast of those days, San Francisco was the only city; and of San Francisco, North Beach. Why? Because partly, totally non-Anglo . . . Italian, Sicilian, Portuguese (fishermen), Chinese (Kuang-tung and Hakka) and even Basque, down from Nevada sheepherding on vacation. . . . Who would not, en-route, stop off in North Beach? To buy duck eggs, drop into Vesuvio, City Lights, get sesame oil or wine, walk up Grant to this or that place. Or liv-ing there: the hum of cable-car cables under the street —lit-up ships down on the docks working all night —the pre-dawn crashes of the Scavengers' trucks. Spanning years from the time when young women would get arrested for walking barefoot, to the barebottom clubs of Broadway now tending tourist tastes from afar.

The emergence of the Beat Generation in the mid-1950s was the cultural phenomenon that focused national and international media attention on North Beach as *the* literary center of San Francisco. The first Beat writing by Jack Kerouac, Allen Ginsberg, and William S. Bur-roughs was done a decade earlier in the apartments and bars around Columbia University in New York, in the Lower East Side and West Side, but it wasn't until Kerouac, Ginsberg, and Gregory Corso came West and became part of the local scene — Rexroth, William Everson, Ferlin-ghetti, Snyder, Philip Lamantia, Michael McClure, Lew Welch, Bob Kaufman, Kirby Doyle, Philip Whalen, and others of the "San Francisco Renaissance" that the Beats finally made their mark. And though the media spotlight shifted from the Beats (and the coffee house hangers-on who became known as beatniks) to the hippies, attention never wavered from the writer who came out of this group as the unques-tioned "King of the Beats." Fifteen years after his death October 21, 1969, and almost thirty years since the publication of *On the Road* in 1957, Jack Kerouac's legend and works live on — the essence, history, myth of the Beat Generation.

Born March 12, 1922, in Lowell, Massachuetts, to a working-class, Catholic, French-Canadian family, Kerouac had a fairly typical all-Ameri-can childhood, playing on the neighborhood sandlots, reading pulp magazine adventures, becoming a high school football hero. He entered Columbia on a football scholarship, but a leg injury took Kerouac out of the action, and he decided he would become a writer. In the next years he met Burroughs, Ginsberg, Lucien Carr, Neal Cassady — the people who would become the cast of his one great work, his romanticized biography of himself and his friends which spanned several novels, books of poetry, and even his non-fiction.

Kerouac first landed in the Bay Area in 1947, staying with his friend Henry Cru in Marin City, hoping to get a merchant marine berth on a ship. The job didn't come through, and Kerouac spent most of his time hanging out in Cru's rooms, bored. But after Neal Cassady came to San Francisco to marry his second wife Carolyn March 31, 1948, the city held new interest for Kerouac—it became a place of romance, of meetings, happenings. Cassady sped across the country several times in the next years to drive his spiritual brother West.

Between these trips Kerouac holed up at his mother's, working on his first novel. *The Town and the City* took about four years to write; modeled on Thomas Wolfe's works, it attracted little notice when it appeared in 1950, and it would be seven years before Kerouac could sell his next book. Inspired by Cassady's energetic monologues, by long frenetic letters Neal wrote on a benzedrine high, Kerouac began to write in what he called "spontaneous prose," completing over a dozen books before 1957. He typed *On the Road* as one long paragraph in twenty days in April 1951. Staying with the Cassadys in their home on Russian Hill for six months in 1952, he broke *On the Road* into paragraphs, and also worked on *Visions of Cody* and *Doctor Sax*. Up on bennies, he knocked out *The Subterraneans* in three days in October 1953. He wrote the poetry cycle *San Francisco Blues* in his favorite skid row hotel, The Cameo, on Third Street, over a few months in 1954, sipping sweet wine and looking out his window on the street scene. After *On the Road* saw print September 5, 1957, it rapidly went through three printings and made the bestseller lists for five weeks—and while it was still at the top Kerouac wrote *The Dharma Bums*, covering his 1956 meeting and mountain climbing expedition with Gary Snyder and Ginsberg's reading of "Howl" at the Six Gallery, in ten marathon sessions on the typewriter, pounding out 15,000-20,000 words at a stretch.

Ginsberg had left New York in December 1953 to travel in Mexico and Central America; he arrived at Cassady's new home in San Jose the next April. He crashed there some weeks before moving to various rooms in the city, and later rented a cottage on Milvia Street in Berkeley. He soon met Rexroth, Robert Duncan, Jack Spicer, and other young poets, finding the encouragement and enthusiastic audience that had not materialized for him in New York. He organized the Six Poets at Six Gallery reading—with Rexroth introducing Ginsberg, Snyder, McClure, Lamantia, and Whalen—on the evening of October 13, 1955. His reading of "Howl" created a sensation. The hundred or so people jammed into the Six Gallery shouted along with him, as Kerouac wrote in *The Dharma Bums*, ". . . by eleven o'clock when Alvah Goldbook was reading his, wailing his poem 'Wail' drunk with arms outspread, everybody was yelling 'Go! Go! Go!' (like a jam session). . . ."

This reading was the catalyst that brought the Beats to public attention, the event that Kerouac described as "the night of the birth of the San Francisco Poetry Renaissance." Before coming back to San Francisco in time to hear the reading, Kerouac had written Ginsberg: "LET'S SHOUT OUR POEMS IN SAN FRANCISCO STREETS—PREDICT EARTHQUAKES!" The sensation created by the publication of *Howl and Other Poems* by City Lights in 1956, and the media attention it got when the book was seized by Customs as obscene, launched the Beats to fame—and the trial which ended in victory for City Lights on September 9, 1957, helped to catapult the just-released *On the Road* high up the bestseller lists.

William S. Burroughs in his foreword to Tom Clark's *Jack Kerouac* (1984) says, "Sometimes, as in the case of Fitzgerald and Kerouac, the effect produced by a writer is immediate, as if a generation were waiting to be written." In her Kerouac biography Ann Charters states: "Kerouac had no idea that he had written a book that would turn on an entire generation. He thought of the book, characteristically, entirely in personal terms of finding his own 'writing soul at last'. . . . But the young people who responded to the book, who read it not as 'literature' but as an adventure, recognized that Kerouac was on their side, the side of youth and freedom, riding with Cassady over American highways chasing after the great American adventure — freedom and open spaces, the chance to be yourself, to be free."

Overnight Kerouac became a media superstar, interviewed on radio, TV, spotlighted in a *Playboy* interview. He became what he had long dreamed of becoming — a legend, a living figure of myth. But Kerouac was not Neal Cassady. When the rebellious generation for which he spoke moved into the 1960s, Kerouac did not move with it. He denounced Cassady and the Merry Pranksters for experimenting with LSD, he voiced support for America's war in Vietnam (even as Ginsberg, Ferlinghetti, and others were marching in antiwar protests). Kerouac moved in with his mother, drinking too much, becoming more reactionary. His last years are an ironic counterpoint to his fame.

But the reasons for Kerouac's fame — his writings — still inspire people at poetry readings today, and in the coffee houses and bars of North Beach it sometimes seems as if a dark-haired figure in a red lumberjack's shirt still watches over the scene where ". . . the only people for me are the mad ones, the ones who are mad to live, mad to talk, mad to be saved."

NORTH BEACH TOUR

Gary Snyder in his essay on North Beach for Deep City Press *wrote, "When we of the Fifties and after walked into it, walk was the key word. Maybe no place else in urban America where a district has such a feel of on-foot: narrow streets, high blank walls and stairstep steeps of alleys and white-wood houses cheap to rent; laundry flapping in the foggy wind from flat-topped roofs." A driving tour is impossible, even parking is difficult — the large garage under Portsmouth Square often fills to capacity, as do the smaller lots scattered in the neighborhood. Riding the 30 Stockton to Broadway and walking over a couple of blocks, or taking the 15 Third or 43 Union to Columbus and Broadway, are the easiest bus routes into the district.*

Begin this tour at 261 Columbus Avenue near the southwest corner at Broadway in a historic building constructed in 1907. For over thirty years the literary center of North Beach, it is the:

1 CITY LIGHTS BOOKSTORE founded in June 1953 by Peter D. Martin and Lawrence Ferlinghetti. The nation's first all-paperback bookstore was conceived by Martin as a way to pay the rent on the second-floor editorial offices of his pop-culture magazine *City Lights*, which featured the early work of Pauline Kael, Philip Lamantia, Robert Duncan, Grover Sales, and Jack Spicer. When Martin left for New York, Ferlinghetti continued to develop the store in a civil libertarian, anti-authoritarian direction.

The store has expanded several times, from the tiny pie-shaped space at the corner of the building next to Vesuvio bar. From the day the bookstore opened, it was full of readers (if not buyers) from noon to midnight, seven days a week. They literally couldn't get the door closed. (There weren't any other paperback stores in the U.S. and in fact there weren't many paperback publishers. The "paperback revolution" was just beginning, and there were readers and publishers who felt that paperbacks "just weren't real books.") The store expanded first to the room above (when Martin departed and his "City Lights" magazine folded), then into the large basement which had once been inhabited by some kind of Holy Roller sect (signs painted on the walls: "Remember Lot's Wife," "I and My Father Are One," "Prayer Room," "I Am the Door," "Born in Sin, Shapen in Iniquity"); and, finally, after 25 years, the old Italian travel agency next door (Fratelli Forte) moved over and let City Lights have a big street-level space, an area four times as large as the original shop.

But Ferlinghetti intended City Lights to be more than a bookstore. Its masthead says *A Literary Meetingplace Since 1953*, and this concept includes the publishing of much contemporary work, both poetry and prose, local and international, along with the re-publication of forgotten or out-of-print classics. With this bookstore-publisher combination, "it is as if," says Ferlinghetti, "the public were being invited, in person and in books, to participate in that 'great conversation' between authors of all ages, ancient and modern."

Within two years of opening the store, Ferlinghetti launched a very modest publishing program, beginning with the Pocket Poets Series. He had in mind the great tradition of publishing by independent international bookstores in England and on the continent, as well as in New York, where often a famous publisher had been a bookstore first. The City Lights list now ranges far beyond poetry, with about a hundred titles in print and a half a dozen new ones appearing every year.

The first authors in the Pocket Poets Series were Ferlinghetti himself, Rexroth, and Kenneth Patchen. But it was the appearance of Allen Ginsberg's *Howl and Other Poems* (PP#4) which really made publishing history and put City Lights on the map.

After Ginsberg's Six Gallery reading of "Howl" in October 1955 Ferlinghetti sent him a note, repeating Emerson's message to Whitman upon reading *Leaves of Grass:* "I greet you at the beginning of a great career." But Ferlinghetti added a line: "When do I get the manuscript?"

Whalen, (?, ?), Ginsberg, Kaufman, Ferlinghetti, Plymell

Printed in England, *Howl* was seized by U.S. Customs in 1957; the charge was obscenity. The ACLU did not agree, and even the U.S. District Attorney in San Francisco refused to institute condemnation proceedings. But when Customs released the printing, local police arrested publisher Ferlinghetti and bookstore manager Shigeyoshi Murao. (Ginsberg was in Tangier at the time, and neither charged nor arrested.) After a long court trial that summer, during which City Lights and *Howl* were supported by poets, editors, critics, and university professors, Judge Clayton Horn ruled the book not obscene, establishing the legal precedent of redeeming social value that in the next decade allowed Grove Press to publish Lawrence's *Lady Chatterley's Lover*, Miller's *Tropic of Cancer*, and other landmark books.

The bookstore is still open seven days a week from ten a.m. to midnight and has become one of the truly great independent bookstores in the U.S. (This was not all its doing — the growth of computerized chain bookstores with their cut-throat business methods has driven more and more of the old-fashioned intimate bookshops out of existence, making those who have survived ever the more valuable to booklovers.) Now cooperatively run, the bookstore has a staff with special book interests in many fields, and you can usually get an intelligent opinion about a book from the clerk — though it may range from weird to esoteric. There is an emphasis on libertarian-left and Third World books and periodicals, but the huge stock includes in-depth collections of fiction, poetry, translations, literary criticism, film, theater, jazz and blues, history, philosophy, and on and on. There's a used book section; and these days City Lights is fast becoming the L. L. Bean of quality books with an expanding mail-order service.

It's been twenty years and more since tour buses first started to pull up in front of City Lights, disgorging passengers eager to eye "beatniks." Randolph Delehanty in his architectural guidebook San Francisco *writes that,*

> In August 1958, North Beach's beatniks, tired of being the object of visitors' curiosity, organized "The Squaresville Tour." One hundred beats in Bermuda shorts and beards, or black slacks and sandals, marched — if that's the word — across Downtown's Union Square to I. Magnin. A bongo drummer led the incursion on a busy Monday shopping night. One marcher brandished a good-natured sign that read "Hi Squares."

Across Adler Alley from City Lights, saloon-keeper Henri Lenoir took the problem in hand by placing a sign in the window of:

2 VESUVIO CAFE announcing "Don't envy Beatniks . . . Be One!" and offering for sale a Beatnik Kit that included a poem entitled "How You Gonna Keep 'Em Down on the Peninsula After They've Seen North Beach?" and the official signature of "Big Daddy" Eric Nord, the big daddy of the beatniks.

Vesuvio, at 255 Columbus, "a gathering place of the people of North Beach since the days of 1949," was founded by Henri Lenoir — his second saloon in North Beach. Lenoir came to the city from Europe in the early 1930s and soon became a familiar figure on the local scene. In

Henri Lenoir

his bars he exhibited paintings by San Francisco artists, as well as comic postcards, racy Victoriana, stained-glass, deco memorabilia, and various odd items. Art critic Allan Temko writes that,

> "It was really a kind of Surrealist or Dadaist architectural environmental 'collages' which people try to concoct today, but no one in San Francisco . . . has come close to matching Henri's wit and boulevardier's elegance, his kindness and humor, his roguish sense of the absurd. Now we have fern bars with imitation Victorian glass, redolent of pseudo-history, but his bars made history. They were spontaneous San Francisco poems, richer, far more delightful, than most of the hundreds of poems that were read there. . . ."

In Vesuvio Dylan Thomas held forth, knocking back drinks during his tours through San Francisco in the early 1950s. Jack Kerouac once spent a long night here in 1960, when he was supposed to head south to Big Sur for a meeting with Henry Miller. Miller had written Kerouac that he admired *The Dharma Bums* and would enjoy a visit, but Kerouac got drunk in Vesuvio and spent the rest of the evening calling Miller every hour or so to tell him he was just a bit delayed in getting out of the city. The two writers never met.

Essentially, Vesuvio — especially in the days when Lenoir owned the saloon — is a place every writer hung out. Even under new management the place continues the literary tradition. To the right of the front door, gouged in wet cement after some repair work on the sidewalk, you'll find an evocative list of major North Beach figures:

Paddy O'Sullivan

White Crombie
Two Dollar Burt
Gregory Corso
Bob Miller
Peter Speer
Janice Blue
Bob Kaufman
Dennis Crisp
Fox Lewis
    —all 86'd
2/3/81

> The emergence of the Beat Generation made North Beach *the* literary center of San Francisco—and it nurtured a new vision that would spread far beyond its bounds. For the fresh rebellious acts and ideas of the Beat writers became the main shibboleths of the counter culture of the 1960s and early 1970s: the hedonism, sexual liberation and liberation of consciousness, the new concepts of ecology, the turning to the Far East for its Buddhist awareness of "the sentience of all beings," the freedom of the Road, the opposition to war, and the general rejection of the materialist values of Middle America—in all these the Beats prefigured the New Left evolution and the impulse for change that swept eastward from San Francisco.
>
> — *Ferlinghetti*

Naturally, many of the hangouts of the Beat Fifties are gone, but a surprising number still exist. As Herb Gold noted in his "Bohemia as Seen by a Survivor" (*California Living*, Oct. 18, 1981), when he takes his "nightly walk in North Beach, down to City Lights, over to Enrico's or the Trieste or the Puccini, I am testing myself against history." The Co-Existence Bagel Shop at 1398 Grant and The Place at 1546 Grant (described by Kerouac in *The Dharma Bums* as "the favorite bar of the hepcats around North Beach") both closed in 1960. The Bread and Wine Mission on the corner of Grant and Greenwich, The Cellar at 576 Green, bars and clubs such as Barnaby Conrad's original Matador and the first hungry i, Mike's Pool Hall (immortalized in many poems) are ghosts of the past. The Coffee Gallery at 1353 Grant lasted longer than the others of its era—only the name was changed (to the Lost and Found Saloon) in the early 1980s.

Before escalating rents forced him out, Lenoir lived in the studio above the bookstore down the street from Vesuvio, and now lives further north on Columbus Avenue. You can find his first saloon directly across Columbus from Vesuvio, in the deadend of Adler Alley, number 12:

3 SPEC'S   Under Lenoir's management in the 1940s, the bar that is now Spec's was called 12 Adler Place. Herb Caen made the rounds here, and in the Black Cat down on Montgomery and other spots, covering the San Francisco scene and, oddly enough, Caen's one immortal coinage came out of his rubbing shoulders with the Beats of North Beach. In 1957 when *On the Road* was at the top of the bestseller lists and the Russians had just launched Sputnik, Caen wrote in his column that both the Beats and Sputnik were "far out" as far as he was concerned, and shot off the term "beatnik." Rumor has it that Bob Kaufman was the first to say "beatnik" but Caen made it a cliché in the popular imagination.

Much of the literary trade migrated to Vesuvio when Lenoir moved across the street, and back again after Lenoir sold *it*. Both bars are full of writers, film and theater people, and musicians now. Just step in and have a beer and you're sure to rub shoulders with a mad poet.

South on Columbus from
Spec's a few steps will put you
in front of the entrance to:

4 TOSCA CAFE Another major watering hole, Tosca's is another favorite North Beach bar and cafe. Once Bob Dylan walked into the bar with Ginsberg, Ferlinghetti, Shig Murao, Peter Orlovsky and Peter's young brother, who had just been released from a mental hospital. As they sat in Tosca's drinking and talking, the crazed brother got up to go to the john and by mistake went into the women's restroom. They were all thrown out immediately, no questions asked. The next day the manager of the bar read in Caen's column that he had unknowingly evicted Bob Dylan. Ginsberg never went back. But that was over twenty years ago, and today it attracts more writers and especially musicians than ever before. Playwright-actor Sam Shepard and his friend Johnny Dark—whose relation to Shepard seems to resemble Neal Cassady's to Kerouac—have been known to shoot pool in the back room.

Continue down Columbus, past
Pacific, to 140 Columbus:

5 THE PURPLE ONION This club, and the original hungry i (for id, or intellectual) around the corner at 599 Jackson, were mainstays of North Beach nightlife in the 1950s, where the Smothers Brothers, Flip Wilson, Rod McKuen, Barbra Streisand, Mort Sahl, The Kingston Trio, Lenny Bruce, Woody Allen, Dick Gregory performed. "Big Daddy" Eric Nord founded the hungry i, and Enrico Banducci took it over briefly, before opening Enrico's Sidewalk Cafe.

Novelist and screenwriter Alvah Bessie worked for Banducci as stage manager for seven years. Bessie fought with the Abraham Lincoln Brigade against Franco in the Spanish Civil War; his non-fiction account of his experiences, *Men in Battle*, was published after Ernest Hemingway recommended it to Maxwell Perkins at Scribners. Bessie later worked in Hollywood as a screenwriter, but was ruined when he refused to talk about possible "Communist affiliations" before HUAC. He went to prison as one of the "Hollywood Ten." He says his novel *One for My Baby* (1961), about a San Francisco nightclub of the 1950s, is *not* about Banducci's hungry i.

Banducci does appear, perhaps a bit larger than life, but nonetheless recognizable in Don Asher's *The Electric Cotillion* (1970). Asher played jazz in the hungry i in the early 1960s as house pianist. His first book, *The Piano Sport* (1966), and most of his other novels feature North Beach scenes, recreating the district as it was before the influx of topless clubs and strip shows later in the 1960s.

Maya Angelou sang and danced at the Purple Onion in the 1950s. A popular performer, she later toured in a production of *Porgy and Bess*, and began to turn out equally popular volumes of autobiography and poetry in the 1970s, beginning with *I Know Why the Caged Bird Sings* (1970). Her screenplay for "Georgia, Georgia" in 1972 was the first script written by a black woman ever filmed by Hollywood.

Return up Columbus half a block and angle north into Kearny. Near the northwest corner of Kearny and Broadway you'll find Banducci's current place:

6 ENRICO'S SIDEWALK CAFE   With its sidewalk tables, Enrico's is the city's best-known European-style restaurant-cafe. Writer-professors and journalists, playwrights and gossip columnists, actors and impresarios: you're likely to find a lively mix at Enrico's. Herb Gold or Ron Kovic might be seen there sitting at tables while the crowd lines up to get into Finocchio's drag show upstairs.

The punk rockers hanging out along Broadway today give the street by night a distinct flavor of rebellion, not all that different from the days of the Beats. As Michael McClure said in an interview with Pat Holt for the *Chronicle*: ". . . I think the performance aspects of the punks are very closely associated with the poetry readings of the Beats. . . . I also think the punks are returning to a level of self-expression that is the same as self-experience— a weird haircut is a statement of feelings and perceptions, just as outward appearances were in the 1960s and 1950s. . . ."

Walk east on Broadway to the northeast corner of Montgomery:

7 1010 MONTGOMERY STREET   is where Allen Ginsberg lived from February 3 to September 6, 1955— and where he wrote "Howl," the definitive poem of the Beat Generation.

Head west on Broadway.
Before you get to the corner
of Columbus you'll cross
Romolo Street, an alley rising
sharply uphill to the right.
Head up Romolo, past the old
Basque Hotel with its huge
dinners (reminiscent of the
days when Basque sheep-
herders came to town).
When the street pitches
sharply up for part of a block
and the sidewalk turns to
stairs, turn left down Fresno
Street. A block down at Grant
turn right. Just up the block on
the southwest corner at 606
Vallejo you'll enter a true time
warp. Founded in 1954 and
still going strong as a
bohemian hangout is the:

8 CAFFE TRIESTE   One of the great wake-up spots in North Beach, the place for morning or midday coffee or espresso, the Caffe Trieste is one of the few places left that has changed little. The poets of the 1950s all came here, poets come here today. You'll probably see them scribbling on the napkins. Gregory Corso and Kaye McDonough are regulars. Ginsberg stops here when he hits town. Bob Kaufman, Jack Hirschman, Kirby Doyle, Tisa Walden, Jack Mueller, Roderick Iverson, Jeffrey Grossman are habitues. Harold Norse in "At the Trieste" writes:

> here in San Francisco
> as I sit at the Trieste
> —recitative of years!
> *O Paradiso!* sings the jukebox
> as Virgil and Verdi combine
> in this life
> to produce the only Golden Age
> there'll be

You also could take a copy of Virgil's *Eclogues* to read over coffee—or Norse's *Beat Hotel*, for that matter.

Saturday mornings, the owners of the Trieste sing *bel canto* and the crowd joins in—sometimes you'll hear a visiting Wagnerian Brunhilde or an aspiring Madame Butterfly flying through to the Met. At a back table here, Ferlinghetti wrote an entire book of one-act "happenings," and Francis Ford Coppola is said to have polished the screenplay of "The Godfather" at the historic cafe.

From the Trieste go east on
Vallejo a quarter of a block. On
the north side of the street
you'll see:

9 MARGRAVE PLACE   Stewart Brand lived here in the mid-1960s, before planning the Trips Festival and launching his Whole Earth spaceship. In 1966 Ken Kesey and Mountain Girl of the Merry Pranksters were arrested on the roof of his apartment house in this alley for smoking marijuana. It was Kesey's second offense, and to avoid jail—to rub "salt in J. Edgar Hoover's wounds"—Kesey fled to Mexico. Prankster Robert Stone ended up in Mexico with Kesey, working as a journalist, and soon Neal Cassady followed to be up on the action. On February 3, 1968, Cassady walked out along the railroad tracks near San Miguel de Allende—another link in the rails he had ridden and worked on most of his life—and was found the next day beside the tracks by a group of Indians. He died later that day—"overexposure" was given as a cause of death. In his biography of Cassady *The Holy Goof* (1981) William Plummer notes that "The apocrypha that has accreted around Neal Cassady tells us that his last words were, '64,928.' Legend has it that Cassady was counting the ties, that he was faithful to his part of the Promethean transaction, right up to the end."

Cassady successfully drove on into a new generation of literature, pictured as the hammer-tossing, rapping "Speed Limit" of the Pranksters in *The Electric Kool-Aid Acid Test*. His death inspired Robert Stone's scene in *Dog Soldiers* (1974), in which Cassady as the anti-hero Hicks, mortally wounded, walks with determination along a railroad line in Mexico.

Thus, Neal Cassady, whom Kerouac dubbed "the Holy Goof," was made a legend.

*Continue up Vallejo, take a left
on Kearny, a right on Green to:*

Patchen drawing

10 **377 GREEN** When Kenneth and Miriam Patchen first came to San Francisco in the early 1950s they stayed with Holly Bye and her husband, the printer David Ruff, in their place at 970 Broadway between Mason and Taylor. The Patchens had several apartments in North Beach before settling at 377 Green Street.

Patchen was born in Ohio in December 1911, went to the University of Wisconsin, and after 1936—when his first collection *Before the Brave* helped him win a Guggenheim fellowship—spent his life writing and painting. His last twenty years were spent in increasing pain from a severe, spreading spinal disease. In the 1950s he used a cane to get around North Beach, and after the Patchens moved to Palo Alto he was confined to the house. His poems of political protest, anger and despair co-exist with some of the most tender love poems in the language. Henry Miller called him a kind of "sincere assassin" and "the living symbol of protest" and Kenneth Rexroth said he was "Laureate of the Doomed Youth of the Third World War." Patchen issued many poetry collections, gathered together later in *Selected Poems* (1964) and *Collected Poems* (1969). *Memoirs of a Shy Pornographer* (1945) is the most famous of his novels.

In 1984 the Sierra Club published a deluxe edition of his "painted poems" under the title *What Shall We Do Without Us?*—a tribute to one of the most important poets of this century, one who was largely ignored by leading literary critics of the Establishment. (Stanford University never acknowledged his presence a mile from its campus during all of the 1960s.)

If you wish, continue to the
corner of Green and
Montgomery.

11 **GARY SNYDER AND PHILIP WHALEN**   lived in this building
on the northwest corner of the intersection for about two and a
half years. With Lew Welch, they were the Northwesterners who became
significant figures in the San Francisco Renaissance. After a big poetry
reading sponsored by Don Carpenter at Longshoreman's Hall in 1964,
they took the money they'd earned and hid some of it in the oven at
Snyder's new place further down Green, "two or three doors east of
Grant, on the south side," before descending on Tosca's for a party with
the rest of the loot.

Return to Grant and turn left.
Next door to the venerable
Fugazi Hardware is:

12 **THE LOST AND FOUND SALOON**   Formerly the Coffee Gallery, this place at 1353 Grant still maintains the character of the
1950s despite the name change. It is still full of beat-looking poets and
artists, as well as an assortment of urban cowboys, skid-row visionaries
and drifters.

Return to Green, turn left.
Stop halfway down the block at:

13 **GINO AND CARLO**   Located at 548 Green, this dark bar was
the chief hangout for another group of poets whose leading talent
was Jack Spicer. It also was a regular stop in columnist Charles
McCabe's rounds of North Beach. For about fifteen years, McCabe's
routine was to rise before eight a.m. in his apartment on Telegraph Hill,
write for an hour, and then walk downhill to the mailbox to send in a finished column. Then McCabe stopped here, where he always sat on the
stool at the end of the bar by the window, ordered a glass of ice water
and a Rainier Ale, and, over four more ales, roughed out another
column. Residents of the neighborhood knew the exact hour his majestic
figure might be seen walking over to Capp's Corner, the New Pisa or
perhaps the North Star before returning home. Around seven p.m. he
returned to Gino and Carlo for a scotch and water, or two . . .

West on Green from Gino and
Carlo's, next to Caffe Sport,
you could once find at 576
Green:

14 **THE CELLAR**   Most famous of the San Francisco clubs that featured jazz poetry, the Cellar sound is captured on recordings
made by Rexroth and Ferlinghetti. Rexroth later turned sour on some
aspects of the Beat movement. He described beatniks as frequenting
"every Greenwich Village coffee shop and bar for about two years, all
kinds of bums with pawn-shop saxophones put together with scotch
tape, and some other guy with something called poetry, were, like, you,

know, blowing poetry, man, dig? And it was absolutely unmitigated crap. It killed the whole thing."

The Cellar played a key part in Rexroth's later break with the Beats, and especially his growing disregard for Kerouac's works. When Gary Snyder left the Bay Area for Japan on May 15, 1956, Kerouac saw him off on the docks. That night, Kerouac and poet Robert Creeley got smashed in the Cellar and were thrown out by the bouncer. Kerouac invited Creeley to stay with him in Snyder's cabin in Mill Valley. Creeley accepted the offer, but he brought with him Marthe Rexroth whom he had talked into leaving her husband. Rexroth assumed that Kerouac had thus helped to take away his wife. Kerouac soon made Rexroth's literary hit list.

Keep walking west on Green
until you come to:

15 **FUGAZI HALL** best known today for the zany review Beach Blanket Babylon, running for over ten years now. But it's also one of the sites of the Poets Follies, held in the mid-1950s. These standout events—featuring Weldon Kees, Michael Grieg, Vincent McHugh, and Sarah "Stripteasedale," to name only a few—rate with the Six Gallery reading and the poetry and jazz sessions at the Cellar as seminal happenings on the North Beach Scene. In 1984 Italian-American writers held a conference here: Dorothy Cavalli Bryant starred.

Many of the North Beach regulars almost never leave the neighborhood—one man told me he had been out of the area (say, over to Fifth and Mission or downtown) only three times in six years. The hotel and apartment dwellers haunt the Savoy-Tivoli at 1438 Grant, Caffe Roma at 414 Columbus, Caffe Puccini at 411 Columbus, Malvina's Coffee House at 512 Union—and literary life goes on day and night. Some people wonder how the writers always in the cafes find any time to write. (Some of them don't.)

Go back to the intersection at
Columbus, where Stockton
angles in. You'll see the
triangular corner building that
houses the:

16 **U.S. RESTAURANT** This old Italian family restaurant once sheltered working-class Italians and writers alike, and they still pour in. Other places—Mario's Cigar Store on Washington Square, Little Joe's on Broadway, the Cafe Americain down the way on Columbus and the Washington Square Bar and Grill all get their share of the local literati.

In spite of rapid gentrification, North Beach continues to attract writers. Literary events are held regularly at City Lights, at the Intersection, and at small theaters or galleries, like Latif Harris's Bannam Place. And the district remains one of the few parts of the city where the streets are full of people at night. As Ferlinghetti says, "one has the feeling of being in a *quartier*, an intimate neighborhood where convivial life goes on at all levels—the real center of the old City."

CHINATOWN

Stevenson galleon, Portsmouth Square

The Jackson Square district boasts pre-Earthquake buildings which once housed San Francisco's first literary journal— *The Golden Era*. And Portsmouth Square, for many decades the city center, is now the hub of the Chinese community. A literary tour of the area ranges from rough-and-tumble gold rush writers through today's Asian-American cultural renaissance.

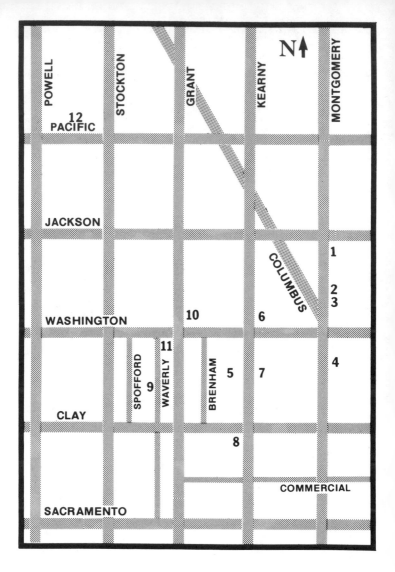

POWELL

STOCKTON

GRANT

KEARNY

N↑

MONTGOMERY

12
PACIFIC

JACKSON

COLUMBUS

1

2
3

WASHINGTON   10   6

4

SPOFFORD

WAVERLY   11

BRENHAM

5   7

9

CLAY

8

COMMERCIAL

SACRAMENTO

Begin at Jackson and Montgomery. The 15 Third and 41 Union will drop you within a block.

The area of four square blocks around the intersection of Jackson and Montgomery preserves several of the oldest structures in San Francisco. The building found fifty feet south on Montgomery from the east corner of Jackson is:

1 **730-32 MONTGOMERY** Research by the Landmark Preservation Advisory Board indicates that "this building was constructed in 1852 on the foundations of an 1849 structure destroyed in the fires of 1851." From 1852-1856 the *Golden Era*, San Francisco's first literary magazine, operated out of this building. Bret Harte worked here as a typesetter. In 1857, after a move to new offices, the *Era* published Harte's first writings, "inconsequential, sugary poems." A vast roster of the city's early writers appeared in the *Era*: Mark Twain, Artemus Ward, Prentice Mulford, Fitzhugh Ludlow ("the American De Quincey," author of *The Hasheesh Eater*), Joaquin Miller and his first wife Minnie Myrtle, called the Sweet Singer of the Coquille.

Next door you'll come to:

2 **728 MONTGOMERY** Lately famous as the office building of flamboyant lawyer Melvin Belli (you can look in the window on skulls, skeletons, hotel keys, and sundry memorabilia he has piled up), this structure dates from 1853-1854. Tradition has it that Harte wrote "The Luck of Roaring Camp" in this building, and that Robert Louis Stevenson and Oscar Wilde came here during their brief stays in the city to visit artist Jules Tavernier in his studio. The artist Joe Strong, with Tavernier a mainstay of the city's early Bohemia (and the man who would marry Stevenson's future step-daughter), also had a studio near here, at the foot of present-day Columbus Avenue. Like many of the claims for a visit by Stevenson, those for stops in this building are suspect. The City Directories for 1879 and 1880 list Tavernier's studio, and sometimes residence, as 729 Montgomery (across the street, no longer standing) — it is unlikely a typo occurs twice in the directory. From 1881 on, however, Tavernier is listed here, so that Wilde's visit in 1882 is certainly more than a "tradition."

A few steps further south will
put you before:

3 **710 MONTGOMERY** The Canessa Park Building housed the famous Black Cat Cafe from the 1930s until its closing in 1963 — a favorite hangout for John Steinbeck when he came to the city, and for William Saroyan, Herb Caen, the artist Dong Kingman, writer Janet Richards, and jazz critic Charles Richards.

*Across Washington Street you'll
see the Transamerica Pyramid
climbing toward the sky. It
stands on the exact site once
occupied by:*

4 THE MONTGOMERY BLOCK   Built in 1853 by General Henry W.
"Old Brains" Halleck, the Montgomery Block was the largest and
most expensive construction west of the Mississippi. Halleck erected the
four-story, block-square building on a raft of redwood logs sunk into the
ground to enable it to ride out earthquakes, and he designed it to be fire-
proof. It survived the 1906 disaster that crumbled or gutted most downtown buildings, but was torn down in 1959 after more than a century, to
clear space for a parking lot. (The modern pyramid was begun in December 1969 and finished by summer 1972.)

Here *S.F. Bulletin* editor James King of William died after his 1855
duel with James Casey. Here, in exile, Dr. Sun Yat-sen drafted the 1911
Chinese constitution which was effected after the overthrow of the Manchu
dynasty. Here in the basement steam baths Mark Twain met the fireman
Tom Sawyer, who later opened a tavern at Third and Mission; after
Twain's popular novel was published Sawyer added to the sign on his
establishment "Ale & Spirits — The Original Tom Sawyer, Prop." Ambrose
Bierce, Frank and Charles and Kathleen Norris, Charles Warren Stoddard,
Joaquin Miller, Gelett Burgess, Sadakichi Hartmann, and W. C. Morrow,
lived in the "Monkey Block." In fact, more than two thousand writers
and artists came to work and play in this single most important literary
locale in the West during the 19th and early 20th centuries.

Literary San Franciscans frequented Pappa Coppa's restaurant on
one corner of the block and drank Pisco Punch in the Bank Exchange
bar on the other corner. *Literary San Francisco* calls Coppa's "the most
important turn-of-the-century bohemian rendezvous," and Mary Austin
in her autobiography said it was "where I met George Sterling and Lafler,
James Hopper, Xavier Martinez, and the two Newberrys . . ." — most of
the cast that later set up the operatic Carmel artist colony. "Sterling had
written me and called. One dined so very well at Coppa's: such platefuls
of fresh shrimps; such sand dabs and crisp salads; such almond tartlets

and dago red. Then there were the intriguing decorations; I recall the black cats and the large gentleman with the motto, 'Paste makes waist.' " Porter Garnett, Martinez and others contributed to these extravagant Coppa murals wi th drawings in crayon, charcoal, & chalk. Names of the greats—Aristotle, Dante, Rabelais, Goethe, Verlaine, Kant—were interspersed with local talent Sterling, Martinez, Lafler, Burgess, Newberry (and Perry Newberry's wife "Butsky," the cigarette fiend).

George Sterling kept a room here too, probably paid for by Mickey Bender, or another of his friends and patrons. One old-time Monkey Block resident recalled that the poet sometimes bothered other roomers by marching up and down the halls reciting poems. This room was for love affairs—none of the hundred or so women who came to his funeral (and Pan knows how many others) would have been allowed into the Bohemian Club, where he lived.

As the bohemians converted into studios the old offices of lawyers and businessmen who had been the block's original tenants, the latter moved into newer offices and replaced in the Bohemian Club all the bohemian writers and artists who had originally founded it, prompting the shrewd observation from "Riptides" columnist Robert O'Brien: "A Montgomery Block residence is the equivalent of a membership card in the poor man's Bohemian Club."

A plaque describing the Montgomery Block may be found in the lobby of the pyramid, and a modern version of the Bank Exchange is open, but the atmosphere of the grand old days is gone, when Mary Austin would make an engagement to meet Sterling here before going "to fill the Stevenson galleon with violets." But you may still follow their route west a block on Washington, across Kearny, to:

5 PORTSMOUTH SQUARE The Spanish custom house inspected shipments coming into the Bay until July 9, 1846, when Captain John B. Montgomery raised the American flag here and began a new era for the city. When Sam Brannan announced in this plaza on May 11, 1848, that gold had been discovered, he created a boomtown—by the year of the Forty Niners the city was spreading rapidly out from the hub of this original town square and is still growing.

In the northwest corner of this small park you'll find the first monument ever erected to honor the memory of Robert Louis Stevenson. *Les Jeunes* mainstays Bruce Porter and Willis Polk were chairmen of the committee that gathered the $1,500 for materials to build this memorial. Polk designed and constructed the pedestal, which features Stevenson's "Christmas Sermon," and Porter cast the model of the galleon *Hispaniola* from *Treasure Island* that rides the bronze Spanish Main atop the column, which Sterling and Austin filled with violets that day in San Francisco before the fire.

Roy Nickerson in *Robert Louis Stevenson in California* (1982) notes that the monument was dedicated October 17, 1897; Stevenson's stepson Lloyd Osbourne (for whom Stevenson wrote *Treasure Island*) and landlady Mary Carson of 608 Bush were among the many people present. Originally the monument stood in the center of the square on the spot where Stevenson sat alone in great depression on Christmas Day, 1879, and where he returned time and again in the next months to write, sitting on a bench in the sun. When the parking garage under the square was being built the monument was dismantled, removed, and later relocated on the present site; Nickerson points out that the movers replaced the *Hispaniola* on "changed tacks"— it now points north instead of south.

This monument has been a lodestone for writers— Sterling made sure he was photographed here, leaning against the pillar with a book of poetry in hand, and Sadakichi Hartmann had his photo made about 1916 as he put a wreath on the monument. Dashiell Hammett was aware of this literary site too: in the Op story "Zigzags of Treachery" the short fat detective is led by a suspect "down Kearny Street to Portsmouth Square" where the shadowed man "stretched himself out on the grass face down, lit a black pipe, and lay looking dejectedly at the Stevenson monument, probably without seeing it."

On the western side of this park the Mormon leader Sam Brannan founded the first newspaper in San Francisco, the *Star* (later the *Alta Californian*), at Washington and Brenhan on the original town square—the site is unmarked. But on the wall next to 19 Brenhan you'll find a plaque on the spot where John Hamilton Still opened the city's first bookstore. He arrived in California September 16, 1849, and soon opened the shop, which he operated until spring the next year, exchanging literature for gold fresh from the hills. Still's granddaughter Mrs. William Ely Chambers and the Society of California Pioneers erected this plaque September 16, 1965.

On the eastern side of the park a footbridge arches across Kearny to the Holiday Inn. Plaques engraved with traditional Chinese aphorisms decorate the walkway walls. Pause halfway across and look from the north side of the bridge down toward the east side of Kearny between Washington and Jackson, the former site of the:

6 INTERNATIONAL HOTEL   One of the great tenants' rights battles in the modern city was fought in the late 1970s by the residents of the I Hotel as they barricaded themselves in the building against a police seige. Like the Montgomery Block before it, the low-level brick structure was razed in 1980 to make way for yet another parking lot—or more likely, with presumed changes in zoning laws and a few political favors, for the inevitable highrise.

The I Hotel was a major Asian American literary center, beginning about 1969 when members of the revolutionary Red Dragon Party moved into the International. With the opening of Everybody's Bookstore, many writers and artists from Chinatown and nearby Manilatown were drawn to the I—which, with its cheap rent, became a natural center of action. In 1972 Jim Dong and Michael Chin founded the now famous Kearny Street Workshop to bring the arts to the youth of the neighborhood, opening photography, printmaking, and potters' studies for community use. That same year George Leong and Al Robles launched the Writers' Workshop. For the first time, Asian-American writers from all over the Bay Area were brought together for various literary activities, and the 1970s saw a phenomenal burst of activity. The Jackson Street Gallery, located at the site of the old hungry i, exhibited works by local Asian American artists during this renaissance. Among the writers who came to prominence, in numerous anthologies and books, readings and performances, were Virginia Cerenio, Jessica Tarahata Hagedorn, Yuri Kageyama, Geraldine Kudaka, Genny Lim, Janice Mirikitani, Richard Oyama, Luis Syquia, Jeff Tagamai, Kitty Tsui, Nellie Wong, Shawn Wong, Merle Woo, Victor Wong, Doug Yamamoto, Frank Chin, Milton Murayama, Norman Jayo, and Alan Chong Lau.

Many of the International Hotel's writer-residents helped man the barricades through the last days, and helped memorialize it after the mass eviction of all its tenants in the collection *Poems from the I Hotel* (1979). Curtis Choy's fine film "The Fall of the I Hotel" documents the final seige and seizure.

Across the street in the building now occupied by the Hunan Village Restaurant was the old Luck M Pool Hall, a historic meeting-place for musicians, political activists, and writers. Here Joaquin Legaspi—painter, writer, merchant seaman—gave legendary readings.

*Continue across the bridge into
the Holiday Inn and:*

7 THE CHINESE CULTURAL CENTER Since the destruction of the International Hotel, the Chinese Cultural Center here in this highrise hotel has provided space for some events sponsored by the now homeless Kearny Street Workshop, and continues to offer its own more mainstream lectures, films, and workshops. The spacious gallery on occasion features displays on the lives and works of Chinese writers, and in the small bookshop you may find a conservative selection of the many books that have come out of the community. The bookstore also hosts autograph parties—such as the gala celebration in 1981 for Yuan-Tsun Chen upon publication of *The Dragon's Village*, a novel based on her experiences in the Chinese cultural revolution.

*Near the southeast corner of
Portsmouth Square at:*

8 CLAY AND KEARNY The Filipino-American poet Al Robles, co-founder of the Writers' Workshop, directs the Manilatown Senior Center, whose facilities are often used for pan-Asian literary events.

Robles, a San Francisco native, evokes Manilatown in *Breaking Silence*;
An Anthology of Contemporary Asian American Poets (1983) as an:

> ifugao mountain wood and rock collector, now involved in collecting carabao
> tales with ragged patches of the first pilipinos, old-timers — manongs, in america —
> in a place called manilatown where the smell of chicken blood fills the air — where
> adobo soaks up your tribal vision — where pig entrails dangle like rosary beads
> from the sky — where carabaos dance on each rice grain — where the taste of life
> is in the heart of fish tales and loincloth rituals — where brown hands meet the
> moon together.

*South half a block on Kearny will bring you to Commercial Street, which
housed the old Mint where Bret Harte worked. The eastmost blocks of
Commercial occupy the position of the Long Wharf, which reached far
out into the Bay from Montgomery before landfill made it a regular thoroughfare. Alonzo Delano ran a produce stall on this wharf in the 1850s,
and wrote humorous articles about the Forty Niners under the penname
"Old Block," collected as* Pen-Knife Sketches, or Chips of the Old Block
(1853) and Old Block's Sketch Book *(1856). The fabulous Emperor
Norton, ruler by his own decree of a much easier (and long gone) San
Francisco, lived on Commercial — a stroll on the few blocks that have
escaped the expanding highrise boom will give you a good look at the city
of his day, before the falling of the concrete shadows.*

*Go west on Commercial to
Grant, right half a block to Clay,
then west again. Off Clay
between Grant and Stockton
Streets run two narrow streets:*

9 WAVERLY PLACE & SPOFFORD ALLEY   In the garishly titled story
"Dead Yellow Women," Hammett does a fine send-up of the nefarious
Oriental masterminds that populate so much pulp fiction, typified by Sax
Rohmer's insidious Dr. Fu Manchu. Hammett's brilliant villain Chang Li
Ching's stronghold is spread throughout buildings, linked by subter-
ranean passageways on Waverly and Spofford, and the plot concerns
murder, illegal immigrants, and Far East political wars. (In another story a
movie theatre owner claims he has been robbed by a group of "creeping
Siamese" — the Op's comment: "Being around movies all the time has
poisoned his idea of what sounds plausible.")

Racist perceptions of Asian language and culture by the 1920s created
a vast literature so fantastic, so spiced with menace, that today it is regarded as a romanticized, archaic sub-grouping of the mystery story.
The so-called "Yellow Peril" novel began with Pierton W. Dooner's *Last
Days of the Republic*, issued by the Alta Californian Publishing House
here in San Francisco in 1880 as propaganda to limit immigration from
China, picturing incoming waves of Asians organizing a military takeover.
Dozens of similar books followed, with Charles Foley's *Kowa the Mysterious* (1909) a "highpoint" in this dubious field for the savagery of its
racist denunciation of Chinese and its bizarre plot — an underground
domed city where the "Oriental menace" is gathering collapses, causing
the 1906 earthquake!

A reverse stereotype to such figures as Fu Manchu is found in Charlie
Chan, created in 1925 by Earl Derr Biggers. This Honolulu police detective sleuthed his way through six novels (several with San Francisco set-

tings) and dozens of films, but Chan is only an example of another kind of prejudice at work.

Even sympathetic writers sifted and stereotyped Asian culture through Western perceptions: the visiting Aesthete Oscar Wilde found Chinatown

> the most artistic town I have ever come across. The people – strange, melancholy Orientals, whom any people would call common, and they are certainly very poor – have determined that they will have nothing about them that is not beautiful. . . .

The restaurants present the bill, he noted, "made out on rice paper, the account being done in India ink as fantastically as if an artist had been etching little birds on a fan."

Dr. C. W. Doyle of Santa Cruz wrote *The Shadow of Quong Lung* (dedicated to Ambrose Bierce, "by his grateful pupil") to attract notice to the plight of slave prostitutes in Chinatown, but this 1900 novel begins with a Chinese woman shrilling in "pidgin English" as her child runs toward a streetcar, "slop him, my lil Moy, slop him!" Erle Stanley Gardner, who often defended Chinese clients as a lawyer in Oxnard, wrote seventy-three stories for *Black Mask* about Ed Jenkins, "the Phantom Crook," most of which take place in Chinatown. But even though Gardner was familiar with Chinese on a workaday basis, he could not resist the commercial allure of presenting the "mystery Chinatown" that so appealed to his pulp audience.

The mysterious allure is a literary creation. As you walk down Waverly Place and Spofford Alley today you'll find that the sheer stairs Hammett pictured leading down to Chang's lair probably led to one of several places along this row that handset the type for the many Chinese-language newspapers. In the 1970s one such paper was the S.F. Journal, *a community journal in which Maurice Chuck published many poems by local authors. Along these thriving commecial lanes you'll find Taoist and Buddhist temples, the Chinese Library of America, the Sinocast radio studios, travel agencies and other businesses. Sun Yat-sen plotted the 1911 revolution that brought down the Empress Tzi Hsi from 36-38 Spofford Alley. Up Sacramento from Grant is the newspaper office of* Cathay Times *and* Young China Daily *where Sun Yat-sen's desk is still in place.*

Sui Sin Far (American name, Edith Eaton) was the first Chinese American author to write with less inclination for sensation or romantic coloring. As early as 1912 her *Mrs. Spring Fragrance* collected realistic stories about Chinese-Americans coping with their status in a foreign country. Several Chinese-American writers have come from Chinatown: poet George Leong, author of *A Lone Bamboo Dress Doesn't Come from Jackson Street*, grew up near the corner of Jackson and Mason; the poet and short-story writer Russell Leong, one-time editor of the KPFA *Folio*, was born here, as were Merle Woo, Victor Wong, and historian-novelist Ruthanne Lum McCunn, acclaimed for *A Thousand Pieces of Gold*, a powerful documentary story about Chinese immigrants in the pioneer West.

An earlier generation of intellectuals and writers has walked these literary streets too. Nobles Alley in North Beach is the home of C. H. Kwock, translator (with Vincent McHugh) of the collection *Old Friend from Far*

Away. He and Nelson Yee, another familiar figure on the scene for decades, might be found in Spec's and Vesuvio—hangouts midway between North Beach and Chinatown.

In the 1950s the first great commercial success for an Asian writer here came for C. Y. Lee's *The Flower Drum Song* (1957), in which Grant Avenue is portrayed as "the Canton of the Occident." The novel was adapted for a Rogers and Hammerstein musical play and later filmed. Lee, who came to American from Hunan province in 1943 and settled in San Francisco in the early 1950s, has written several other novels, memoirs, and a history of the Tong wars. Books by Jade Snow Wong, such as *Fifth Chinese Daughter*, have sold hundreds of thousands of copies; her Jade Snow Wong Studio and travel agency is something of an institution over at 2123 Polk Street.

The genteel novels about Chinatown that were the rule until the new ethnic militance of the 1970s are considered by some to be sell-outs to the still romanticized Western market. Playwright and novelist Frank Chin, author of *The Chickencoop Chinaman* and *The Year of the Dragon* (1981) says the polite novels about Chinatown are "sucking white fantasy and telling lies for a buck." Chin detests the quaint tourist view of Chinatown, and portrays it as a physically and psychologically oppressive ghetto where, as one critic notes, "a satisfactory masculine identity is hard to come by." Chin has stirred up controversy—and once was punched out in an argument with Alex Hing over *The Chickencoop Chinaman*.

For some hangouts of young Asian writers you can walk along Grant, past Washington, to where the false cavern front at 916 Grant opens on the sidewalk, leading into:

10 LI PO'S BAR   Named after the great Chinese poet, Li Po's is an active literary bar today. Filmmaker Wayne Wang, whose "Chan is Missing" received great critical acclaim (and awe from many quarters, because he made the film for only a few thousand dollars, instead of the millions usually sunk into movies today), is setting his next film in Li Po's—to capture this place in celluloid.

Other highlights of literary Chinatown include obvious places such as the local branch of the San Francisco Public Library at 1135 Powell — and not so obvious places such as St. Mary's Park, a meeting-place of the intellectuals, especially the old-timers who call themselves Longtime Californ'.

You could do a literary eating tour through Chinatown, too — with good food at relatively low prices, it has always been a place writers come for chow. After the Six Gallery reading, the Beat Generation Poets and their friends headed for 813 Washington Street to:

11 SAM WO'S — along with Woey Loy Goey, a haunt of the Beats. Here, according to Kerouac biographer Dennis McNally, "Gary Snyder showed Jack Kerouac how to order and use chopsticks, all the while telling humorous Zen anecdotes." Along Jackson Street today you may find writers from the Kearny Street Workshop in some of their favored places — Red's at 672 Jackson, the Lun Ting Cafe (known as Pork Chop House among the writers) next door at 670. When the night gets old and places begin to close their doors, hungry writers migrate down the street to Woey Loy Goey, called by some "The Hole." If it's really late, they head for the Ocean Sky — an act nearing desperation. For a late drink they may adjourn to Li Po's, or Spec's or Vesuvio, or Mr. Bing's at 201 Columbus, down the street.

North Beach and Chinatown merge culturally in many ways, and as Chinatown moves north into the area once known as Little Italy some wits are calling the area the Marco Polo Zone.

One last site on this tour is now a Chinese housing project, though you should be aware that at 848 Pacific Street, between Stockton and Powell, was once found:

12 IZZY GOMEZ'S SALOON "The old honkytonk," where whores and lowlife mixed with "society people" was dramatized by William Saroyan as Nick's Waterfront Saloon in *The Time of Your Life*, winning the New York Drama Critic's Circle Award and a Pulitzer, which Saroyan refused to accept. The bar is long gone now, but the play lives on — and the saloon too, in memory and local legend. In *The City at the End of the Rainbow* (1976) David Siefkin describes the celebrities come to visit the 1939 World's Fair on Treasure Island, writing that a "look into Izzy Gomez's saloon on Pacific Street revealed not only the 300-pound Gomez preparing his steakburgers and beakers of red wine but, in a corner, sipping his wine, Somerset Maugham." An immortal literary watering hole.

MISSION

Roberto Vargas and Alejandro Murguía on Mission Street, 1976

Covering an area larger than the entire downtown, including North Beach, Russian Hill, Nob Hill, and the Tenderloin, the Mission sweeps from South of Market on its northern face to Army Street on the south — encompassing the most active literary scene in 1980s San Francisco. Writers and multi-media artists have taken over warehouses for work space where the Mission joins South of Market and over toward Potrero Hill, and the coffeehouses, clubs, and galleries along Mission and Valencia are the center for an especially active movement among women and Latino writers.

The easiest way to tour the Mission and surrounds is by car, but an enterprising walker with a bus map in hand for covering the long stretches can search out these sites — perhaps making a couple of trips of it.

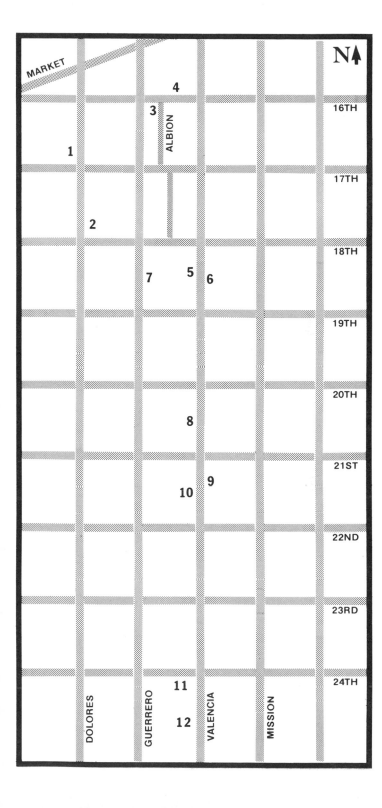

*Begin the tour on Dolores
between 16th and 17th streets
three blocks south of Market
at the:*

1 **MISSION DOLORES**   The first writing done in this city was by Father Francisco Palóu here in the Misión San Francisco de Asís — the sixth mission founded as the Spaniards staked their claim to California. It was named for Saint Francis of Assisi, founder of the Franciscan Order, whose name the city itself now bears. Palóu founded this mission June 29, 1776, and Father Junípero Serra dedicated it October 9th of that year. Construction on the present building was begun April 25, 1782, and completed in 1784.

In this building Palóu wrote his biography of his friend Serra, who had lived in the same religious house on Mallorca before they left Spain to colonize the New World. In *Literary San Francisco* Nancy Peters notes: "In promoting his friend for beatification, Palóu so embroidered upon Serra's real achievements — distorting facts, slandering secular explorers, and supplying miracles — that this part of his book may be said to qualify as imaginative literature." *Relación Histórica de la Vida y Apostólicas Tareas del Venerable Padre Fray Junípero Serra* was published in Mexico City in 1787. Palóu also wrote *Noticias de la Nueva California*, covering his nine years in San Francisco, as well as other points in this new land. He records the opening ceremonies for Mission Dolores, which featured firecrackers and the explosion of ships' rockets, saying in summation: "The day had been a joyful one for all. Only the savages did not enjoy themselves on this happy day!" (Indeed, the Indians were afraid to return to the vicinity of the mission for several days, and we know now that those fireworks sounded the death-knell for their culture.)

As late as winter 1835-36, when Richard Henry Dana sailed into the Bay on the *Alert*, he found only one shack built by a trader and this mission situated in the entire area, as he recorded in his maritime classic *Two Years Before the Mast* (1840), a book that has never gone out of print.

For the nominal fee of 50¢ you may tour this historic mission, the oldest structure in San Francisco. It is closed on Thanksgiving and Christmas, but open from 9 a.m. to 4:30 p.m. May 1-October 31; 10 a.m. to 4 p.m. November 1-April 30; 10 a.m. to 1 p.m. New Year's Day and Easter; 10 a.m. to noon on Good Friday.

*In the next block, past 17th,
you'll find:*

2 **569 DOLORES**   The anarchist writer Emma Goldman lived here with her lover Alexander Berkman in 1916; she had come to the city to show support for Tom Mooney, on trial "for a bombing he did not commit." Mooney and Warren Billings both spent decades in prison on the charge that they planted the bomb in the 1916 Preparedness Day parade on Market Street, before they were finally pardoned and released. The liberated Goldman also gave lectures in the city, on feminism and birth control, inspiring by her example later groups such as the Sexual Freedom League.

San Francisco novelist Herbert Gold notes in his preface to *The Records of the San Francisco Sexual Freedom League* (1971) that the book is "dedicated to Emma Goldman, the famous anarchist who once dandled on her copious lap a baby who became my former wife. She bounced her on her knee. If only she had dropped her, how different my life would have been!"

Return to 16th Street and turn right, walking past Guerrero and pausing within a quarter block at:

3 ALBION STREET In the last block of this two-block-long street the poet Harold Norse, author of *The Beat Hotel*, lives now.

Another quarter block will put you before 3120 16th Street, across the way from the Roxie Theatre, the:

4 CAFE PICARO This combination cafe-restaurant-bookstore is the scene for many evenings of readings or performances, a place where you can sit at the old oak tables and read the used books in stock over coffee or a hearty, simple meal.

Another place is found about a block away: go on to Valencia, turn right, and stop at 766 Valencia:

5 THE VALENCIA ROSE RESTAURANT-CABARET You can't miss this iron-balconied stucco building, painted rose madder with blue trim. With a full schedule of events, including poetry readings, the Valencia Rose is one of the district's hottest literary night spots.

Other literary venues in this area include the Artemis Cafe, Baha'i Center, the Clarion Cafe, EYE Gallery, New Langton Arts, Newspace, Noe Valley Poetry, Southern Exposure Gallery, Project Artaud, Studio W, the Victoria Theatre, Talking Leaves Bookstore, The Women's Building, San Francisco Socialist School, Studio Rhino, Studio Eremos, and 544 Natoma. For a schedule of the proliferating literary events here – and all over the Bay Area – pick up a free copy of Joyce Jenkins and Steven Abbott's monthly Poetry Flash *in bookstores, cafes, ice cream shops; you can't miss this widely distributed, invaluable and up-to-the-minute calendar.*

Across the street from the Valencia Rose at 777 Valencia you'll find:

6 NEW COLLEGE OF CALIFORNIA Robert Duncan, a longtime resident of the Mission who now lives on 20th Street, is director of poetry here – permanent poetry teachers also include Duncan

McNaughton, editor of *Mother* and *Father*, author of *Shit on My Shoes*;
leading language-poet and critic Michael Palmer; kabbalist-poet David
Meltzer; Lois Patler; and Diane diPrima.

Two blocks south on Valencia
will bring you to:

7 MODERN TIMES BOOKSTORE This cooperatively-run bookstore at 968 Valencia carries one of the city's best selections of radical and progressive books, magazines, posters, and records, with
especially strong sections in sociology, media, and political economy—
though they stock a bit of everything here, and even have a children's
book nook.

Here you may find books by several of the radical writers who have
lived in San Francisco, such as Emma Goldman, or Al Richman, author
of *A Long View from the Left* (1972). If they have them in stock, the early
writings of Mike Gold might be of interest. Gold came to the city in the
mid-1950s and lived here until his death in 1967. In the 1920s he was a
prominent literary critic, and was very influential in directing other
critics—Edmund Wilson, for one—toward a leftwing sensibility. Gold's
Jews Without Money (1930) is considered a classic. (Unfortunately, by
the 1940s Gold lost the critical distance necessary for such writing—in
his years in San Francisco he basically served as a literary hack for the
Stalinists.)

In the next block at 1009
Valencia you'll come to:

8 OLD WIVES TALES This bookstore, like Modern Times, provides
several weekly book-related events: lectures, slide shows, readings,
and autograph parties. Old Wives Tales carries an astonishing array of
books by, about, and for women, and is one of the major centers for the
women's literary movement in the Bay Area.

Shameless Hussy Press, the Women's Press Collective, and others
are publishing an impressive number of books by women poets such
as Janice Mirikitani, Pat Parker, Susan Griffin, and Kathleen Fraser.
Parker has said: "The response of women to poets was so great after
coming out of that male competitive scene in poetry. Women are very
supportive and not into putting people down." This movement also has
spearheaded renewed recognition for older, well-known Bay Area
writers (past and present) such as Tillie Olson, Josephine Miles, Kay
Boyle, and Ruth Weiss; in a local radio interview Meridel Le Seuer said
of her literary reputation: "I call myself 'Mrs. Lazarus'—I was buried and
the women's movement dug me up."

Dorothy Bryant is one of the major figures to emerge from the
flourishing small press scene in the Bay Area. Born in San Francisco in
1929, Bryant grew up here in the Mission District, and later taught
school in the city and in the East Bay for almost twenty-five years before
becoming a full-time writer. Her *Writing a Novel* (1978) is a how-to-do-it
book by an author who tackles any kind of novel she feels like—mainstream, science fiction, mystery. *The Kin of Ata Are Waiting for You*
(1976) is a utopian novel originally issued by Bryant's own Ata Press,
following Bryant's first book *Ella Price's Journal* (1972). *Miss Giardino*

Dorothy Bryant

(1978) is set in the Mission, and the main character of Bryant's controversial *A Day in San Francisco* (1982) is Clara Lontana, fifty years old, who also grew up in this neighborhood, and returns to the city to confront her gay son at the annual Gay Freedom Day. Of the writers who have used San Francisco in their fiction, Bryant is one of the most accurate in evoking a specific place. Her most recent "novel of ideas" *Killing Wonder* (1984) makes use of a whodunit format to explore some intriguing aspects of the women's writing and publishing scene. Her protagonist Jessamyn Rebecca Posey takes the F bus to visit the Latina writer-publisher Yolanda Dolores, heads into the Mission:

> lurching past Mexican restaurants next to big chain stores, huge old movie houses hollowed out at the bottom to make parking lots, furniture stores with windows full of puffy-glittering junk, brand-new bank buildings and empty old store buildings. The first time I took the bus down Mission Street, they were planting little palm trees along the sidewalks. The trees were still there, but they hadn't grown much. They looked dry and stunted, pathetic little gray-tan poles. I got off at Twenty-fourth Street.

Most of the action takes place in Berkeley (Bryant's present home); through the East Bay and in various San Francisco neighborhoods Posey pursues writers suspected of murdering an Anais Nin sort of figure.

Off Valencia at 3410 19th
Street you'll find the San
Francisco branch of the:

9 HENRY GEORGE SCHOOL OF SOCIAL SCIENCE This school and twenty-one other offices throughout the world continue the teachings of that radical economist and author, whom Miriam Allen deFord in *They Were San Franciscans* (1941) described as the one American who "has been the father of an economic theory which has commanded and continues to command world-wide adherence, which possesses devoted disciples whose efforts to introduce their system into cities, states, and even nations are unabating. . . . And the father of the single tax was an American, born in Philadelphia, but resident for the best years of his life in San Francisco. His name was Henry George. He is the only American analogy of that other great system maker, Karl Marx."

In 1871 George proposed his single tax by which rent would derive from *land* instead of from individuals, swinging the weight of taxes from the greater populace to the relatively few landowners. He developed this theory in *Progress and Poverty*, published the year before he left San Francisco for New York in 1880. When the home where Henry George wrote *Progress and Poverty* was demolished several years ago, the local Georgists salvaged the plaque which had been erected on the building in honor of the economist. The plaque is being held in the school offices until the day it may be replaced in an appropriate site in this city where the single tax was born.

Continue down the block to
Mission and turn right. Two
blocks south, past 21st Street,
you'll find:

10 LIBRERIA LA LATINA It is perhaps ironic that the district that has grown up around the original Spanish Mission should once more be full of Spanish-speaking people, but bilingual bookstores such as this one at 2548 Mission Street reflect the fact that the Latino settlement did not grow up in the Richmond or Sunset Districts. Much of the Latino literary movement has been fired by the political situation in Central America over the past decade and a half. You'll find this alliance of literature and politics reflected in the offerings of most Mission bookstores. . .

As at 2848 Mission two blocks
further south, past 24th, in:

11 BOOKWORKS This store hosts a variety of events such as autograph parties and poetry readings, with an emphasis on Latin America and the political scene. Recent distinguished visitors have included John Nicols, Victor Navasky, Juan Rulofo, Ariel Dorfman, and Victor Perrera.

A few doors further south at
2868 Mission is the:

12 MISSION CULTURAL CENTER Much of the initial impetus in the local literary-political scene was created by this center, which served as a *locus* for the Latino writers, sponsoring readings for the poet-priest Ernesto Cardenal — now the Minister of Culture in Nicaragua, the pro-Allende poet Fernando Alegria of Chile, and the Nicaraguan poet Roberto Vargas. Lawrence Ferlinghetti observed that the "San Francisco Latino writers were much more active politically in the 1970s, and in fact more effective, than their Anglo counterparts in town." This active political involvement continues today with the support of lobbying movements, educational publications, and refugee programs, as the center hosts visiting Latin American authors and serves as a forum for films, concerts, and theatrical pieces. Over 75,000 people took part in its programs and classes in 1983 alone.

With the explosive growth of both Latino writing and women's writing in this neighborhood, it is no exaggeration to say that the Mission is the center for the most active poetry scene in San Francisco since the Beats ruled North Beach.

One of the most active sites may be found at 2851 24th Street, at Bryant, some eight blocks east of Mission Street:

13 **THE GALERIA DE LA RAZA AND STUDIO 24** This gallery and next door studio offer for sale many artworks and sponsor shows by traditional and contemporary artists. They are a favorite hangout for Mission District writers Francisco Alarcón, Juan Felipe Herrera, Victor Hernández Cruz, Tina Avila, Magaly Fernández, Alejandro Murguía, Tina Alvárez-Robles, Margarita Robles, and Wilfred Castaño.

Continuing east to Potrero, then right for a couple of blocks will bring you to 1499 Potrero hidden away under the freeway interchange:

14 **THE FARM AND CLOUDHOUSE** The Farm is a working farm, with various crops, lettuce gardens, and cows, here next to one of the major industrial areas of San Francisco. The various rooms and floors of the main building, a converted warehouse, have been used for any number of multi-media events and benefits, from Mark Pauline's dynamic exhibits of motorized dead animals and explosive scenarios to a Memorial Party for Gary Warne. Within the Farm you'll find Cloudhouse, managed by Kush, a familiar non-stop poetry reader you'll probably see reciting on some street corner around the city one day — flamboyant impresario for many a wild literary event down on the Farm.

Rising to the northeast above The Farm you'll see the southern heights of:

15 **POTRERO HILL** The major literary sites are on the northeast slopes of this hill, the side where it climbs up above the railroad switchyards South of Market where Jack Kerouac worked as a brakeman for Southern Pacific. It is an area offering an impressive view of the high-rise skyline of downtown San Francisco and the Bay.

Lawrence Ferlinghetti moved to Potrero Hill in 1958 with his wife Kirby, buying the small Victorian at 706 Wisconsin, between 20th and 22nd streets. Over the years they watched the skyscrapers go up. Originally they had had a view of Telegraph Hill and Coit Tower. Literary visitors to this house included Kerouac, Ginsberg, Cassady, Orlovsky, Snyder, McClure, and other writers and poets of the Beat Generation and many others published by City Lights. Lord Buckley, Robert Duncan, William Saroyan, and Kenneth Rexroth were other authors who stopped by during Ferlinghetti's residence, and for a few years in the 1970s Jerry Kamstra, author of *The Frisco Kid* and *Weed*, lived in the basement flat. In 1972 Ferlinghetti left this house and moved into an apartment over the City Lights publication offices in North Beach.

Kenneth Rexroth, before his move to Scott Street in the 1950s, lived only two doors downhill from Ferlinghetti's place, in the house fronted by the small yard behind the tall wood fence. His first poetry collection, *In What Hour,* appeared in 1941; by the 1950s Rexroth was the literary lion of the city — an era documented in the memoir *Common Soldiers* (1979) by Janet Richards, another Potrero Hill writer. Rexroth was an erudite poet and critic who came to the city from Chicago the day San Francisco's unofficial poet laureate, George Sterling, killed himself in 1927. David Meltzer described Rexroth as "an early progenitor of what many consider the archetypal California poet: naturalist, classicist, mountain-climber, orientalist, anarchist, polyglot, down-to-earth mystic, autodidact, at ease in most elements of society." However, Rexroth's work in more than twenty volumes of poetry and translations, and in his collected criticism in *Assays*, goes beyond that of a mere regionalist: some feel that Rexroth is one of the great American *littérateurs* of his generation.

About seven blocks away at 412 Mississippi, near 19th Street, Frank P. Herbert lived in the late 1950s and early 1960s. Herbert worked for the Hearst *Examiner* as an editor on *California Living*, writing science fiction on the side. His early novels such as *Dragon of the Sea* (1956) — also known as *21st Century Sub* and *Under Pressure* — established Herbert in that field, but it was *Dune* (1965) that proved to be his masterpiece, a massive novel that won both the Hugo and Nebula Awards as best of the year and became a multi-edition cult classic, the basis for a multi-million-dollar film. This novel, which has sold more than ten million copies, made *The Book of Lists* #2 as one of "11 Bestselling Books Rejected by 13 or More Publishers" — it was deemed "too slow," "too long," and "confusing and irritating." (The several sequels with which Herbert has followed *Dune* routinely take their place at the top of the bestseller lists.) Herbert now lives in the Pacific Northwest and on Maui.

Lawrence Swaim wrote the novels *Waiting for the Earthquake* (1977) and *The Killing* (1980) on this hill at 1225 De Haro, and in his place on Missouri Street Larry Gonick wrote and drew a *Cartoon History of the Universe*, published in comic book format by Rip-Off Press and issued by Morrow in book form in 1982.

South of the Mission rises
another series of ridges
known as:

16 BERNAL HEIGHTS   Novelists Frank Browning, Steve Chapel, and Gordon De Marco have made their homes here, and young Jack London once lived on a farm in this area with his mother and step-father John London. David Mason finished *The Return of Kavin* (1972) at 618 Gates, which was in near-ruin when he stayed there in 1969, and also wrote the science fiction novel *The Shores of Tomorrow* (1971) and three porno novels. (One of these, *Devil's Food*, is a science fantasy porn book set in San Francisco.) Bret Harte lived even further south at 40 Silver Avenue in 1864; Kate Douglas Wiggin, famous for *Rebecca of Sunnybrook Farm* (1903), established the first free kindergarten on the West Coast on Silver Avenue later in the 1800s.

Working your way toward Noe
Valley and the Castro you can
stop off at Valencia at Army,
where you'll find on the wall of:

17 **1538 VALENCIA** a plaque marking the original site of the Bancroft Library, collected by Hubert Howe Bancroft in order to write his monumental history of the West. First kept in Bancroft's "history factory" on Market Street so that he and his assistants could use it for research, the library was moved to this site in 1881. In 1905 it was purchased by the University of California and moved in 1906 to the campus in Berkeley.

On Sanchez between 30th Street and Randall you may see:

18 **1715 SANCHEZ** On October 23, 1927, a midwife delivered Philip Lamantia in the garret of this two-story wood-frame house. When Lamantia was fifteen André Breton published his first poems in the surrealist journal *VVV*, and this San Francisco native has become a major voice in that field. Dropping out of high school, he moved to New York when he was sixteen, then lived in Morocco, Greece, Spain, and Mexico until his return to the city fourteen years ago. Lamantia has been an editor on *Arsenal, Cultural Correspondence*, and *Free Spirits: Annals of the Insurgent Imagination*, contributing poems and essays on surrealism, occultism, Amerind myths, and pop culture. His books include *Selected Poems 1943-1966, The Blood of the Air, Becoming Visible, Touch of the Marvelous, Erotic Poems*, and *Destroyed Works.*

On Jersey near Diamond you'll find:

19 **471 JERSEY** The place Don Carpenter was living at the time he put together the poetry reading for Gary Snyder, Philip Whalen, and Lew Welch in Longshoremen's Hall in 1964 — in this period Carpenter was working on early fiction and plays, setting many of them in North Beach. His first novel *Hard Rain Falling*, featuring an extensive San Francisco scene, was published in 1966.

Following Diamond north to 18th, and dropping down east two blocks will put you at:

20 **18TH AND CASTRO** The heart of the Castro area, a major center for the gay bar scene, this intersection is where the first home stood in Kathryn Forbes' bestselling *Mama's Bank Account* (1943) made into both a play and a movie under the title "I Remember Mama," and a TV show as "Mama." Frank M. Robinson used his share of royalties from the epic disaster film "The Towering Inferno," starring Paul

Newman and Steve McQueen, to buy a house near here at Noe and 20th; the film, shot here in the city, was based in part on *The Glass Inferno*— one of several novels Robinson has co-authored with Thomas Scortia. The poet and science fiction writer Emil Petaja also has lived in this area, up on Diamond, for decades, and Armistead Maupin moved to the Castro from Telegraph Hill recently. A few blocks north on Castro, journalist Warren Hinckle lives in a black-painted house.

From Castro and Beaver you may head west up the steep hill to the bare knob of rock known as:

21 CORONA HEIGHTS   More easily approached from Roosevelt and Museum Way, Corona Heights is where the ashes of the sorceror Thibaut de Castries are buried at midnight in Fritz Leiber's novel *Our Lady of Darkness* (1977) by a party consisting of writers Clark Ashton Smith, Dashiell Hammett, and two companions. Pictured as a place of demonic enchantment, Corona Heights offers a magnificent view of downtown, especially by night— one of the least used vantage points in the city.

If you walk down Beaver Street to Noe you'll pass #69, where Leiber has the decadent poet Jaime Donaldus Byers (modeled on his friend Donald Sidney-Fryer) living in the horror novel. A jog right on 17th a quarter-block to Market will bring you to:

22 THE CAFE FLORE   At 2298 Market, this cafe is a crossroads for the literary populations of the Castro and Noe Valley, the Mission, and the Haight-Fillmore. A real sidewalk cafe, tables shaded by umbrellas, you might stop for coffee among the writers with notebooks and pens in hand often found scribbling away.

A return to the north on Noe and right on Duboce past Belcher will put you before one last site:

23 475 DUBOCE   After Fritz Leiber's wife died September 2, 1969, in their home in Venice, California, his friends Donald Sidney-Fryer and the film critic Margo Skinner talked Leiber into moving to San Francisco that Christmas. In this basement flat Leiber crashed with the Hippie household called the Family Sunshine (Sidney-Fryer, his wife, a musician named Pasha, and a gay man named Peter) until he moved to 811 Geary the following February. Leiber recalls that this mini-commune was into the typical hippie health food trip, except Pasha, who outraged their sensibilities by flourishing on a diet of Dr. Pepper and potato chips. During this period Sidney-Fryer was completing his book of romantic fantasy poetry, *Songs and Sonnets Atlantean* (1971).

HAIGHT-FILLMORE

The Straight Theater, Haight-Ashbury, 1967

The adjoining neighborhoods of the Haight-Ashbury and the Fillmore offer a wide spectrum of literary action. After World War II, Blacks moved to San Francisco to work in the shipyards and defense plants, and the Fillmore became a center for Afro-American culture. Today the Western Addition Cultural Center at 760 Fulton sponsors events; and the Lorraine Hansberry Theater and the Buriel Clay Theater present top plays by Black playwrights. The Haight-Ashbury became in the 1960s internationally famous as a center for the hippie counter culture. This neighborhood has seen all manner of writing from Zen Centered poets to Tillie Olsen's feminist fiction to Hunter S. Thompson's gonzo journalism, born on the hill near U.C. Medical Center.

The map shows streets running vertically: SCOTT, PIERCE, STEINER, FILLMORE, WEBSTER, BUCHANAN, LAGUNA. N↑ compass. Horizontal streets: OAK, PAGE, HAIGHT. Markers: 2 and 1 near Buchanan/Oak, 3 near Scott/Page.

Begin at the corner of Page and Laguna. The 7, 6, and 71 Muni lines all stop a block away at Laguna and Haight. The brick building on the northwest corner of Page and Laguna is:

1 THE ZEN CENTER OF SAN FRANCISCO Poet Philip Whalen has lived here as a Buddhist monk since 1973, and though he once told Don Carpenter, "I had a job once, and I don't ever want another one," he can be found teaching (with Judy Grahn and Lyn Hejinian) a course on Gertrude Stein at the New College of California. Whalen has been around the San Francisco literary scene since 1951, coming south from Reed College in Portland where he roomed with Gary Snyder and Lew Welch. Among his books are *Heavy Breathing, Severance Pay, Off the Wall*, and *Diamond Noodle*.

Diane di Prima, who lives on Laguna a block away, also has ties with the Zen Center, having lived and taught here off and on since she first came to San Francisco in the 1960s. She has published twenty-one books of poetry, plays, and prose—*War Poems* (1968), *Revolutionary Letters* (1974), the porn classic *Memoirs of a Beatnik* issued by the Olympia Press, and most recently *Selected Poems 1956-1975*. Di Prima is the only major woman poet of the Beat Generation, miraculously flourishing during that macho era as a kind of anarchist-Zen-den mother, and a power on the New York literary scene, with her Poets Press and *Floating Bear*, a magazine she began in 1961 with Leroi (Amira Baraka) Jones. She and Alan Marlowe formed the New York Poets Theatre, which performed works by Robert Duncan, Wallace Stevens, Michael McClure, Frank O'Hara and others. In San Francisco she is a founding member of the New College poetics faculty, and works with the San Francisco Institute of Magical and Healing Arts.

A block north on Laguna and left a quarter-block up Oak will put you before an impressive Victorian with a rare (for the city) front yard, at:

2 **457 OAK**   Jan Kerouac lived here all of 1968, after the Summer of Love had put the adjoining Haight-Ashbury district on the cultural map. Jack Kerouac's daughter, like others of her generation who tried life on the road, had twice the experience in half as many years. At an age when Jack was at Columbia University hoping to be a football hero, Jan Kerouac had traveled farther, faster than her father would his whole life. At twelve years, she and her twenty-two-year-old lover were dropping acid; by fourteen, a junkie and seller, she had been committed to Bellevue's psych ward; and at fifteen, pregnant, she set out for South America, working her way as a waitress, hooker— "anything that paid the rent." Her autobiographical novel "Everthreads," published under the title *Baby Driver: A Novel About Myself* (1981) records this odyssey — with sections on her year here at 457 Oak.

The Western Addition beyond Fell Street has seen more than fifty percent of its Victorians and other fine old buildings fall before urban renewal. Eric Hoffer's place at 1438 McAllister near Pierce is only one of many that have been torn down. He lived there seventeen years but finally left when the neighborhood became too noisy to bear. In his Working and Thinking on the Waterfront *(1969) Hoffer mentions that a prostitute had moved into the room below his late in 1958: "First night she did a gold-rush business which kept me awake until past midnight. Tonight, the moment I hear somebody knocking on her door I open the window and call out into the dark: 'She don't live here any more!'"*

In The Imagined City: San Francisco in the Minds of Its Writers *(1980) Tillie Olsen recalls, "I must have worked in at least a hundred different San Francisco places. I have a family and work knowledge of San Francisco that few writers have." She had sold a first chapter of her novel* Yonnondio *to* Partisan Review *in the 1930s, and then did not write for two decades. She was raising a family and working too, getting the experience for her award-winning stories that feature a Fillmore District setting in* Tell Me a Riddle *(1961). Olsen was jailed in the General Strike of 1934 as she marched with fellow union members, and remained active in the labor movement in the following decades.* Yonnondio: From the Thirties *was released in 1974, and another book,* Silences, *in 1978.*

Six blocks west on Page from the Zen Center, on the southwest corner at Scott, stands another Victorian-style building. The first floor once housed Jack's Record Cellar over which Kenneth Rexroth lived in the second floor flat at:

Mother to
Daughter
Daughter
to Mother

TILLIE OLSEN

A FEMINIST PRESS
DAYBOOK AND
READER

3 **250 SCOTT**   Rexroth lived here in the 1950s and early 1960s before he left the city to teach at U.C. Santa Barbara. He did a weekly radio show over KPFA, wrote a column for the *Examiner*, and in this flat organized "Friday soirées" that were attended by artists, anarchists, writers, and film makers. William Everson, Robert Duncan, James Broughton, Muriel Rukeyser, Thomas Parkinson, Philip Lamantia, and Richard Moore were the principal poets who sat in on these informal gatherings, which introduced diverse radicals and artists to one another as well as to many international visitors.

In a 1969 interview, published in *The San Francisco Poets* (1971), Rexroth told David Meltzer this now-famous literary anecdote concerning 250 Scott: "I have always said that the greatest shock Kerouac ever got in his life was when he walked into my house, sat down in a kind of stiff-legged imitation of a lotus posture, and announced he was a Zen Buddhist . . . and then discovered everyone in the room knew at least one Oriental language." Rexroth, who never missed an opportunity to knock Kerouac after their feud began in 1957, doesn't mention that he himself didn't know any Oriental languages— all the Chinese and Japanese poems he "translated" were versions made from earlier *French* translations. Called by some the literary "godfather" of the scene, he was a man with encyclopedic knowledge, a photographic memory and great charisma, but he had a definite tendency to elaborate on the truth. His publishers made him call his autobiography "an autobiographical *novel*."

Go south on Scott one block to Haight, and turn right. A walk four blocks west will bring you abreast of Buena Vista Park, rising high to your left. Continue to the western edge of the park and climb the curving street that runs along the margin of the woods to:

4 737 BUENA VISTA AVENUE WEST   This Queen Anne mansion was built in 1898 for sugar magnate Floyd Spreckels. Now a bed-and-breakfast inn, it preserves the tradition that the top floor served as a studio for both Ambrose Bierce and Jack London, though since the imperious older writer and the dynamic young Jack got along about as well as Rexroth and Jack Kerouac, presumably they did not share the studio at the same time.

Return to Haight and turn left, heading west along the couple of blocks that will take you to the famous corner of:

5 HAIGHT-ASHBURY   The hippie flowering of the 1960s saw its most natural and best literary expression in the underground comix, especially those by R. Crumb and Gilbert Shelton's Fabulous Furry Freak Brothers. The last third of Emmett Grogan's novel *Ringolevio*

(1972) features a Haight scene. Among hippie-era readers, Richard Brautigan's novels became incredibly popular. However, the few novels to come out of the Merry Prankster group are more substantial: Ken Kesey's *One Flew Over the Cuckoo's Nest* (1962) and *Sometimes a Great Notion* (1964), written in the forefront of the movement before Kesey threw himself into *living* his art, and Robert Stone's *A Hall of Mirrors* (1967) and *Dog Soldiers* (1975).

Allen Ginsberg and Gary Snyder had become by 1967 poet-gurus for this new counter culture. Volume one, number seven of Allen Cohen's newspaper *Oracle* featured a wide-ranging interview with Ginsberg, Snyder, Timothy Leary and Alan Watts. Lew Welch regularly contributed to the *Oracle*. After his friend Lenore Kandel's poetry collection *The Love Book* was branded obscene in 1966, it became the object of a censorship controversy rivaling that over *Howl* in 1957. (*Zap Comix* was also jumped by the censors.) Invoking the "redeeming social value" precedent set in the *Howl* trial, Kandel won her case and was acclaimed as "the Love Poet" (or, by some, the fuck poet). Ashley Brilliant created his pithy "Pot Shots" postcards in this psychedelic milieu, and in 1967 Rod McKuen—invoking Stanyan Street (and Other Sorrows) at the end of Haight Street—hit some massive popular chord that made him the best-selling American poet of modern times.

If you head north on Ashbury a block, then jog right half a block, you will come to the two-block-long:

6 DOWNEY STREET   Joanna and Michael McClure have been residents of the Haight for over two decades, living on Downey. One of the migrants from the Wichita Vortex, McClure came to prominence in the 1950s and was one of the poets at the landmark Six Gallery reading. His scandalous play *The Beard* (1965), which features pop mythology icons of Jean Harlow and Billy the Kid, was busted for obscenity every night of its San Francisco run. In the 1970s McClure established a niche for himself in American poetry with his "mammalism"—the theory and exposition of poetry as biology. He has published many books of poems, essays, and plays. His play *Josephine the Mouse Singer* won an Obie as best play of 1979. Among recent books are *September Blackberries, Jaguar Skies, Scratching the Beat Surface*, and *Fragments of Perseus*.

From Downey continue west half a block to Clayton, downhill two blocks to Page, then left two blocks to Shrader, where you'll see a grand Victorian on the southwest corner at:

7 1901 PAGE   Built for a sea captain in 1896, this mansion later fell into the hands of Kathleen Thompson when she and her siblings moved to San Francisco from Mill Valley, after the sudden deaths of their parents. Kathleen tried writing, unsuccessfully, for the *Evening Bulletin*; an editor for Associated Press bluntly told her that writing was not her forte. But after she married Charles Norris, brother of Frank Norris (her sister married William Rose Benét), and moved to New York she became one of the most successful novelists of the 1920s, and possibly the most prolific. She conceived her books as she played solitaire and did the actual writing very quickly. Her husband, an editor, helped with many of her early novels. When Kathleen insisted that Charles accept a co-author credit on the title page, he declined and instead began to turn out novels of his own, typified by one-word titles (*Hands* takes place in San Francisco).

After she moved east a caretaker kept this house for her for twenty years, and then Mary Fairfowl, a pensioner of Kathleen Norris, took it over, operating a workshop here for St. Joseph's Catholic Church in the 1940s and 1950s. Kathleen and Charles Norris eventually returned to California, living in Palo Alto, but her period in New York provides the best stories about this writer. In *While Rome Burns* (1934) Alexander Woollcott recalls a day when an acquaintance spotted "the slightly majestical figure of America's favorite author" strolling down Fifth Avenue and decided that an unexpected pinch on her rear might be fun. The quick-witted Norris turned on the fellow among the crowds passing on the sidewalk and cried out: "Not one penny. Not one penny more. . . . Only last week I gave you a hundred dollars to buy medicine for your poor, sick wife . . . Did she get a penny of it? Not she! No, you spent it on the drink, my lad. You guzzled it, Frank Sullivan, and they found you in the gutter." Sullivan, who wasn't even married, fled through the shocked crowd that had suddenly gathered about them; Kathleen Norris continued with her shopping.

Head south on Shrader four blocks to Frederick and turn left to:

C. Norris, F. Hurst, K. Norris, Atherton

8 419 FREDERICK   Novelist and poet Kay Boyle owned this home when she was teaching at San Francisco State College in the 1970s. An American expatriate who lived largely on the Left Bank in Paris and in southern France between the world wars, Boyle has just reissued *Being Geniuses Together.* Her first novels, *Plagued by the Nightingale* (1930) and *Year Before Last* (1931), and story collections, *Wedding Day* (1929) and *The First Lover* (1932), established her as one of the finest writers of that era, and she has sustained that reputation with many other novels and collections. Her poetry—*A Glad Day* (1938), *Selected Poems* (1962)—later earned equal acclaim. She sold this place a few years ago before moving to the Pacific Northwest.

Continue on Frederick east to Cole Street, turn right one block to Carl, and take another right on Carl. About four blocks west on Carl, between Willard and Arguello, you'll find:

9 **348 CARL**   William Saroyan lived at this address in the early 1930s, writing in the small front room on an oak table he bought for four dollars in 1930 when he was twenty-four years old. Saroyan bought it for use in an uncle's flower stand on Geary, but the stand folded within two months. Saroyan ended up making better use of the table at which he wrote his first professional stories. Afterwards he took it with him every time he moved.

Saroyan dropped out of high school at fifteen, confident he could become a writer; he began sending stories out at age seventeen, but they were bounced. Saroyan vowed he would write only for himself until he was thirty, but he sold his second published story "The Daring Young Man on the Flying Trapeze" when he was twenty-six. He got only $15 from *Story* magazine; however, the tale made him an overnight sensation, "the most significant talent to appear in San Francisco since Frank Norris and Jack London."

He wrote the play "The Time of Your Life," based on the scene in Izzy Gomez's Pacific Street saloon, in six days. He refused the Pulitzer Prize that this play won in 1940, saying that his art did not need patronage from the wealthy— he suggested the $1000 prize be given to "young writers who need it." In his famous novel *The Human Comedy* (1943) the protagonist Homer holds a job Saroyan once had as a teenager in his native Fresno, as a telegraph messenger, but Homer delivers telegrams which tell families that their sons have died in action during the war. Saroyan was always a flamboyant figure, later sporting a trademark handlebar mustache— he called himself "The World's Greatest Writer." During his last years he returned to Fresno, where he died May 18, 1981, seventy-two years old.

Return to Willard, and climb some three blocks uphill to the last block between Belmont and Woodland. Screened by ornamental trees is the home of Ruth Witt-Diamant at:

10 **1520 WILLARD**   Witt-Diamant founded the San Francisco Poetry Center at State College in 1954— one of the most significant venues for poetry in the city's history. The Poetry Center has brought to San Francisco virtually every major poet to read and lecture; and many of them were put up in the guest room of this house. Witt-Diamant had talked Dylan Thomas into visiting the West coast in 1952, and after his first visit he returned several times, always staying here. Anais Nin, W. H. Auden, Stephen Spender, Theodore Roethke, Elizabeth Bishop, Robert Lowell, and many others were also guests in this house. Allen Tate, William Carlos Williams, Louise Bogan, Malcolm Cowley, and Randall Jarrell all read on the Center's programs under Witt-Diamant. The poet Kathleen Fraser directed the Center for many years after the founder retired, and it continues today, with solid programs by Bay Area and visiting poets.

Follow Willard back downhill to Parnassus and turn left. Up the block you'll come to:

11 **318 PARNASSUS**   The now-famous gonzo journalist Hunter S. Thompson lived here in the mid-1960s when he was researching and writing his book *Hell's Angels* (1967). The Angels inspired a good deal of literary activity with their motorized outlaw existence. Allen Ginsberg dedicated "To the Angels" to them as a plea to keep them from trashing anti-war demonstrators in Berkeley. Michael McClure helped Angel secretary Frank Reynolds write his autobiography *Freewheelin' Frank* (1967), and Reynolds appeared, playing harmonica, with McClure in a few musical gigs about San Francisco. Thompson's book gives the best coverage of this cultural phenomenon, and you can see the first indications of the definitive Hunter S. Thompson in the pages where he describes his research methods, inviting Hell's Angels over for late night drinking and doping. His neighbors often complained about the choppers ranked on the sidewalk, but Thompson states in his book that "one of the worst incidents of that era caused no complaints at all: this was a sort of good-natured firepower demonstration, which occurred one Sunday morning about three-thirty. For reasons that were never made clear, I blew out my back windows with five blasts of a 12-gauge shotgun, followed moments later by six rounds from a .44 magnum."

Just a couple of blocks further west on Parnassus will put you in the midst of the:

Ishi

12 **U.C. MEDICAL CENTER**   A great cultural symbol, who seized the public's imagination and much press coverage, spent his last years at the Museum of Anthropology in what today is the med center. Ishi, "the last of the Stone Age Men," the last wild Indian in North America, was found August 1911 near Oroville. He had never seen a white man and knew nothing of civilization. Anthropologist A. L. Kroeber of U.C. Berkeley rescued Ishi and found him work, and his wife Theodora wrote Ishi's biography, *Ishi, Last of His Tribe* (1964), from his own words. Indicative of Ishi's impact as an imaginative symbol is the futuristic novel *Earth Abides* (1949) by George R. Stewart, a fellow-professor of the Kroebers at Berkeley. In this book Stewart kills off most of the earth's population with a viral plague. His hero ultimately realizes that he is "the Last American": his name is Isherwood Williams, but he is known by his nickname *Ish*. Ironically, Stewart has the country re-populated by descendants of the few survivors, who know nothing about civilization or how to rebuild it. They hunt and fish and live their lives as Ishi and his people did for centuries before white men came into their world.

*If you walk through the med
center to where Parnassus
crests the ridge at 4th Avenue
you can look downhill over one
of Ishi's favored haunts, on
whose trails he spent many
hours:*

13 **GOLDEN GATE PARK**   Adjoining the Haight-Ashbury, running
to the Pacific between the Richmond and Sunset Districts — some
1040 acres, fifty-two blocks long, eight blocks wide — Golden Gate Park
has a wealth of literary associations. A walk from the east end of the park
to the Pacific will take you past several significant areas.

Begin on the northwest corner of Stanyan Street and John F. Kennedy
Drive at McLaren Lodge. From 1895 when he was appointed Superintendent until his death in his nineties, "Uncle John" McLaren ruled
Golden Gate Park, converting it from a wasteland of sand dunes into the
largest man-made park in the world. From his lodge this short, gruff
gardener from Scotland managed his magnificent empire, and also
wrote such books as *Gardening in California — Landscape and Flower*,
which A. M. Robertson published in 1924. McLaren had absolute
power over park employees — to become a gardener under "Uncle
John" you had to score ninety percent or better on a test identifying
one hundred plants — and you had to *spell* their names correctly too.

A short walk from McLaren Lodge is Hippie Hill, on the north side of
the large field opposite the Children's Playground. The name comes
from the heyday of the Haight-Ashbury, when this gentle rise was
covered with longhairs, playing music, tossing frisbees, smoking pot.
Ashley Brilliant trooped over to this hill with a handheld bullhorn and
rapped for hours on end. The major hippie event in Golden Gate Park
was the "Human Be-In Gathering of the Tribes" held in the polo fields
deeper in the park January 14, 1967.

An outgrowth of the Trips Festival and neighborhood Free Fairs, the
Be-In launched the Haight-Ashbury into the Summer of Love and led to
many other free concerts in the parks, and to the Monterey Pop Festival
and other epic outdoor concerts that were hallmarks of the 1960s rock
scene. An estimated 20,000 people came to hear the Jefferson Airplane,
Grateful Dead, Quicksilver Messenger Service, and Dizzy Gillespie.
Ralph J. Gleason in his *The Jefferson Airplane and the San Francisco
Sound* (1969) said: "Everybody came. There were state assemblymen,
reporters, clergy, university professors, advertising agency executives,
a Los Angeles music business lawyer, jazz musicians, little old ladies in
tennis shoes, hordes of kids, Berkeley political types and old-line anarchists." Poets Allen Ginsberg, Gary Snyder and Maretta Greer led
chants on the stage. A couple of mounted police patroled the area, but
the Hell's Angels acted as the unofficial police force. "A lost child has
been delivered to the stage by the peace officer and is now below the
stage being cared for by the Hell's Angels," Gleason reported in the
Chronicle. Ferlinghetti observed, "To the participants it truly seemed a
new age had arrived, with a new vision of life and love on earth," but he
adds that Ginsberg turned to him and whispered "What if we're all
wrong?"

The Shakespeare Garden near the Academy of Sciences is a
charming spot, dedicated as "The Garden of Shakespeare's Flowers"
in 1928 (so marked by a footstone at the western entrance to the glade,

which is planted with flowers mentioned in the Bard's plays). On a wall at one end of the garden you'll find a number of large plaques with botanical quotes — the Bohemian Club, the Creative Writers of California, the P.E.N. Club, and other groups presented them as gifts. The bust of Shakespeare which they flank was a present from Stratford-Upon-Avon — one of only two copies cast in 1914 by George Bullock from a bust carved by sculptor Garrett Jansen sometime before 1623. It is thought that this bust was modeled by Jansen from either a life or death mask of Shakespeare, and hence the best likeness of the playwright known to exist.

Off John F. Kennedy Drive as you turn toward the De Young Museum there is a bust of Cervantes, with Don Quixote and Sancho Panza kneeling at its base, and in the Rhododendron Dell nearby is a lifesize statue of the short John McLaren himself, who detested the monuments that the City fathers insisted on placing in his park — you'll notice that many of the statues in Golden Gate Park are virtually buried in foliage, per Uncle John's instructions.

George Sterling led Theodore Dreiser and his companion Mrs. Helen Richardson (who lived with Dreiser until his death) on long midnight walks through the park in 1921. Dreiser said that Sterling hovered over San Francisco "like a burnished black Holy Ghost." As they strolled along the Chain of Lakes, Sterling suddenly stripped and swam to the middle of the lily pond to pluck a flower for Helen, who said his action was a beautiful "water dance that Nijinsky or Shankar or Mei Lan-fang might have dreamed up." A passing policeman questioned them, but let them proceed when the famous Romantic identified himself.

It is said that Sterling repeated his midnight swim several times in the next years, as one of his just duties as King of Bohemia, and that one night another officer nabbed him. This policeman wasn't impressed when he learned who Sterling was, and did not believe that the poet had "special permission" to swim in the park lakes whenever he so wished. Sterling was arrested, but soon freed — and the officer was chewed out for molesting the poet.

Eric Hoffer spent many hours in this park. Calvin Tomkins notes in *Eric Hoffer: An American Odyssey* (1968) that "Although many of Hoffer's ideas came to him first while he worked on the docks, virtually all of them took their finished shape and definition in Golden Gate Park. Two or three days a week, when he did not feel like going to the docks, he would take a bus to the 10th Avenue entrance to the park and then follow his favorite path down to where the park met the ocean . . . , sit on a bench facing the Pacific and write it out in his notebook, sentence by sentence."

The quiet introspection Hoffer nurtured in this park contrasts dramatically with the use Hunter S. Thompson made of it as he was writing his book on the Hell's Angels. The bad press the biker gangs were getting put pressure on all motorcyclists, and though Thomson ended up with no insurance, his driver's license in jeopardy, he had a compulsion to take his machine out on the road. "So it was always at night, like a were-wolf, that I would take the thing out for an honest run down the coast. I would start in Golden Gate Park, thinking only to run a few long curves to clear my head . . . but in a matter of minutes I'd be out at the beach with the sound of the engine in my ears, the surf booming up on the sea wall and a fine empty road stretching all the way down to Santa Cruz. . . ."

OTHER CITY SITES

Alice Walker, 1984

From Golden Gate Park you might do a whirlwind tour of the widely scattered sites in the Sunset and Richmond Districts, working your way back toward downtown through Pacific Heights. Neal Cassady could do this drive in thirty minutes (or less), but you might wish to take your time and see the sites a bit more closely. By bus or foot this tour will have to be made in several installments.

*In the Sunset you'll find an
address for William Saroyan at:*

1 2727 TARAVAL, a studio flat where the novelist and playwright lived in 1948.

*The largest concentration of
writers in this area are
connected with:*

2 SAN FRANCISCO STATE UNIVERSITY W. H. Auden was on hand to dedicate the Poetry Center which Ruth Witt-Diamant founded here in 1954. Witt-Diamant, aided by her secretaries Ida Hodes and Lola Chardon, and by assistant director Robert Duncan, presented scores of poets over the next years. S. I. Hayakawa was president of this college in the 1960s, wearing his trademark tam-o-shanter and infuriating the Left with his policies—his rise in conservative political circles has obscured his many books on semantics. Don Carpenter took his Masters degree here; Ernest J. Gaines earned his Bachelors. Kay Boyle was a professor at State for a number of years. Leonard Wolf, Stan Rice, the Greek poet Nanos Valaoritis, and Jeff Chan, chairman of Asian-American Studies are among the writers who have served on the faculty.

*Near State College on the
circular Urbano Drive you'll
find:*

3 128 URBANO Leonard Clark lived in this house in the 1950s—an oddly tame neighborhood for one of the most adventurous literary figures in San Francisco's history. An explorer and world traveler, Clark roamed Sumatra, the Malay peninsula, the Philippine islands, the Celebes, Ceylon, Tibet, India, Burma, Mongolia, China and Chinese Turkestan, Mexico, Yucatán, the Amazon and served as an American intelligence officer behind Japanese lines in World War II.

A real-life Indiana Jones, Clark gained international fame for the fabulous objects of his quests. His book *The Rivers Ran East* (1953) recounts his exploration of the Amazon rain forests in search of the mythical Spanish treasure city of El Dorado; *The Marching Wind* (1954) details his journey into the Himalaya range in search of Amne Machin, a mountain sacred to the Ngolok tribes who live at its foot, and rumored to be higher than Mount Everest. This last expedition was described as "the greatest field expedition of modern times," as Clark entered previously unexplored regions on horseback with a party of hundreds of scientists and troops provided by the Chinese Nationalist Government. His earlier expedition into the heart of the Gran Pajonal in the Amazon was accomplished with only one companion. When Clark finally returned to civilization after months in the jungle he learned that the U.S. State Department had been informed by the governments of Peru and Ecuador that, regrettably, the explorer had been killed by Huambiza head-hunters.

Clark's *Explorer's Digest* (1955) was a book for teenagers about six modern explorers, but Clark's personal adventures did not necessarily appeal to the juvenile imagination—in 1949 he returned from his quest for Amne Machin, and was arrested in Canton after a drinking party celebrating the wedding anniversary of Willard Freeman. Freeman, a British trader, and Harold Harris, an American businessman, were killed by shots from Clark's pistol and the explorer himself wounded in an argument over Freeman's wife. (She slept through the gun battle in an adjoining room!) Clark, whose wartime services had earned him the Legion of Merit, the Bronze Star, and other honors, was saved by intervention of the State Department and got out of the area just before the Red Chinese rushed in. His 1937 autobiography *A Wanderer Till I Die* proved prophetic: the forty-nine-year-old Clark and two companions drowned May 4, 1957, in a boating accident on the Caroni River in Venezuela. He was searching for diamond mines.

From the area around State College you might head over to the San Francisco Zoo, where the small Leon's Bar-BQ opposite the entrance to the zoo is a great place to have lunch—and a legitimate literary site, a place many writers stop to eat when they get out to the beach.

Here you can get onto Great Highway northbound and travel quickly past the edge of the Sunset District, past Golden Gate Park, and over to the Richmond District, where you may stop at:

4 SUTRO HEIGHTS PARK   Overlooking the Cliff House and the Pacific, this is the place in John Dos Passos' novel *The 42nd Parallel* where Mac the Wobbly liked to bring his girl—still a great place, a park that is little used.

At the south edge of the park you'll find Sutro Heights Avenue, which runs for two blocks between 48th and 46th Avenues, between Anza and Balboa, and where Eugene Cunningham lived in:

5 120 SUTRO HEIGHTS AVENUE   Cunningham wrote twenty-one western novels under his own name and the pseudonym Leigh Carder, beginning with *The Trail to Apacaz* in 1924. Among his other westerns are *Riders of the Night* (1932), *Pistol Passport* (1936), *Texas Triggers* (1938), and *Riding Gun* (1956). His non-fiction book on true western gunfighters, *Triggernometry* (1934), is a classic—and one of his most successful books, going through many editions under the original title and under the 1941 reprint as *Gunfighters All*. Cunningham was born in 1896 in Helena, Arkansas, but grew up in Texas near Dallas-Fort Worth. He served in the Navy in the Mexican Campaign and World War I, and re-enlisted in World War II, after which he lived in this house until his death in 1957.

*From Cunningham's last
address head north to Geary
and take Geary east toward
downtown by car or bus. At
19th Avenue head north to:*

6 121 19TH AVENUE David Dodge lived here in the 1940s. He had worked as an accountant for McLaren, Goode and Company in the Financial District, but rose quickly to literary fame by creating one of the best detective series set in San Francisco, four novels featuring James Whitney, a hard-boiled Certified Public Accountant. The series began with *Death and Taxes* in 1941, a fast funny book along the lines of Hammett's *The Thin Man*, but the last novel featuring "Whit" is now the most famous. Upon returning from wartime service Dodge's mood darkened, and he wrote *It Ain't Hay* (1946), a classic anti-marijuana tract with Whit going on the vengeance trail against pot smugglers. It features such memorable remarks as: "Look at some of these musicians that use it. It excites them, makes them high and hot, so they can beat the music out faster, get in extra licks they couldn't handle otherwise. They're in the groove, and the groove is boogie-woogie—for them. For somebody else, the groove is rape or murder or arson." At one point a seventeen-year-old, after smoking "two reefers he bought in a pool hall," clubs to death his father, mother, and fourteen-year-old sister with a baseball bat. One suspects that Dodge's contact with marijuana must have been limited—or else they had some superpowerful dope in the Forties. Dodge left San Francisco to travel in Central and South America, and set a number of mysteries south of the border (*Plunder of the Sun* about Inca treasure is the best known of this group), and then moved to Europe where he wrote international caper novels. Alfred Hitchcock's *To Catch a Thief*, starring Cary Grant and Grace Kelly, was based on the novel by David Dodge.

*From Dodge's place continue
on the remainder of the block
to Lake Street, and turn east
until you come to:*

7 454 LAKE Between 6th and 5th Avenues, this is one of several places where the juvenile fiction writer Howard Pease, creator of the Todd Moran books, lived; the San Francisco City Directory lists Pease here in 1931.

Alice Adams

A few more blocks east takes
you to:

8 CLAY & PRESIDIO Alice Adams lives in this neighborhood midway between Pacific Heights and the Richmond. Winner of numerous

O. Henry Awards for sophisticated short stories that appear in magazines like *The New Yorker* and *The Atlantic Monthly*, Adams makes liberal use of San Francisco locales. Her characters—generally professionals and prosperous artists—shop in Jackson Square, lunch on ferny Union Street or in Chinatown, live in pretty Victorians and spend vacations in summer homes on Lake Tahoe. In "True Colors" from *To See You Again* (1976), mad lovers meet in the Washington Square Bar and Grill in North Beach, "the sort of place mentioned in columns, locally," then come to a strange end in Las Vegas. Other books by Adams are *Beautiful Girl, Rich Rewards,, Careless Love*, and *Families and Survivors.*

The neighborhood with the international flavor just west of Arguello is called "The Clement" and centers between 2nd and 9th Streets on:

9 CLEMENT STREET At 506 Clement Street you'll find one of the city's finest used book stores, Green Apple Books, well worth a visit for that out-of-print book you've been unable to find. This is a center for the literati of the Inner Richmond. Janice Mirikitani, author of *Awake in the River* lives here, as does jazz critic-poet Richard Oyama and performance poet Yuri Kageyama. Filipino-American poet Luis Syquia grew up in the neighborhood and still can be found here when he's not working as a broadcast journalist for KPFA or a King Crab butcher in the Aleutians.

Over on California Street at Sixth Street the Asian American Theater was (until it shut down in 1984) a catalyst for many Bay Area playwrights including Lane Nishikawa (Life in the Fast Lane), Philip Gotanda, Genny Lim (Paper Angels), Bernadette Cha, and Hiroshi Kagigawa

Return to Geary and head east again. In the 1960s, Richard Brautigan lived on Geary near Masonic, across from Sears. Past Masonic it is only some three blocks to Divisadero and another cluster of sites, beginning with:

10 LOUISIANA ON DIVISADERO Since 1963 the award-winning novelist Ernest J. Gaines has lived on Divisadero, spending part of the year here, part in his native Louisiana, where he sets his books. His most famous title is *The Autobiography of Miss Jane Pittman* (1971), made into an outstanding film for television starring Cicely Tyson. Among his other titles are *Catherine Carmier, Of Love and Dust, In My Father's House,* and *Bloodline.*

There is another literary association of Divisadero Street also connected with Louisiana. Though much of the action occurs in New Orleans in the 1800s, the actual interview in Anne Rice's bestselling *Interview With the Vampire* (1976) is recorded in a building overlooking

Divisadero. Rice was born in New Orleans in 1941. Her first novel is a *tour de force* in which the 200-year-old vampire tells his horrific story to an eager young reporter — one of the best of the hundreds of tales about the Undead since J. Sheridan LeFanu's classic *Carmilla* of 1871. Rice followed her first book with *The Feast of All the Saints* (1979), based on the brilliant society of "The Free People of Color" (mulattoes who were not slaves but had no political freedom) in 19th century New Orleans. In 1982, she published *Cry to Heaven*, chronicling the history of the castrati and their place in European music.

From the intersection of Geary and Divisadero head north two blocks to Sutter, where you will see near the northeast corner at Divisadero:

11 **2378 SUTTER** In the third-floor flat in this building the Saroyan family lived in the late 1920s. Twenty-one-year-old William Saroyan returned here in January 1929 from his first, unsuccessful assault on literary New York. He said that he could look out his window at the back of Mount Zion Hospital across Sutter — a building now greatly modernized.

Go to the corner at Divisadero and look across the street. Near the northwest corner, where a more recent building is today, once stood:

12 **1707-A DIVISADERO** In his *Places Where I've Done Time* (1972) William Saroyan notes: "For a while after 1929, after my return from New York, the five of us in the family moved across the street from 2378 Sutter Street to 1707-A Divisadero. I worked wherever there was a job, and for $10 I bought an enormous old-fashioned baby-grand piano — sometimes I put a blanket on top of it and stretched out up there for a nap."

One block north to Bush and two blocks east, past Pierce, will bring you before:

13 **2377 and 2381 BUSH** Both of these buildings were designed by the architect Albert Pissis, renowned for creating the Flood Building and the Emporium which face each other across Market Street. Punk-Romantic poet G. Sutton Breiding lived at 2381 and at 2377 the doomed fantasist David Mason lived his last days. Mason wrote in the sword-and-sorcery genre pioneered by Robert E. Howard.

In the novels *Kavin's World* (1969), *The Sorcerer's Skull* (1970), and *The Return of Kavin* (1972), Mason added some excellent entries into a field that otherwise has become rife with bad writing. His books have especially good scenes of ships and sailing, based on years Mason worked in the merchant marine. In December 1969 he moved onto a fifty-foot tugboat berthed near the Yacht Club, but on a trip down the coast to Santa Barbara the following June the boat sank several miles offshore, just south of Half Moon Bay. Mason and his pet wolf swam through the choppy waves to safety. (Another San Francisco master of sword-and-sorcery, Fritz Leiber, shouted in envy: "*Damn* the man!")

This adventurous writer also dabbled with the occult, here and earlier in Greenwich Village. On his next boat, *The Sea Hag* (moored in the Marina next to Fort Mason), a weird doom like the awful curses in stories by Clark Ashton Smith overtook Mason. *The Sea Hag* was a thirty-two-foot fishing trawler converted from a WWII LCP hull, with a big cabin on top that looked like a large crate, all painted black and strange to see among the sleek sailboats — this "one dreadful boat that never put to sea." *The Sea Hag* began to ship water and had to be pumped out every few days, even as Mason developed some mysterious disease in which his body became allergic to itself.

By the time he came to this flat on Bush Street *The Sea Hag* was awash at its moorings, his manuscripts and files waterlogged, and Mason himself had to make frequent trips to the hospital to have excess fluid pumped from his abdomen. His pet wolf was given to the San Francisco Zoo, *The Sea Hag* was towed out into the Pacific by the Coast Guard and exploded, and Mason died. A couple of years after his death the paperback company that had published his major novels, Lancer Books, went into receivership, casting Mason's work itself into a sort of limbo. Copies can be found only by scouting the used bookstores, with the result that Mason, one of the more interesting writers to live in San Francisco, has been almost completely forgotten.

Circle the block to Pine Street and go back west to Broderick, and then north two blocks to Sacramento. On the northwest corner you'll find:

14 1921 BRODERICK Or rather, what remains of 1921 Broderick, the place where Frank Norris died in October, 1902, of peritonitis from a ruptured appendix, at the age of thirty-two. To judge from older maps of the city, this same building stood in 1902 but in the intervening years it has been raised and a lower level added. The entrance to what would have been 1921 Broderick is now a window (the size of a doorway) on the Broderick side of the building, on the second-floor level. While this building is the same basic structure, it has been so greatly renovated both inside and out that it no longer evokes the day when one of the city's major writers met his death within its walls.

Continue north on Broderick to Broadway, where you'll find, between Broderick and Baker:

15 **2840 BROADWAY**   Willis Polk designed this building for Mrs. Andrew Welch, and Polk used the courtyard on a broadside Christmas card in 1919. He had his assistant draftsman R. B. Owen design the card, and his friend George Sterling compose a five-line "thought" for the seasonal greeting.

Follow Broadway east to Fillmore, then plunge north down the sheer slope as Fillmore drops down into Cow Hollow from Pacific Heights. Between Filbert and Greenwich you'll see:

16 **3119 FILLMORE**   Currently the Museum Shops, this converted auto-repair garage was once the Six Gallery, where Allen Ginsberg gave his sensational first public reading of "Howl" on October 13, 1955.

If you return on Fillmore to Union, a block up, and turn east you'll find:

Jessica Hagedorn

17 **2157 UNION**   On this high-pressure street of boutiques, antique shops, and singles bars Collin Wilcox had his own shop at this address in the 1960s where he sold designer lamps. In off hours, he tried to write the Great American Novel. Wilcox finally broke into print with a mystery novel, *The Black Door* (1967), featuring Stephen Drake, a psychic detective who lives on Telegraph Hill. His *The Lonely Hunter* (1969) introduced Lieutenant Frank Hastings of the SFPD, who investigates a murder in the psychedelic "Hashbury" in his debut case; the popular Hastings series now numbers over a dozen novels and has freed Wilcox from the lamp business, though Wilcox keeps a sentimental attachment to his old trade by writing some mysteries under the pseudonym Carter Wick. (Wilcox has a story about how he once was paying a bill with a credit card and the woman noticed his name. "You're not *the* Collin Wilcox!" she exclaimed. The prolific mystery writer dusted off his modesty routine and admitted, well, yes, he was *the* Collin Wilcox. "Oh, Mr. Wilcox," said the woman, "I just adore your lamps!")

This stretch of Union Street also is part of the scene in "The Blossoming of Bong Bong" by Jessica Tarahata Hagedorn, a wild tale that winds through the singles bars, over to Twin Peaks, down Market, and into the Fillmore. Hagedorn once lived in the Fillmore but was born in the Philippines, and her story gives us San Francisco as seen through the eyes of a dazzled young man newly arrived from Manila. Her work was first heralded by Kenneth Rexroth in the *Four Young Women: Poems*, and she has won high praise for *Dangerous Music* (1975) and *Pet Food and Tropical Apparitions* (1981). Ishmael Reed calls her "one of the queens of the marvelous Ditty-Bop school of poetry."

If you travel a few blocks
further on Union to Van Ness
and head south you'll come to:

18 **2128 VAN NESS**   Near Pacific, this is the building where Ella Leffland wrote her first novel, *Mrs. Munck* (1970).

Follow Van Ness south to
Sutter. If you head east on
Sutter you'll come to the:

Ron Kovic

19 **YORK HOTEL**   On Sutter near Leavenworth, this hotel was home for a few months for Vietnam vet Ron Kovik, author of *Born on the Fourth of July* (1976) and *Around the World in Eight Days* (1984). In this place Kovik wrote three novels — in thirty-eight days. He'd often spin his wheelchair down to the Plush Room at two in the morning after the evening's theatre was over, park at a cocktail table, and write until dawn as the custodian cleaned the place up.

If you head west on Sutter and
drop south a block at Laguna
to Post Street you'll be at:

20 **JAPANTOWN**   The Kinokunya Bookstore in the west wing of the Japan Trade Center features handsomely produced books from Japan, as well as an excellent selection of titles by Japanese-American authors. Book parties, poetry readings, and concerts are often held at the Japanese-American Workshop at Buchanan and Octavia, and Japantown has several literary hangouts — the Jigoku is gone now, but the Kanzaki Lounge and Japan Town Bowl are still favorites.

One block south of Post will
bring you to Geary again.
Between Laguna and Gough
you'll see several highrise
apartment buildings on the
north side of Geary; in one of
these George R. Stewart lived
until his death in 1980.
Directly across Geary from
these apartments is:

21 **ST. FRANCIS SQUARE**   In this longshoreman-run co-operative lives Alice Walker, winner of the American Book Award and the Pulitzer Prize for Fiction for her phenomenally popular novel *The Color Purple* (1982), which dominated the best seller lists for years. Walker, who writes winningly of women and blacks, has published a score of books: poetry, stories — *You Can't Keep a Good Woman Down* (1972), *In Love and Trouble* (1967) — biographies, such as her fine *Langstone Hughes: American Poet* (1974), novels, and a collection of essays *In Search of Our Mothers' Gardens* (1983).

JACK LONDON

Jack London in Oakland, 1900

"I would rather be a superb meteor, every atom of me in magnificent glow, than a sleepy and permanent planet. The proper function of man is to live, not exist. I shall not waste my days in trying to prolong them. I shall use my time."

—*Jack London, September 1916*

One unquestionable world-class writer comes from the San Francisco Bay Area: Jack London. With Nietzschean determination and raw talent London, who had been a factory-hand, sailor, hobo, janitor, and prospector, wrote book after book to become, before his death at the age of forty, the most popular writer in America and ultimately one of the most widely translated and reprinted authors of all time.

London was born in San Francisco January 12, 1876, to Flora Wellman, seamstress, piano-teacher, and medium in the spiritualist circles of the city. His father was William H. Chaney, "a wandering astrologer" who had abandoned Flora, the latest in a succession of wives and common-law wives, soon after he learned she was pregnant.

Flora resented her bastard son the rest of her life. The baby was given to a black woman, Mrs. Alonzo Prentiss to wet nurse for most of his first year. Only after Flora married a farmer named John London on September 7th was the baby returned to its mother — and only then was he given a name.

The rearing of young "Johnny London" was left to his stepsisters and his stepfather, who was devoted to his adopted son. Flora increasingly spent her time thinking of schemes to raise the family above its working class status — and to holding seances in which she served as the medium for an Indian Chief called "Plume" who spoke from the Spirit World. From a farm on San Francisco's Bernal Heights the Londons moved to apartments south of Market, and then worked other farms in Oakland, Alameda, and San Mateo County. John London managed to save enough money to mortgage an eighty-seven-acre chicken ranch in Livermore by the time Jack was eight, but an 1884 epidemic killed the flocks and the Londons lost the ranch in foreclosure.

By 1885 the family returned to Oakland, where they lived in a large number of houses while John London tried to support them by working as a night watchman and special policeman. The further down the economic scale the Londons slid, the stronger grew Flora's tantrums, which often climaxed with masterly fake "heart attacks."

From doing chores on the farms, ten-year-old Jack became a child laborer in urban jobs — delivering newspapers, doing any work that came to hand to help support the family. He found some relief from drudgery, and from his domineering, hysterical mother, in books. As Russ Kingman notes in *A Pictorial Life of Jack London* (1979), "He read everything he could lay his hands on, principally history and adventure, and all the old travels and voyages. He read mornings, afternoons, and nights. He read in bed, he read at the table, he read as he walked to and from school, and he read at recess while the other boys were playing."

In a letter to Houghton, Mifflin and Company dated January 31, 1900, London wrote of his beginnings in Oakland, saying, "Here, most precious to me was a free library." The stacks of the Oakland Public Library became a haunt for the boy, who lionized poet-librarian Ina Donna Coolbrith. She guided Jack London in his reading; twenty years later, when he was a world-famous writer, he credited her with being the most influential woman in his life.

"Naturally, my reading early bred in me a desire to write," London continued in the letter to his publishers, "but my manner of life prevented me attempting it." In the next few years London went from one job to another, often working sixteen hours a day in canneries and jute mills. He dropped out of high school after the first year, and at the age of fifteen left the family home to live on the waterfront. Borrowing money from "Aunt" Jennie Prentiss, the former wet-nurse he regarded more fondly than his natural mother, London bought a sloop called the *Razzle Dazzle* and at the age of sixteen became an oyster pirate on San Francisco Bay. The daring night raider of the tideland oyster beds soon earned the title "Prince of the Oyster Pirates," but after a few months he switched his allegiances and became a deputy in the Fish Patrol, a marine law enforcement body. He worked as a longshoreman, salmon fisher, and many other jobs with far less adventure and glamor than his months as a marine privateer and patrolman.

In the waterfront saloons and on the boats the teenage London developed his great acquaintance with "John Barleycorn" and began thinking about the inequalities of the capitalist system, which allowed children to slave hours a day for bare sustenance in order to further enrich the wealthy. He listened to socialist speakers in the Oakland town square, and felt compelled to speak out on these issues himself. A seven-month sealing expedition on the *Sophia Sutherland* in 1893 had taken him to Japan and the Russian coast, and a march east with Coxey's Army in 1894 had started him on the road as a hobo, riding rails, being jailed for vagrancy, seeing the underside of American life, and fully discovering his virile identity. "I loved life in the open," London said, "and I toiled in the open, at the hardest kinds of work. Learning no trade, but drifting along from job to job, I looked on the world and called it good, every bit of it . . . this optimism was because I was healthy and strong, bothered with neither aches nor weaknesses, never turned down by the boss because I did not look fit, able always to get a job shoveling coal, sailorizing, or manual labor of some sort."

London determined that he would succeed, developing his personal philosophy that exulted in his ability "to hold my own at work or fight, I was a rampant individualist. I was a winner. Wherefore I called the game, as I saw it played, or thought I saw it played, a very popular game for men. To be a *man* was to write *man* in large capitals on my heart. To adventure like a man, and fight like a man, and do a man's work (even for a boy's pay) — these were things that reached right in and gripped hold of me as no other thing could. And I looked ahead into long vistas of a hazy and interminable future in which, playing what I conceived to be a *man's* game, I should continue to travel with unfailing health, without accidents, and with muscles ever vigorous. As I say, this future was interminable. I could only see myself raging through life without end like one of Nietzsche's *blond beasts*, lustfully roving and conquering by sheer superiority and strength. . . ."

London crammed enough intensive study into a few months to pass entrance exams for U.C. Berkeley, but left the college after a semester to head for the Alaskan gold fields in 1897. In the Yukon, London's health failed him· he was forced to return to Oakland or die from scurvy. But as was the case with Mark Twain's failed mining ventures in the Washoe and the Sierra, London found his true riches in the tales he heard and experiences he had at the northern frontier.

He returned home to find that his stepfather had died while he was away, and that the burden of paying the rent for the London family now fell to him. London realized the futility of working without a trade, with old age sure to overtake him one day as it had John London, forcing him to scrape along to make ends meet. The trade that Jack London decided to master, however, was not that of ship's navigator or machinist or anything that might have been expected of him. He decided to earn a living by writing.

London set out to conquer writing by sheer effort. He wrote everything — stories, poems, jokes — that he thought could find a market. He struggled the rest of 1898 after his return home without making a single sale, and in 1899 collected hundreds of rejection slips, but the January issue of the *Overland Monthly* published an Alaskan tale, "To the Man on the Trail," paying London $5.00. London almost gave over the idea to continue as a writer, but then a second story sold for more money, and a third, and a fourth.

In 1900 his first book collected several of these stories under the title *The Son of the Wolf*. London was well into the work routine he would continue the rest of his life: sleep for four and one-half hours, rise at dawn, and write at least one-thousand finished words each day.

London's talent for publicity, which had landed him in the papers on earlier occasions as Oakland's youngest socialist leader, served him well. By the time *The Call of the Wild* (1903) and *The Sea Wolf* (1904) — his two adventure classics — appeared, London's every move called for coverage. His purchase of the "Beauty Ranch" in the Valley of the Moon and his two-year around-the-world cruise aboard the *Snark* were only highlights in the life of one of America's most popular, and highest paid, writers — the first writer to rise from the working class in this country to a major position in its literature.

London's achievement is distinctly American. Eclectic, he amalgamated the thoughts of the major philosophers he liked — Nietzsche, Darwin, Haeckel, Spencer, Marx — with a Horatio Alger-like work ethic. He used a multitude of fictional and non-fictional formats for his books — autobiography, adventure, science fiction, society novel, social essay, sports, swashbuckler — and invested them with a simple sweeping style to show Nature red in tooth and claw as the great arena for the struggles of Man.

London died on his Glen Ellen ranch November 22, 1916. The official report states he died of uremic poisoning, but some suspect he may have died from an overdose of morphine — in his major autobiographical novel *Martin Eden* (1909) the character based on London commits suicide. He left behind forty-odd published books, and others which appeared posthumously, and the record of a life of struggle and success that made him a legend before he was thirty.

JACK LONDON SITES

Jack London lived in a succession of homes in San Francisco, Oakland, and other Bay Area cities. As an oyster pirate he cruised throughout the Bay and along the coast, and sailed extensively while working with the Fish Patrol out of Benicia. The majority of homes occupied by the London family have been destroyed, some in the 1906 earthquake and fire, many more in the waves of urban renewal which have swept through Oakland in the last decades. No London dwelling stands in San Francisco today, but you can find a plaque on the building at 601-605 Third Street at Brannan marking his birthplace; it is the first stop in the South of Market tour. In the San Leandro marina you may visit a state historic site that young Jack London often visited by night — the San Leandro oyster beds. According to tradition, Moses Wick was the first man to bring seed oysters around Cape Horn from the East to implant in these tidal beds. At the time the "Prince of the Oyster Pirates" was raiding them, the oyster industry was the most profitable fishing enterprise in the state, but pollution in the Bay killed the industry five years before London's death.

JACK LONDON IN OAKLAND

Heading north or south bound on Highway 17 (the Nimitz Freeway) in Oakland, take the Broadway exit and follow Broadway west to what today is called Jack London Marina, where you'll find:

1 JACK LONDON SQUARE This group of waterfront restaurants was named Jack London Square May 1, 1951; with the more recent Jack London Village which it adjoins, it is the largest dining and shopping area named after a writer in the state of California—and one of the largest and most famous you will find anywhere in the world. Restaurants such as The Sea Wolf overlook the Oakland estuary and the sailboats moored in the marina, and the shops offer the usual stock— though it is ironic that the bookstore in the square has gone out of business. But whether or not you are interested in the commercial fare, this Square is a necessary stop for London fans on two counts.

First, you will find a major haunt of London's waterfront days still standing in authentic and admirable dilapidation: Heinold's First and Last Chance Saloon. Legend has it that here the sixteen-year-old London purchased the sloop *Razzle Dazzle* from "French Frank" to begin his career as an oyster pirate and make his first step toward financial independence. Here Jack could get a small loan from barkeep Johnny Heinold, and here—among other places—Jack London met "John Barleycorn" head-on, developing a dependence on alcohol that would become monstrous, a craving for the "white logic" only liquor could provide. London's autobiographical *John Barleycorn* (1913) gives the history and degree of his drinking with a frankness that appalled many readers who had not suspected his alcoholism.

If Heinold's is open when you visit—it is still an operating bar, and not merely a museum piece—it is a great place to test your own Nietzschean might against John Barleycorn (though in the long odds, Nietzsche doesn't have much of a chance). If it is closed you need only take a few steps to the second major attraction of Jack London Square, the cabin London occupied when he was prospecting in Alaska.

The cabin was discovered in the Yukon in the late 1960s and a party made up of Fred Reicker, Public Relations Director of the Port of Oakland; Russ Kingman, Executive Director of the Jack London Square Association; Sgt. Ralph Godfrey of the Oakland Police Department; actor Eddie Albert; and film maker Jack Williamson went North in 1969 to authenticate the cabin on Henderson Creek. The log cabin was brought to the square and restored; the unveiling of the cabin and its plaque took place July 1, 1970. London's daughter Becky Fleming was one of many people present at the ceremony.

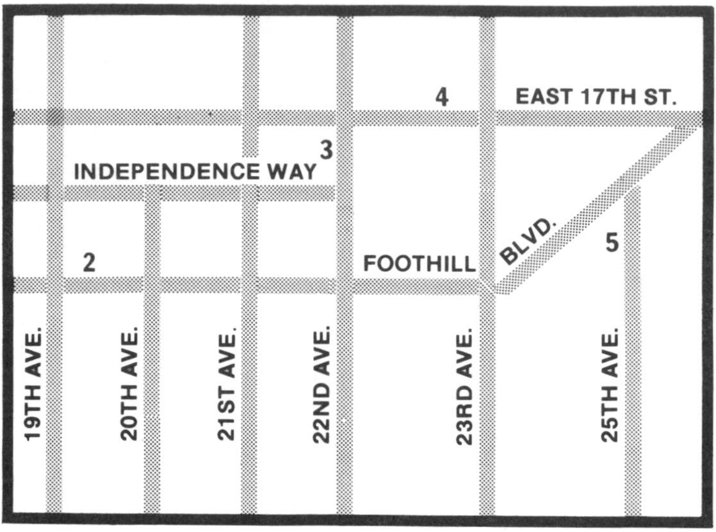

4

EAST 17TH ST.

3

INDEPENDENCE WAY

2

FOOTHILL   BLVD.   5

19TH AVE. 20TH AVE. 21ST AVE. 22ND AVE. 23RD AVE. 25TH AVE.

From Jack London Square it is only forty blocks or so to the largest concentration of still-standing London homes in East Oakland. You might go by car up Broadway to 7th Street, turn right, and follow 7th until it ends at 14th Avenue. You'll turn right from 14th Avenue into Foothill Boulevard to begin the tour. If you decide to go up Broadway to 14th Street, go right and follow 14th Street around Lake Merritt to 15th Street to 14th Avenue and then right on Foothill (this route allows you to make a side stop on the way by turning left on 10th Avenue and going two blocks up to 1640 10th Avenue, the only Gertrude Stein home left in modern Oakland).

On Foothill between 19th and 20th Avenues you will find:

2 1914 FOOTHILL BOULEVARD   Formerly 962 East 16th Street, this is the place Flora London moved after the death of her husband John, while Jack London was in the Klondike prospecting. When he returned to Oakland, disabled by scurvy, London settled here to work supporting the family. In this building he did the massive amount of early writing in 1898-1900 that led to his first sales to the *Overland Monthly* and other magazines, and to the publication of his first book, *The Son of the Wolf*. In this house Jack London became a professional writer.

Continue to 22nd Ave.

3 **1639 22nd AVENUE** Jack London lived here circa 1895-96, the only year he spent attending high school. He contributed stories and sketches to the school paper, the *Aegis*, indicating an early interest in becoming a writer. The front portion of the current building is an old store, which was added years after the Londons had moved on. In the 1890s the modern Garfield School which you see across the street from this house was a cow pasture.

Continue up 22nd Avenue the rest of the block to East 17th Street, and turn right. In the middle of the block you'll find:

4 **2262 EAST 17TH STREET** When the Londons returned to Oakland in the middle-1880s after losing their chicken ranch in Livermore they mortgaged two houses in this block, No. 2262 and another next to it (the current house at 2258 East 17th Street is at the location of the second house but, granting it is the same building, it has been so greatly renovated that it is unrecognizable as the place where the ten-year-old Jack London lived).

These buildings were only two blocks from the home of Jack's step-sister Eliza, who had married a middle-aged Civil War captain named Shepard when she was only sixteen to escape the oppressive atmosphere Flora created in the London home. Eliza had been largely responsible for raising Jack, and he delighted in being close to her again. Several of the London moves within Oakland in the next years would not only be dictated by finances, but also by the desire to be near the Shepards.

Here the Londons boarded girls who had been brought from Scotland to work in California's cotton mills until Flora, in one of her plans to strike it rich quickly through a lottery, lost their money and they had to forfeit both the houses on this street. London attended grammar grades at the four-room Garfield School directly across the street, but found education more to his liking in the stacks of the Oakland Public Library, about thirty blocks away.

Go on to 23rd Avenue, turn right and return to Foothill Boulevard. Take a left on Foothill, a right on 25th Avenue, and stop at:

5 **1645 25TH AVENUE**   Formerly 1327 25th Avenue, this is the building where London lived when he attended college in 1896-1897. From here he left for the gold fields of the Klondike, and it was in this house that his stepfather John London died, unknown to Jack until his return in 1897.

That so many photographs of London's Oakland homes exist is due to London himself. While waiting for the *Snark* voyage, he and Charmian bicycled around the East Bay and took photographs of every house in which London could recall living.

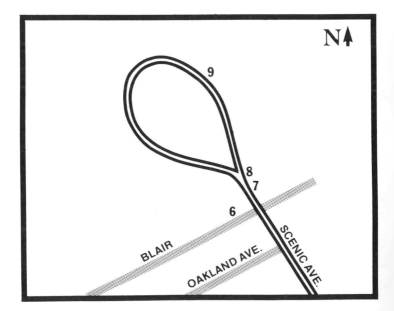

These homes in East Oakland, many of which no longer exist, represent the years before London rose to fame. In the Piedmont hills another cluster of sites shows London's haunts after he became one of the highest-paid writers in publishing history. Follow Foothill back to Lake Merritt, and take Lake Shore Avenue to the right around the lake. When you reach Embarcadero Street and Lake Shore Park, jog left a block to Grand Avenue, and turn right up Grand to Oakland Avenue. Follow Oakland to where it ends at Scenic Avenue.

Turn left on Scenic, and bear left on Blair a fraction of the block to:

6 575 BLAIR Jack and his first wife Bessie moved here in 1901, renting the house for $35.00 a month. The newly successful London was meeting more and more people in the Bay Area's literary and social circles, and it was George Sterling—who would become London's closest friend and companion—who told him that this house, then a one-story bungalow, was available to let. London stayed here off and on the next three years, traveling to the East End slums of London in 1902 to research and write *The People of the Abyss* (1903), spending some weeks at summer retreats or sailing. Here London wrote what would become his most popular book, *The Call of the Wild* (1903), and began work on his next major novel, *The Sea-Wolf* (1904).

The Londons threw Wednesday night parties to which Sterling, Herman Whitaker, Frank Atherton, and many of their other friends regularly came. This crowd in the Piedmont hills consisted of many of the same people who frequented Coppa's restaurant in San Francisco's Montgomery Block, and many were the artists and writers who founded the colony in Carmel. The men were also active in the Bohemian Club; and London was drawn into their private society. Whatever his stance as a socialist and advocate for the poor and downtrodden, London could not help earning respect from the businessmen who came more and more to populate the Bohemian Grove gatherings. After all, in sixteen years as a writer London earned more than a million dollars.

London's mother lived in a small cottage on these same grounds—then well into the country. On this site too were a barn, creamery, laundry, pigeon houses, and other buildings.

In the history of Bay Area architecture this house, now remodeled beyond recognition from London's day, is of great significance as the first shingle-style house built in northern California. It was built by Joseph Worcester, whose use of natural local building materials later became fashionable, especially in the East Bay and on Russian Hill. London noted in a letter dated February 23, 1902, that his new house had "a big living room, every inch of it, floor and ceiling, finished in red-

wood. We could put the floor space of almost four cottages into this one living room alone. The rest of the house is finished in redwood too, and is very, very comfortable. . . ."

In this house London's marriage to Bessie Maddern deteriorated, soon to dissolve in divorce in 1905. If you return to Scenic Avenue and turn left you will come to another shingle-style house London had built later to house his ex-wife and two daughters, at:

7 206 SCENIC AVENUE   This home is the second London built for his family after the divorce. The first house still stands at 519 31st Street off Telegraph Avenue. In 1904, as part of the divorce settlement, London bought that lot and had "One Nail" McGregor build the house you find today — one of a nice line of old buildings in a cul-de-sac. But the area the first house stood on was considered unhealthy for the children after awhile, so London had this home on Scenic Avenue erected in 1913 — at the same time he was financing his $70,000 "Wolf House" on his ranch in Glen Ellen. London's large expenditures — constructing the *Snark* for his around-the-world cruise at a time when wood in San Francisco was at a premium because of the devastating 1906 fire, buying homes for his mother, supporting his huge ranch — kept him in constant debt, and made his one-thousand words a day a *necessity* if he expected to keep up with his bills.

A bit further up the street will put you before:

8 **270 SCENIC AVENUE**   London's good friend Herman Whitaker built this home for his family. It was Whitaker who convinced London to join the Socialist Party, who coached London in boxing and fencing, and London in turn encouraged Whitaker in his efforts at writing. Whitaker wrote seven novels and many essays and stories. London, Whitaker, and George Sterling were all charter members of the Ruskin Club in Oakland, a socialist group.

Still further up the street will put you before another home built by one of London's Piedmont circle:

9 **324 SCENIC AVENUE**   This was the studio and home of the painter Xavier Martinez — one can only admire his choice of view, one of the best in the Bay Area from the top of this ridge. Martinez designed and painted the frieze of black cats that circled the ceiling at Coppa's restaurant above the ingenious murals, and was a major figure in the second wave of San Francisco's Bohemia. London undoubtedly was a frequent visitor here, as well as in Whitaker's home down the street.

Head back down Oakland Avenue to Grand, and follow Grand back to Lake Merritt. Shortly after you go under the Interstate 580 overpass you will come to Staten Street. Turn right. Turn right again on Palm to the last stop remaining on the Oakland leg of the London tour:

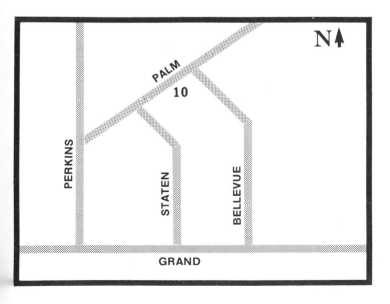

490 27th St.   then   360 Palm Ave.   now

10 **360 PALM**   This building, another now greatly remodeled, originally stood at 490 27th Street off Telegraph Avenue, about two blocks from the first home London built for his ex-wife. He bought this two-story house on 27th Street for his mother, but reserved the upper rooms for himself and his second wife Charmian to use when they came down from Glen Ellen. The Londons lived in these rooms when they were in town until his death. Later the building was moved to this current site.

London's other East Bay residences are either gone or so completely remodeled as to be unrecognizable. But the major Jack London site is not found in Oakland—you'll find it to the north in Sonoma County:

JACK LONDON STATE HISTORIC PARK

London moved to Glen Ellen from 490 27th Street in 1905 when he was twenty-nine years old. His divorce from Bessie had gone through, followed by a wedding with Charmian. He bought 130 acres of land in the Valley of the Moon on which he planned to settle down, but he interrupted his plans to voyage on the *Snark* from 1907 to 1909. When he returned to California, London threw himself into developing his Beauty Ranch, buying more land so that ultimately he owned 1400 acres on which to raise livestock and develop and test his theories of agriculture. He continued his regular writing schedule, publishing several novels about ranch life in California— *Valley of the Moon* (1913), *Little Lady of the Big House* (1916), and others. In addition to this and his ranch work, he did a stint as a reporter covering the Mexican Revolution— taking on a typically superhuman workload. No other literary site in this state gives the visitor the feeling of commercial success that Beauty Ranch does—the realization that a man by virtue of his *writing* transformed one of the most magnificent areas in the state into a personal Shangri-La.

Heading north on Highway 101 you may take 116 out of Petaluma over to 12 and then north to Glen Ellen. The entrance to the park is found in the downtown area on an S curve, with signs marking the turn. The entrance is on Arnold Street, the main drag, into London Ranch Road. There is a $2.00 vehicle fee to enter the park ($1.00 for seniors) and a 50¢ fee if you bring your dog. The park is open daily from 10 a.m. until 5 p.m. except Thanksgiving, Christmas, and New Years; for more information you may write Jack London State Historic Park, P.O. Box 358, Glen Ellen, CA 95442 or phone (707) 938-5216.

Wolf House ruins

This state park was created in 1959 when Irving Shepard, London's nephew and an heir to the estate, arranged for forty acres, including the major buildings London had erected, to be opened for public use. Another ten acres were acquired in 1960 and 1970, and in 1980 the park expanded to include 800 acres of London's original holdings. The park first opened on a limited basis September 1, 1960, and was officially dedicated September 24, 1960, to coincide with the Valley of the Moon Vintage Festival being held in Sonoma.

From the parking area it is only a short walk to the House of Happy Walls, built by Charmian in the years 1919-22. Today it houses a wealth of London memorabilia — London's desk and other furniture, much of it custom-built, many photographic displays on all the important events in London's life, even a brief film clip of the author taken at the ranch not long before his death in which London mugs and hops about with the electric animation of Douglas Fairbanks. Charmian lived in this house until her death in 1955, and directed in her will that it be used as a museum and memorial to her husband's life and work.

From the House of Happy Walls clearly marked trails lead the way to London's grave under an enormous boulder among the trees. His immediate family, his ranch hands, and his great friend George Sterling were the only ones London wished to see his ashes buried, and were the only people at the ceremony November 12, 1916.

Beyond London's grave the trail leads on to the ruins of Wolf House, the dream building from which London planned to guide his empire — incredible in ruin, it cost about $70,000 to build and burned in a fire the night of August 23, 1913, the day before the Londons were planning to move their furniture into the new house.

Another trail leads off to the barns and stables, and the original ranch house where London actually lived while Wolf House was underway, and after his dreams had burned. If you follow the trail past this house into the hills you will come to a reservoir where London fished and swam. It is said that George Sterling helped him build the dam at one end of the lake on one of his many visits.

Beauty Ranch is a fine place for hikes, picnics, family outings, a place that can be enjoyed by London buffs or people who may never have heard of London (if there are any people who have never heard of London) — one of the truly great literary sites in northern California.

Leaving the London Park you might wish to turn right on Arnold Street and go about a mile to 14300 Arnold — The World of Jack London Bookstore run by London biographer Russ Kingman. More London memorabilia is on display in the store, and you'll find the largest selection of London's books available for those who come away from the park with a passionate curiosity to read more Jack London — an almost inevitable effect this well-run park has on the hundreds of thousands who visit each year.

If you go left on Arnold, around the S curve, you'll find a number of shops which nod toward London's great presence, such as The Hungry Wolf restaurant. Going north on Highway 12 to the next town of Kenwood can provide another notable souvenir. The Kenwood Winery offers Jack London Wine, actually made from the grapes grown on the working portion of London's ranch still operated by the Shepards, from vineyards begun by London himself. A chance to make London's acquaintance through a cousin of "John Barleycorn" directly sired by this still enormously popular writer.

Jack and Charmian London

POINTS EAST

The Abbey, Joaquin Miller Park, Oakland

Across the Bay Bridge by bus or car or under the Bay via BART you come to Oakland, whose literary history is dominated by the towering figure of Jack London, but which also boasts a surprising array of writers and some curious haunts. And there is Berkeley, where the University of California has been from its beginnings a locus for writers. Further east are sites for John Muir, Eugene O'Neill, Ella Leffland, and Maxine Hong Kingston.

Heading south into Oakland on Highway 17 you'll see a sign on the freeway that marks the exit to Jack London Square.

This square and other East Bay sites for London are covered in his own chapter, but Highway 17 runs next to another literary shopping area of note:

Bret Harte

1 THE BRET HARTE BOARDWALK In a row of buildings at 567-577 5th Street off Clay, this small set of shops features the usual boutiques and a restaurant called "Eat Your Harte Out." The name derives from the days when Harte lived with his uncle — but his uncle's home was on the opposite side of the street, where Highway 17 carries southbound traffic today.

Many other writers have lived in the city of:

2 OAKLAND Jessica Mitford, the witty, muckraking author of *The American Way of Death* and other books, now lives here. Norman Jayo — poet, screenwriter, and musician — lives in East Oakland. Franklin Walker lived on Majestic Avenue near Mills College. He was professor *Emeritus* of American literature at the college, author of biographies of Frank Norris, Ambrose Bierce, and seminal works on California's early literary history — *San Francisco's Literary Frontier, A Literary History of Southern California*, and *The Seacoast of Bohemia*, on the founding of the Carmel artist colony. The pulp great E. Hoffmann Price was born in Fowler, California, in 1898, but lived in his early teens in Oakland. He recalls sitting on the roof of the back porch at 5314 East 12th Street on the corner of 53rd Avenue in June 1910, watching Haley's Comet sweep across the skies.

Novelist Alfred Coppel grew up in Oakland and Berkeley, and studied at Stanford until joining the Air Force in World War II. He has used northern California settings in several books (such as *Hero Driver*, about stock car racing in Monterey), but of special note is his *Dark December* (1960) — one of the first mainstream novels about nuclear war. The U.S.A. and U.S.S.R. exchange an initial round of warheads, and draw back in horror at the overwhelming devastation wrought by this limited engagement. Coppel's hero is stationed with the Air Force in Alaska and is mustered out as the system collapses. He begins an overland trek to his family home on the peninsula south of San Francisco, with the climax of the novel occurring as he works his way across the wreckage of the Golden Gate Bridge.

Eldridge Cleaver, who served nine years on a one-to-fourteen-year indeterminate sentence for rape, writing *Soul on Ice* behind bars, was a contributing editor on *Ramparts* and the Minister of Information for Oakland's Black Panther Party in 1967. He ran against Dick Gregory for the Presidential nomination on the Peace and Freedom Party ticket in 1968, and on April 6th of the same year was involved in a shoot-out with police in West Oakland in which two officers were wounded and a black youth killed. Cleaver fled the country to Algiers, the French Congo, and other points, sent back messages (ELDRIDGE SPEAKS— FIRST WORDS FROM EXILE was the headline on the *Berkeley Barb* for June 27-July 3, 1969), and became a modern folk hero to a small part of the radical left. He returned to face charges in 1975, but lost much of his particular charm when he became a Moonie a few years ago.

Ishmael Reed has written seven novels, beginning with *The Freelance Pallbearers* in 1967, two essay collections, two poetry collections, two plays, an experimental television soap opera series called "Personal Problems," and a teleplay titled "Mother Hubbard" about a feminist-terrorist organization. Reed was raised in Chattanooga, Tennessee, and Buffalo, New York, but moved to Oakland from New York several years ago to become one of the most active writers and editors in the Bay Area. With Al Young, Shawn Wong, and William Lawson, he founded and edited the annual *Yardbird* from 1972-1976, and currently co-publishes another annual, *Quilt*. He was instrumental in launching the Before Columbus Foundation, which disseminates books of ethnic diversity around the country, with the intention of fostering a multicultural literature. His anthology *Calafia: The California Poetry* (1979) is the best historic gathering of verse from the Gold Rush era through our contemporary poets.

Ishmael Reed

In a KQED TV documentary "*There* with Ishmael Reed" he calls Oakland "a beautiful city," and says (tongue-partly-in-cheek): "If Gertrude Stein had remained, she would have learned to write a straightforward, clear sentence."

The title of the Reed documentary of course refers to the most famous (or infamous) literary quote about Oakland, a remark that San Franciscans have long used to knock the East Bay city: Gertrude Stein's "There is no there there." John Krich says in his *Bump City: Winners and Losers in Oakland* (1979), a history of Oakland written in novel form:

> "Oakland could bear its ugly sister status with quiet pride because of its one great secret: it has always done the dirty work that keeps San Francisco young and beautiful. . . . Oakland was on the mainland. It was a natural warehouse, a storage depot, the end of the line. With the completion of the Transcontinental Railway in 1869, Oakland became the Pacific railhead. First and always, Oakland is a railroad town. There is still no place in Oakland to escape the sounds of the train whistle."

(When Jack Kerouac began work for Southern Pacific, he trained in the Oakland switchyards.) Today Oakland, in Krich's words, "has won its industrial arm-wrestle with San Francisco many times over"— shipping, mail to Asia, interstate commerce, all mostly go through Oakland, which continues to endure the brickbats of the urban chauvinists.

"There is no there there" has occasioned remarkable controversy, and formed a strong association between:

Gertrude Stein

3 GERTRUDE STEIN AND OAKLAND Stein came to this city with her family as a child, and went East in 1891 to attend college at Radcliffe, Harvard, and Johns Hopkins — and then, bored with America, she left for Europe in 1901. The Steins arrived here in 1880, staying in the Tubbs Hotel on East 12th Street. Soon they rented "the old Joseph Stratton Place" on 13th Avenue — a ten-acre farm, the house situated on a hilltop (described in Stein's *The Making of Americans,* 1925). The family moved in 1885 to the Italianate building that is now 1640 10th Avenue, where they lived until her father died in 1891.

In her circle in Paris, Stein met Isadora and her brother Robert Duncan, also formerly of Oakland; Robert told her he had stolen apples from the Stein orchard when they lived on 13th Avenue. And in 1906 Stein's brother Michael and his wife Sara visited San Francisco to assess the damage done to property he owned at 834 Turk Street. They met twenty-nine-year-old Alice B. Toklas, and told her of life in Paris. Toklas borrowed money and left the country, and in 1909 she was invited to join "the Stein menage" in 27 rue de Fleuris. When Stein and Toklas came to New York in October 1934, Stein began a cross-country lecture tour. When they got to San Francisco, they came over from the Mark Hopkins to see her old haunts of forty years before.

Today there is an annual event (usually on the anniversary of Stein's birthday, February 3, 1874) for Oakland sympathizers to explain to the public that she was not downgrading her old home when she wrote (in typical, unstraightforward Steinese) of her American tour in *Everybody's Autobiography* (1937): "what was the use of my having come from Oakland it was not natural to have come from there yes write about it if I like or anything if I like but not there, there is no there there." Stein seemed to be expressing culture-shock over finding the well-remembered farm replaced by stucco tract houses. Even greater changes have visited Stein's Oakland since 1935. The Tubbs Hotel, Oakland High School, which she attended one year without graduating, and other places she knew have long vanished. (Many Stein biographies have her attending an "Oakwood High School," which never existed — they misread her loose handwriting in a 1914 letter to Harriet Lane Levy now in the Beinecke Manuscript Library at Yale. Similarly, on her gravestone her birthplace in Allegheny, Pennsylvania, is misspelled "Allfghany" and her birthdate is off by two days — the French couldn't decipher her script too well either.) The lone Stein site at 1640 10th Avenue is located between East 16th and East 17th streets — cars must approach via East 16th.

*Unknown to Stein, she crossed
paths in 1880 with another
famous writer:*

4 ROBERT LOUIS STEVENSON IN OAKLAND In March, 1880, R.L.S. was also briefly a guest in the Tubbs Hotel. The Tubbs and its grounds occupied an entire block fronting on East 12th Street, between 4th and 5th Avenues. R.L.S. was brought here from 608 Bush when he became too ill for Mary Carson to care for. In his room at the Tubbs his condition further deteriorated, and Fanny Osbourne— with permission of her husband Sam— took Stevenson into her home to recover. The Osbourne house stood in grounds occupying half a block on the northeast corner of East 18th Street and 11th Avenue. Anne Roller Issler in *Happier for His Presence: San Francisco and Robert Louis Stevenson* (1949) wrote: "It was a charming, romantic, storybook sort of home. The low, white, frame cottage stood well back from the street, its peaked roof and gabled lines pleasantly vague, what with the profusion of vines and shrubbery." When Stevenson's health became somewhat better, on May 19, 1880, he and Fanny Osbourne were married in San Francisco after her divorce, and soon left on their honeymoon excursion north to Silverado.

*Another major literary site in
Oakland that is long gone is
the:*

5 OAKLAND PUBLIC LIBRARY This small building stood at 14th Street and Washington— the site of Oakland's modern City Hall, and here Ina Donna Coolbrith served as the first library director from 1878-1892, guiding the early reading of Isadora Duncan and Jack London, offering them "the big books" and inspiring them with a vision of Art. London wrote her in 1906: "No woman has affected me to the extent you did."

*A short drive through the tube
from downtown Oakland will
bring you to:*

6 ALAMEDA The poet Daniel Moore, author of *Dawn Visions*, was born here July 30, 1940. During the 1960s counter culture, Moore enchanted large gatherings in the parks with his Floating Lotus Magic Opera Company's theatricals. After publication of his anti-war poems *Burnt Heart* in 1971, he turned to Sufism and vanished into the deserts of North Africa.

The poet Robert Duncan was born in Oakland January 7, 1919; his mother died in childbirth and he was put out for adoption. He spent his childhood in 1700 Pearl Street in Alameda, a building still standing, with his adoptive parents Edwin Joseph Symmes and Minnehaha Harris. Symmes designed this building, where they lived until October 1927, when the family moved to Bakersfield.

At the age of six, Jack London lived at 211 Pacific Avenue here— one of dozens of places in the East Bay where the London family camped as they moved from house to house.

*Heading into the Oakland hills
toward Piedmont (and the tour
of Jack London sites in that
area) you should stop at the
corner of Pleasant Valley
Avenue and Howe Street and
enter:*

7 THE CHAPEL OF MEMORIES   This large columbarium houses ash-filled funeral urns of all sizes and descriptions, including that of London's great friend, the poet George Sterling. The King of San Francisco's Bohemia is found in a top row on the second floor of the columbarium in the Cypress wing — ask for directions to Cypress B-5-1C. Sterling's vault is very small and nondescript, reflecting the fact that the poet died broke. In his last years in the Bohemian Club he was allowed a charge account courtesy of his various patrons, to which he could bill food, liquor, and other expenses — but one from which he could draw no cash. Sterling rid himself of money as if it burned his pockets. On the mortuary card Sterling's death by suicide is described under Cause of Death as "stomach to chemist."

*Nearby in the Oakland hills, off
Highway 13, is found:*

8 BROADWAY TERRACE   This neighborhood is home for a sizable colony of science fiction writers — Jack Vance, Terry Carr, Marta Randall — and the home of Charles N. Brown, editor and publisher of the sci fi newspaper *Locus*, is often used for book parties and other sci fi gatherings. Robert Silverberg also bought a huge house in this area when he migrated from New York in the 1970s. Recently Silverberg's name has appeared on the bestseller lists courtesy of *Lord Valentine's Castle* (1980) and its sequels, but these books are only a small part of his output. As a teenager Silverberg rented a cheap office in New York and went there during regular work hours to write. For years he produced well over a million words each year, and his output far surpasses that of Jack London, Kathleen Norris, Erle Stanley Gardner, and other prolific writers who have lived in the Bay Area. In fact, Silverberg may even rival John Creasey, now considered the greatest one-man Fiction Factory of all time, who wrote over five-hundred books under fifteen different names ("J. J. Marric," "Jeremy York," and "Gordon Ashe" are only three of his pennames). Silverberg has written short stories, articles, juvenile fiction, non-fiction on ancient civilizations, dinosaurs, and many other subjects, some eighty sci fi and fantasy novels, and — in his spare time — for several years he turned out a soft-core porn novel each week, fifty-two weeks of the year — about two hundred of these appeared under the name "Don Elliot."

*South on Highway 13 from the
Broadway Terrace neighbor-
hood you'll see an exit for
Joaquin Miller Road and:*

9 JOAQUIN MILLER PARK This is a fine place for a hike on the many trails that wind back into the hills, or a picnic at one of several barbecue units and fire circles, in memory of the flamboyant poet Joaquin Miller.

Cincinnatus Hiner Miller's birthdate is sometimes given as 1837, or 1842—one account has him delivered in 1841 in Illinois as his family traveled by wagon en route to Oregon; other accounts make him an Oregon native. He was an authentic western character—a miner, pony express rider, and Indian fighter, and he later served as a lawyer, judge, and publisher. Yet his overriding wish was to be a great poet.

Bret Harte rejected his submissions to the *Overland Monthly*, but Harte's co-editor Ina Donna Coolbrith (who raised Cali-Shasta, the daughter from Miller's brief union with an Indian woman whose tribe lived at the foot of Mount Shasta) gave Miller advice that would make him a living legend. First, she suggested he change his name to the more Californian "Joaquin" (after Joaquin Murrieta, the famous bandit, whose exploits Miller had commemorated in verse); second, *dress* the part of a wild west poet; third, go to England, where characters were appreciated, to seek his fame. Julian Hawthorne said that Miller in London was a "picturesque barbarian, booted, spurred, red-flannel shirted, and sombreroed"; his visit created a sensation and terrific notoriety. He met the Rosettis, Tennyson, the Brownings, Trollope, and saw *Pacific Poems* and *Songs of the Sierras* published.

By the time Miller bought eighty acres of land here on the Oakland hills in 1886 he was known as "The Poet of the Sierras." Gertrude Atherton described him wearing "a black broadcloth suit, the trousers tucked into boots—with high heels!—that reached almost to his waist. His shirt had no collar but his neck was encircled by a lace scarf. On his head was a sombrero, which he removed with a sweeping bow as I entered, and I saw that his long hair, touching his shoulders, was grey on top, and ended in a series of stiff 'rat tails' that were dyed a bright orange." Miller dubbed his land "The Hights," disdainful of proper spelling, and here he entertained Bierce, London, Edwin Markham, Frank Norris, and other literati of the day. Poet Yone Noguchi lived here and worked as a gardener. Before he became a poet, George Sterling met Miller on the Hights; there is no doubt that the flamboyant poseur Miller inspired Sterling's own great role-playing as a Romantic poet later, or that he wore well the mantle of California's Romantic poet, handed down from Miller.

Here Miller devoted himself to his four "great loves": women, whiskey, poetry and trees, until his death in 1913. Most of the trees you see standing in these hills owe their existence to Miller. He personally planted thousands of Monterey pines, cypress, olive, and eucalyptus, and wrote articles for the *Golden Era* (after returning from a second trip to England in 1885) about the worth of trees that so fired the public's enthusiasm they led to the first Arbor Day on November 27, 1886.

You'll find the home he built, The Abbey, still standing at the entrance to the park. A plaque erected September 9, 1928, by the Native Sons of the Golden West details Miller's history. Here he wrote his most famous poem, "Columbus," a favorite with school-age orators on Columbus Day. Here he entertained his lady devotees, performing mystic rain ceremonies (greatly aided by a sprinkler on the roof of the house).

From the front of the Abbey looking to your right you'll see a primitively carved statue by Kisa Beeck depicting Miller astride a horse, on the hill across the road that leads into the park. The statue marks the site of a cottage Miller built for his mother to live in. (His wife Abbie— whose name may have inspired the name of his dwelling—and daughter Juanita spent most of the time in the East; and an earlier, abandoned wife, the poet Minnie Myrtle Dyer, went on the lecture circuit damning the philandering "Poet of the Sierras.")

As you follow the road winding up into the hills you'll find on separate overlooks the large monuments of piled stones Miller erected to honor favored figures: a pyramid to Moses (1892), a pile to Robert and Eliza-beth Barrett Browning (1894), and a pile to General John C. Fremont (1904). The Moses monument affirms Miller's belief in the Ten Com-mandments (not that he always acted on his beliefs) and the Fremont pile marks the site Miller romantically proclaimed as the exact spot where the general first saw the sunset over the Bay, before the Bear Flag Revolt and the creation of the Republic of California. You'll also find the stone pyre Miller built on which he wanted his body cremated, but the Oakland city fathers refused to allow Miller his just, barbaric funeral, though his ashes— cremated in more orthodox fashion— were scattered nearby after a ceremonial bonfire on the pyre.

Oakland bought the Hights for park land in 1919, and in 1930 the California Writers Club, a later version of Coolbrith's California Liter-ary Society, continued one of Miller's finest traditions, in Cascade Grove near the Abbey, with a memorial planting on October 15th of young red-wood trees to Miller, Mark Twain, Jack London, Bret Harte, Charles Warren Stoddard, Edward Rowland Sill, journalist-archaeologist Charles Fletcher Lummis, Edwin Markham, and Ina Donna Coolbrith. John Muir's tree was planted September 26, 1931; Father Palóu and R.L.S. followed on May 24, 1942, and on October 7, 1945, trees for Mary Hunter Austin and Hubert Howe Bancroft. September 28, 1947, the Norris writers— Frank, Charles, and Kathleen— had a "family group" planted in their honor. George Sterling's tree was placed next to that of his great friend "Wolf" London October 8, 1950. Herbert Eugene Bol-ton, author of the California history *Outpost of Empire* (1931) and Cleveland Doyle received trees at some now lost date. Gertrude Ather-ton's tree was planted October 4, 1954, and a last tree in honor of the club itself placed October 14, 1956.

The tradition faded from practice until, in the 1980s, the club revived it, re-planting trees for Miller and Mark Twain, whose original trees had been removed in 1941 to make way for the park's Woodminster Outdoor Theatre. Trees for Robinson Jeffers and John Steinbeck came next, and on June 16, 1984, Dashiell Hammett got the honor (having won out in the club's annual vote over Gertrude Stein). The grove is a short walk northeast from the Abbey. At its base you'll find the Gertrude Mott Fountain, dedicated June 2, 1955, in honor of the author of *The Hand-book of Californiacs* and chairperson of the committee that planted the first trees in 1930 (and no doubt clearance for the planting was made easier because her husband was mayor of Oakland). On the east side of the Cascade (about midway up towards the back of the amphitheatre) there is a bench dedicated to Charles and Ormeida Keeler on October 14, 1956 (Keeler was on the committee for the original planting)— on the opposite side, a bench dedicated September 21, 1958, to poets Derrick and Eunice Lehmer.

In Bay Window Bohemia *(1956) Oscar Lewis recounts the best tale about Miller, down from the Hights to attend a banquet in the Bohemian Club. Miller greatly disliked Bret Harte — perhaps for the early rejection of his poems, or because Miller, a genuine frontiersman, considered the city-slicker Harte a fake in his secondhand accounts of mining life. Lewis writes: "He arrived togged out in his usual outfit, complete with bearskin, partook liberally of the food and drink, and remained in high spirits until the speaker of the evening launched into a paean of praise of Harte's early California tales. Thereupon he rose to his feet and stalked majestically from the room. A little later, questions from the floor having been invited, someone asked: 'What has become of the old, picturesque wild West?' and the speaker brought down the house by replying: 'Didn't you notice? He just walked out.' "*

Berkeley adjoins Oakland on the north, and its literary history in great part centers on the:

10 **UNIVERSITY OF CALIFORNIA CAMPUS** U.C. established its permanent campus here after the Charter Act of 1868 made it the first state-operated college. The first class graduated in 1873, and over the years an astounding number of writers have taught or studied here. Literary faculty members have included Mark Schorer, author of *Lawrence in the War Years* (1968), novels, and criticism; Thomas Parkinson, a poet and editor of *A Casebook on the Beat* (1961); Ishmael Reed, who teaches creative writing; James D. Hart, director of the Bancroft Library and author of a number of reference works; Eric Hoffer; George R. Stewart; Elaine Kim; Alfred L. Kroeber; and many others.

Stewart, author of over forty books in his sixty-three-year writing career, was thought to have created a new form for the novel in *Storm* (1941) and *Fire* (1948), in which raging elemental forces — a Pacific storm, a sweeping forest fire — became the central focus and in effect the leading *characters* in the books. Stewart did extensive research for these novels: manning fire lookouts, working with wilderness firefighters, spending hours on the Bay taking notes as storms rushed in. Both books were very influential. The American Forestry Association made Stewart an honorary vice-president for his encompassing, realistic portrayal of the devastation caused by *Fire*, which was filmed as "Red Skies of Montana," and his naming the *Storm* "Maria" is thought to have influenced the practice of giving ocean-born storms feminine names (as well as inspiring the song "They Call the Wind Maria"). Stewart also wrote a biography of Bret Harte, a history of the Donner Party, the novel *Earth Abides*, and dozens of other books, but his favorite projects came out of his research as an onomastologist, exploring the origins of *names*. His *Names on the Land* (1945), *American Place Names* (1970), and *Names on the Globe* (1975) are invaluable reference works that earned him the the title "Onomastician-in-Chief" of the American Names Society in 1979, the year before he died at age eighty-five. Stewart once said: "Writing was always an escape for me, because I had so much university work to do." He retired from active teaching in 1962, after thirty-eight years in the English department at U.C. (And of some note is the fact that Stewart was another local writer who campaigned to save the Rincon Annex murals when they were threatened with removal in the 1950s.)

Anthropologist A. L. Kroeber's writing on California Indians ultimately was overshadowed by the immense popularity of his wife Theodora's *Ishi in Two Worlds: A Biography of the Last Wild Indian in North America*, published the year Kroeber died, 1961. Theodora met Kroeber, her second husband, while attending his classes at U.C.; they married in the mid-1920s. In *The Imagined City: San Francisco in the Minds of Its Writers* (1980) — a book based on a photographic exhibit by John van der Zee and Boyd Jacobson — Julie Smith provides brief biographies of the thirty-seven local writers encompassed by the project. She says that Theodora Kroeber "was an inspiration to late-blooming writers and aging women." Her first book, *The Inland Whale* (1959) — "nine stories retold from California Indian legends" — appeared when she was sixty-two, and seven years later in 1966 "she married her third husband, a young man of twenty-seven." She also wrote *Ishi, Last of His Tribe* (1964), *Alfred Kroeber: A Personal Configuration* (1970), and other books. Kroeber served a year on U.C.'s Board of Regents but resigned in 1978 because of ill health; she died July 4, 1979, age eighty-two, in her home at 1325 Arch Street.

The Kroeber home, a Bernard Maybeck design from 1907, is also of note as the place where Ursula Kroeber Le Guin, second child of A. L. and Theodora Kroeber, born in 1929, grew up. Le Guin, a resident of Portland, Oregon, for several years, is one of the most respected writers of speculative fiction. Her science fiction novels *The Left Hand of Darkness* (1969) and *The Dispossessed* (1975) each won both the Nebula Award presented by the Science Fiction Writers of America as best of the year and the Hugo Award for Best Novel given at the annual World Science Fiction Convention. She has written other sci fi, historical, and juvenile books; her fantasy trilogy about the water-world Earthsea is a modern classic in that genre.

The poet Robert Duncan dropped out of U.C. in 1938 before getting his B.A., but he was about to be dismissed anyway for not attending drills or section meetings in Military Science and Tactics. After a few years in New York, where he had close connections with Anais Nin and Kenneth Patchen, he returned to the Bay Area. He had first stayed at the Acacia Fraternity House at 2340 Piedmont in the 1930s, then at 1542 Hawthorne. Using his adoptive father's surname, Symmes, he edited the magazine *Epitaph* from 2012 Durant Avenue. Covering his early years in the biography *Young Robert Duncan: Portrait of the Poet as a Homosexual in Society* (1983), Ekbert Faas notes that Duncan's return to Berkeley from New York in 1946 struck William Everson as "the big news"; Duncan immediately organized a weekly literary discussion group.

> "Everson was genuinely impressed. 'In San Francisco Rexroth was our group's *paterfamilias*,' he remembers, 'but on the Berkeley side Duncan was its energy. He was indefatigable in his arrangement of poetry readings as our key creative outlet, since the dominant centers of publications were largely closed to us.'" These meetings were held in the dining room of a communal house, a Victorian mansion at 2643 Telegraph Avenue known as Throckmorton Manor. Thomas Parkinson, Leo Levy, Rosario Jimenez, Robin Blaser, Philip Lamantia, Robert Berg, and others attended, to lecture or talk on Garcia Lorca, H.D., William Carlos Williams, Ezra Pound, and other writers who at that time "were still barely mentioned in academic circles."

In this connection, it might be mentioned that when Gertrude Stein came to speak at U.C. Berkeley on her lecture tour the committee in charge of campus events, according to Lois Rather in *Gertrude Stein and California* (1974), "was torn by dissension, with some hint that Miss Stein's talents were perhaps too trivial for this honor." (She lectured at the International House, April 15, 1935.)

When Eldridge Cleaver was banned from speaking on campus in the 1960s, the protests made headlines. And the famous anti-war marches in Berkeley in the 1960s drew hundreds of writers—Ginsberg, *Realist* editor Paul Krassner, Kesey and the Merry Pranksters, and others. The long Berkeley radical tradition—from the old-time anarchists and Wobblies through the 1960s New Left to the anti-nuke protestors of today—is part of the overall literary scene in the area. Few ultra-conservative writers have come from Berkeley.

The cottages and houses around the campus have been home for any number of writers:

James Broughton, Madeline Gleason, Robert Duncan

11 **2029 HEARST** was another communal house in which poet Robert Duncan lived for about a year. While here, his first poetry collection, *Heavenly City, Earthly City* (1947), appeared. Duncan and one of the other residents of "New Athens" (as the place was called), Jack Spicer, were the two most active younger poets in the Bay Area at the time. When E. M. Forster on a visit to Berkeley asked where he could meet some "non-academic writers," he was directed to Duncan's place.

When On the Road was published in 1957 Jack Kerouac was staying in:

12 **1943 BERKELEY WAY** Now gone, this is the place where Jack and his mother were living briefly when he got his first copies of the finished book from Viking Press. Neal Cassady was there when he opened the package, and saw himself in print for the first time as Dean Moriarity, after years of seeing the novel lugged about America and Mexico in Kerouac's duffel bag.

Allen Ginsberg and Gary Snyder
also lived in cottages in
Berkeley, a year earlier, at the
time of the Six Gallery reading:

13 **1624 MILVIA STREET**   was where Ginsberg moved in September, 1955, after he wrote the poem "Howl" at 1010 Montgomery Street in San Francisco. Berkeley was the east side of the Berkeley-San Francisco Renaissance which had begun in the mid-1940s with the Magazines *Circle* and *Ark*. Here he wrote "A Strange New Cottage in Berkeley," and Kerouac described it—and Snyder's cottage—in *The Dharma Bums*, as residences of "Alvah Goldbook" (Ginsberg) and "Japhy Ryder" (Snyder):

> "In Berkeley I was living with Alvah Goldbook in his little rose-covered cottage in the backyard of a bigger house on Milvia Street. The old rotten porch slanted forward to the ground, among vines, with a nice old rocking chair that I sat in every morning to read my Diamond Sutra. . . . About a mile from there, way down Milvia and then upslope toward the campus of the University of California, behind another big old house on a quiet street (Hillegass) Japhy lived in his own shack which was infinitely smaller than ours, about twelve by twelve, with nothing in it but typical Japhy appurtenances that showed his belief in the simple monastic life . . ."

Soon after moving to the East Bay, Ginsberg—at Rexroth's suggestion—walked over to meet Gary Snyder. The date was September 8, 1955, but the address of Snyder's cottage on Hillegass is lost to memory. Snyder was fixing the bicycle he used for transportation. He was interested in simple living, in American Indian culture, and was studying Oriental languages at the university to prepare himself for a trip to Japan, where he planned to study Buddhism in a monastery. Snyder's lifestyle and ecological concerns pioneered some basic tenets of the counter culture that would follow in the 1960s and beyond. When he, Ginsberg, Leary, and Watts were interviewed by *The Oracle* in 1967, he revealed how he'd been able to live outside the mainstream of American life, surviving off the urban landscape: "Yeah, we used to go around at one or two in the morning, around the Safeways and Piggly Wigglies in Berkeley, with a shopping bag, and hit the garbage cans out in back. We'd get Chinese cabbage, lots of broccoli and artichokes that were thrown out because they didn't look salable anymore. So, I never bought any vegetables for the three years I was a graduate student at Berkeley."

A major figure in the literary
history of Berkeley lived for
several years in:

14 **2805 ELLSWORTH STREET** and later in a home on Dana near Derby. William Anthony Parker White, a.k.a. "Anthony Boucher," was born in Oakland August 21, 1911, and died in Berkeley April 29,

1968. He was a graduate student in languages at U.C., and stayed in several places near the campus— the Sequoya Apartments on Haste Street, the I House, in 1932-1934. He set his first mystery novel *The Case of the Seven of Calvary* (1937) on and around the campus, using many places you can still find today.

From his Berkeley homes he struck what he considered to be "a blow against the insularity of the East" by using three rubberstamps, rows of orange-crate bookshelves, and a typewriter to do all his editorial and critical work. He wrote several novels and story collections of his own, but is perhaps more famous as the founding editor of *The Magazine of Fantasy and Science Fiction* from 1948-1958. He raised the literary standards of American science fiction; Fritz Leiber says Boucher was an acute and demanding editor— he even made Ray Bradbury do re-writes. Boucher also produced the largest critical body of writing on mystery fiction to date, contributing 852 "Criminals at Large" columns for the *New York Times Book Review*, as well as reviews for the San Francisco *Chronicle* and *Ellery Queen Mystery Magazine*. It was Boucher who introduced Jorge Luis Borges to American readers in 1948 by translating a story for *Ellery Queen*. He published the first stories by the now renowned Richard Matheson, and suggested in 1966 that Joe Gores, then working as a private eye, should try his hand at detective fiction.

Boucher also gave a steady market to another now famous writer, when he was living in Berkeley working as a disc jockey and writing his first stories and novels:

15 **1126 FRANCISCO** Found between San Pablo and Curtis, this house was one of several Bay Area homes for Philip K. Dick. His novel *Martian Time-Slip* (1964) of course is set on Mars, but stems from the politics and interactions of the Berkeley Co-Op, of which Dick was an early member. His *The Man in the High Castle* (1962), winner of the Hugo as best novel of the year, spins off from the notion that the Axis powers won World War II (the Japanese ruling San Francisco develop an obsession with collecting Old West six-shooters, a tidy send-up of Westerners' interest in collecting Samurai swords). *Do Androids Dream of Electric Sheep?* (1968) features police bounty hunter Rick Decard stalking eight Nexus-6 androids through a depopulated future San Francisco Bay Area. When this novel was filmed as *Bladerunner*, starring Harrison Ford, the action was shifted to an overpopulated future Los Angeles. Just before the release of this film in 1983 Philip K. Dick died, when he was finally reaching financial independence after writing over one-hundred stories and fifty books. In the sci fi newspaper *Locus* a cheering theory was put forth that Dick's death was a hoax, that he had taken his film royalties and retired secretly in grand fashion South of the Border (possibly to sip tequila by the mummified remains of Ambrose Bierce).

The androids Roy Batty and Pris are modeled on Ray Nelson and his wife Kirsten, who live in El Cerrito. Nelson co-authored The Ganymede Takeover *(1967) with Philip K. Dick, and uses a future Berkeley in his sci fi novels* Then Beggars Could Ride *(1976) and* The Prometheus Man *(1982). Berkeley resident Richard A. Lupoff set the sci fi novel* The Crack in the Sky *(1976) in this city, as well as the werewolf novel* Lisa Kane *(1976), in which Anthony Boucher appears as a character (in homage to Boucher's fine story "The Compleat Werewolf," a tale of lycanthropy largely set on the U.C. campus). The East Bay has been a center for a huge population of science fiction and fantasy writers — Boucher, Dick, Lupoff, Nelson, the writers living on Broadway Terrace in Oakland. Poul Anderson, a prolific and award-winning author (*The Broken Sword *of 1954, *War of the Wingmen *of 1958, and *Tau Zero *of 1970 are three of his many novels) has lived in Orinda — through the Caldecott Tunnel, for decades. Avram Davidson, Randall Garrett, Grania Davis, Elizabeth Lynn, and Chelsea Quinn Yarbro are among other sci fi writers who have made their homes in Berkeley — such a large number, in fact, that a critic once remarked that if California slid into the sea after a big quake America would lose at least half of its sci fi writers.*

*In the first block of El Camino
Real in Berkeley stands a
house called:*

16 GREYHAVEN Named after the elf city in Tolkien's *Lord of the Rings*, this house is a communal sanctuary for numerous fantasists — residential evidence that Berkeley has been a major site in the development of modern science fiction and fantasy. Diana Paxson, Paul Edwin Zimmer, John De Cles, and others live or have lived here. In 1983 Marion Zimmer Bradley, author of the popular Darkover series and more recently *The Mists of Avalon* (an Arthurian fantasy told from a feminist viewpoint), edited a collection of the commune's fantasy writings — stories, poems, plays — and titled it *Greyhaven* after their home.

*Originally found at 2054
University Avenue, now
located in 2207 Shattuck on
the southeast corner at Allston, is:*

17 KPFA Since its founding in 1949, KPFA FM 94 has been the greatest radio outlet for writers and literature in the West. Other stations have had literary programming — Joseph Henry Jackson, book editor for the *Chronicle*, did a book review program for KGO that was also aired nationally in the 1940s — but nothing approaching the amount of air time KPFA has offered. Anthony Boucher began a weekly "Golden Voices" program with his monumental collection of historic opera recordings in KPFA's original studio, and continued this and other programs until his death in 1968. Kenneth Rexroth had a weekly program in which he reviewed books of all kinds—poetry, fiction, even science fiction ("In the McCarthy period when the only expression of any kind of radicalism was confined to science fiction, I used to review science fiction for KPFA," he said.) Today Richard Lupoff hosts a weekly program devoted to science fiction, "Probabilities." The poet Stephen Ronan, editor of *Ammunition*, is a sometime host of KPFA's wildest after-midnight serendipity "Over the Edge," with random narrative, music, maniacal insomniac call-ins, and other audio-enigmas.

Jaime de Angulo first broadcast in 1949 the myths and stories he had gathered and recorded while living with native peoples of California. Here were the tales as they were actually told, not as "translated" into sentimental fairy tales, and audiences were mesmerized. De Angulo mastered seventeen different Native American languages, compiled invaluable observations and made dictionaries of disappearing languages. He had first arrived in San Francisco just in time for the 1906 earthquake, then lived in Alturas and Big Sur before earning a degree in Medicine at Johns Hopkins. He first settled in Berkeley in 1923. His Maybeck home on Buena Vista Way after 1935 became a center of local Bohemia, drawing musicians, artists, writers, anthropologists, and visiting Indians. "Jaime de Angulo is the American Ovid," said Ezra Pound. Among his books are *A Jaime de Angulo Reader* (1979) and *Indian Tales* (1953). He settled in Big Sur in 1940, where he saw almost no one—except Harry Partch, Robinson Jeffers and occasionally Henry Miller. He captures the menacing and lonely Big Sur country in a strange gothic novel called *The Witch*, collected in *Jaime in Taos* (1984), edited by his daughter Gui de Angulo.

The appreciative study of Native Californian cultures is a long Berkeley tradition. Academic anthropologists pioneered it—A. L. Kroeber, Harrington, Heizer and others—but invaluable contributions have been made by brilliant mavericks like De Angulo, by writers like Theodora Kroeber with her perennial favorite, *Ishi*, and recently by Malcolm Margolin with such books as *The Ohlone Way* (1978).

Alan Watts did many programs discussing philosophy—his tapes are still regularly played on Bay Area stations today. KPFA was also responsible for now historic recordings by Dylan Thomas; *Literary San Francisco* says that Thomas "recorded special programs twice when he was in Berkeley; and other participants from elsewhere included Robert Frost, William Carlos Williams, Richard Eberhart, Robert Lowell, Marianne Moore, Theodore Roethke. Practically every important writer in the Bay Area appeared on KPFA sooner or later." Erik Bauersfeld and Padraig in McGillicuddy produce regular readings of fiction and poetry as well as live interviews with writers and the station goes on sending out (as Kerouac writes in *The Subterraneans*) "loud suddenly turned-up KPFA symphonies of Vivaldi harpsichord intellectuals performances boom blam the tremendous sound of it . . ."

Many other writers have lived in the Berkeley-East Bay area: Nellie Wong, Merle Woo, feminist and poet Susan Griffin, who wrote the popular *Woman and Nature*; Don Carpenter, a native of the city, raised in the Berkeley hills. Dorothy Bryant is a resident, transplanted from San Francisco's Mission district, and presides over Ata Books, 1928 Stuart Street. After innumerable difficulties with editors and publishers, as she recounts in "My Publisher/Myself" / *Myths to Lie By* (1984), she decided to publish her own books: "Ata Books is solvent. My net income is somewhere below the government-designated poverty level, but double the average annual income from writing in the United States. And all my books are in print. So I have finally found my Publisher." (She goes on to say she has no intentions of becoming *anyone else's* publisher.)

South and east of Berkeley
and Oakland you'll find places
such as:

19 SUNOL Here Ambrose Bierce stayed for a time, and here Gertrude Atherton visited him early in 1891 — a somewhat daring act in its day. The two were drawn together by a perverse attraction, but Atherton was repelled by Bierce's lofty dictums and arrogance. She had him escort her back to the train station which, in those days, happened to adjoin a pigsty. In her *Adventures of a Novelist* she records that as they waited for the train, "We walked about the station and the malodorous grunting pigsty when he suddenly seized me in his arms and tried to kiss me. In a flash I knew how to hurt him . . . I threw back my head . . . and laughed gayly. 'The Great Bierce! Master of style! The god on Olympus at whose feet pilgrims come to worship — trying to kiss a woman by a pigsty!' " Bierce shoved her on the train and they never met again, though they later taunted each other in letters with talk of spending weeks together in her apartment or at his retreats.

North of Berkeley you'll find
the city of:

20 MARTINEZ Ella Leffland grew up on the Carquinez Straits, the setting for *Mrs. Munck* (1970) and *Rumors of Peace* (1979). This second novel ends with the famous World War II munitions explosion at an arms stockpile in Fort Chicago, a blast that was heard throughout the Bay Area.

The major literary site in Martinez is found by following Highway 4 into town — and noting that you are traveling along "John Muir Parkway." The look of the landscape between Interstate 80 and Martinez will give you an idea of why this country appealed to Muir as the place to live his last years, though you'll find that the area immediately around his ranch today would appall the naturalist with its modern construction, its "John Muir Inn" offering "Air Conditioned, Heated Pool, TV" or the "John Muir Business Park" that the ads proclaim is "Finally Here."

Follow Highway 4 to Martinez,
exiting into the Alhambra
Valley Road; turn left under
the freeway and park in the lot
at 4202 Alhambra. As you turn
off on the exit you'll see to
your left the Italianate bell
tower of the:

21 JOHN MUIR HOUSE A 50¢ admission fee lets you enter for a self-guided tour of this National Historic Site which includes the Muir house and gardens, as well as the nearby Martinez adobe of 1849. A film about Muir is shown on the hour, and this site is open every day of the year except Thanksgiving, Christmas, and New Year. Groups may arrange tours by phoning (415) 228-8860. Despite the massive changes to the surrounding area, the Muir house and the grounds are still much as Muir knew them. Most of the windows in his home still retain their original hand-rolled glass panes.

Muir was born in Dunbar, Scotland, in 1838, but migrated with his family to Wisconsin in 1848. He attended the U.W. in Madison, but later decided to study in the "university of the wilderness." He explored Alaska, the High Sierra (where you may now follow his route along the John Muir Trail), Yosemite, making "all the wilderness his home," as he wrote in *Steep Trails*. When he was in his forties he married Louise Strentzel and here in the Alhambra Valley he managed their own ranch as well as her father's. As a fruit rancher from 1880-1890, Muir became wealthy enough to devote his time to exploring wilderness areas, his writing, and preservationist causes.

The Muir house was built by Dr. John Strentzel in 1882, and Muir moved in only after his father-in-law died in 1890. The stove and table in the kitchen are the originals he used, and in his study upstairs you may see his "scribble desk" where he wrote most of the books and articles that appeared after 1894, describing his explorations and calling for preservation of wilderness areas. One room upstairs is decorated with a photographic display on Muir's childhood in Scotland; another shows his founding of the Sierra Club in 1892. He was president of this influential organization until his death in 1914, and was instrumental in saving the Grand Canyon and Yosemite for public use as National Parks. The Spanish-style fireplace in the east parlor was put in by Muir after the original chimney collapsed in the great 1906 earthquake. Otherwise, the building reflects the taste of his father-in-law, and the furnishings are period pieces installed to recreate the look of his day.

The house itself is exeptional, and well worth the visit. His study is cluttered with rocks and pieces of bark such as he himself would bring up from the fields, and manuscripts are flung on the floor in rolls just as was his practice. You may explore the house thoroughly, even up to the bell tower for a look over the valley — and a pull on the bell rope. Muir's belief that "Wilderness is a necessity," expressed in so many books, is still a great cause today. In practical terms, Muir may well be the single most influential author who has ever written in California.

Muir's books are still in print after almost a hundred years; the park office offers a selection of both hardcovers and paperbacks. Leaving the Muir site you might wish to drive past his earlier home, where he made a fortune raising fruit before moving into the Strentzel mansion in 1890, achieving the financial freedom that enabled him to realize so many of his dreams. For ten years he, his wife Louie, and daughters Wanda and Helen lived in a Dutch colonial style house built in the 1850s that still stands at 5031 Alhambra Valley Road about a mile south of the official historic site. This house is falling into disrepair today, and in a small private graveyard secluded in the fields beyond this house Muir's grave lies unknown to most people passing on the highway. But his legacy — our National Park system as well as Yosemite, Muir Woods, and other sites named for him — is perhaps memorial enough to his life and work. Even the Muir House, made a national historic site in 1964, is a minor attraction compared to the vast wilderness areas he helped to preserve.

In Danville, south of Martinez on Highway 680, you'll find another National Historic Site of literary interest:

22 TAO HOUSE Playwright Eugene O'Neill and his wife, the actress Carlotta Monterey, came to San Francisco in December 1936. The previous month O'Neill had become the first American playwright to win the Nobel Prize. With the $40,000 award from the Nobel Committee, $75,000 from the sale of his home called "Casa Genotta" on Sea Island off the Georgia coast, and $3,000 from the sale of other property, O'Neill decided to build a new home for himself in northern California. He was impressed with the Lucas Valley in Marin County when he visited the area his first month in the city. But then O'Neill was hospitalized for removal of his appendix, and on a convalescent excursion around the area in March he came to the San Ramon Valley, "more beautiful than Lucas." O'Neill decided he would live here, and purchased fifteen acres, hiring contractors to begin construction of a Spanish or Mission Revival style home. The O'Neills had been staying in the Fairmont, but soon moved to Berkeley for a couple of months, where they rented the home of Mrs. J. B. Havre. In June they rented the home of the Walter Wood family in Lafayette until they moved into the completed Tao House on December 30, 1937.

The O'Neills lived here until February 25, 1944, when they sold Tao House. O'Neill destroyed ideas for seven plays, including "Testament for Tomorrow," and burned most of his "Cycle" plays, but he completed the last five plays he would write, in his study: "The Iceman Cometh" (1939), "Hughie" (1940), "Long Day's Journey into Night" (1940-1941), "A Moon for the Misbegotten" (1941), and "A Touch of the Poet" (1942). From here they moved to the Fairmont and then to the Huntington in San Francisco, and spent the remainder of O'Neill's life in hotels. O'Neill died in 1953 in a Boston hotel room.

O'Neill raised chickens on the side. The grave for his beloved Dalmatian, Blemie, who died December 17, 1940, is on the property. The loss of the dog was a great blow to O'Neill, who was becoming more and more an outsider. When his seventeen-year-old daughter Oona married Charlie Chaplin, then fifty-four, on June 16, 1943, O'Neill broke all connections with her.

Tao House was made a national historic site in 1976, but has yet to be opened to the public at regular hours. Restoration work to recreate the O'Neill residence is underway, and materials are being gathered to present an overview of O'Neill's life, from his birth in New York City on October 16, 1888, and his early success in the East, to his last period of creativity here in Danville. One magazine stated: "Before O'Neill, the United States had theatre. After O'Neill, it had drama."

Eugene O'Neill at Tao House

Tao House is located at the end of Kuss Road, off Bradford Place, in Danville. Area residents are disputing the access road clearance to the site. Proposals for opening an access road through adjoining wilderness areas have been put forth, but at this writing the matter is still under heated discussion. Until the problem of access is resolved, Tao House will not be open to the public. Write to the Golden Gate National Recreation Area, Information Office, Fort Mason, San Francisco 94123 for updates on the opening of this great literary site. The Eugene O'Neill Foundation which is overseeing the restoration of his last home hope the problem will be resolved, at least by O'Neill's centennial in 1988.

Further east you'll find:

23 **STOCKTON AND MODESTO**   These cities may seem unlikely places for literature, but Stockton is the setting for Leonard Gardner's *Fat City* (1969), and the place where novelist Maxine Hong Kingston grew up. Kingston's novels offer sensitive portrayals of people in changing cultures, of Chinese adapting to new customs after immigrating to this country. She uses her home area in Stockton's Chinatown as one of many California settings in *The Woman Warrior* (1976), following the lives of three generations of Chinese women through the cultural transitions necessary to living in America. This book and *China Men* (1980) both capture the emotional truth of the Chinese-American experience.

The poet and filmmaker James Broughton was born in Modesto. Possibly the Great Modesto Novel is Louise Baker's *Party Line* (1945), about an actual party-line phone operator in the town; it uses most of the people in Modesto under slightly different names. The phone operator who inspired the novel is still a legendary figure, in Modesto.

Further east you come to Calaveras and Tuolumne counties, with their Mark Twain sites. Prentice Mulford spent many years prospecting in the Tuolumne River country. His authentic background contributed to the realistic descriptions in Joaquin Miller's Life Among the Modocs, *which Mulford rewrote before publication. There is no doubt that Miller, if he wasn't the best writer around, at least was a genuine frontiersman. Bret Harte's wilderness expertise is still under debate. Roy F. Hudson in the* Pacific Historian, *published by the University of the Pacific in Stockton, argues in the August 1962 issue that the original of Harte's "Poker Flat" is Sandy Bar in Tuolumne County, and that Harte "strove for accuracy in the setting of his locales." In the July, 1936, issue of* Westways *(formerly* Touring Topics*) Idwal Jones wrote: "The only man I ever met in the foothills who had known Harte at all well was William Sloniker, a mild, bearded Austrian carpenter in Jamestown. Harte joined up with him for a couple of days, and dug in his claim at the foot of Table Mountain, then left, and never more appeared in that part of the world. Harte never visited Rough and Ready, nor Coarse Gold nor Grass Valley. He was a city lover, a dandy, a born* flaneur, *and never left San Francisco if he could help it, unless to drive down to the Santa Cruz mountains with his friend Anton Roman, the bookseller, who had a roving disposition, did a big trade in the foothills, and supplied Harte with most of his story ideas."*

POINTS SOUTH

Robinson Jeffers' Tor House, Carmel

Heading south from the city toward the many literary sites in Monterey, Carmel, and Big Sur, with Steinbeck Country in the nearby Salinas Valley, you'll pass several places with literary associations. And if you keep on to the California midlands before reaching the L.A.-Hollywood regions you'll hit William Saroyan's Fresno, or Mary Austin's Inyo County home in the city of Independence—now a state historic site—where she wrote her classic *The Land of Little Rain*.

*The Peninsula below San
Francisco offers several sites
and associations. As you pass:*

1 BURLINGAME remember it as home for Kathryn Forbes, author of
the immensely popular *Mama's Bank Account* (1943), who lived
here under her married name Kathryn Anderson McLean. It was home
too for Edward Stewart White who lived here after 1903. His *Story of
California* trilogy of novels were once popular: *Gold* (1913), about the
gold rush; *The Gray Dawn* (1915), about the Vigilantes; and *The Rose
Dawn* (1920), on the southern California land boom.

The signs along 280 or 101 for:

2 REDWOOD CITY should evoke the name of E. Hoffmann Price,
who has lived in the hills above this town for some forty years. Price
sold over five hundred stories to such pulp magazines as *Weird Tales,
Black Mask*, and *Argosy*, and was the star contributor to the risque
Spicy Detective and *Spicy Western* titles. He "bailed out" of the fiction
business in the early 1950s and worked as a microfilm technician for
many years in the Redwood City courthouse. A grand raconteur, Price
can hold forth for hours as he drinks 151 proof Demerara rum and recalls the old days, when he drove across America and became the only
man to meet all three of the great writers who made *Weird Tales* a literary treasure trove: H. P. Lovecraft, Clark Ashton Smith, and Robert E.
Howard. Now in his eighties, Price still motors across country, and has
returned to writing fantasies, space operas, westerns, and mysteries.

Samuel W. Taylor also lives in Redwood City; he describes himself as
"a professional Mormon" and is a major writer chronicling the history of
that sect. His first novel, *Heaven Knows Why!* (1949), is a whimsical
fantasy about Mormonism, and is unique in that it is still *the only humorous Mormon novel*. Walt Disney based his comedy films "The Absent-
Minded Professor" and "Son of Flubber" in the early 1960s on "A Question of Gravity" which Taylor wrote for *Colliers*. Also, Taylor wrote the
fine suspense novel *The Man With My Face*, set in Redwood City and
San Francisco— his other San Francisco book is *The Grinning Gizmo*
(1951).

*Traveling south on 101 or 280
you'll come to:*

3 PALO ALTO In the late 1920s Kathleen and Charles Norris built a
home at 1247 Cowper in this peninsula city, but still spent the summers on their fifty-six-acre ranch near Saratoga, which they had purchased in 1919 upon returning to California from New York. The ranch
was sold after Kathleen's death in 1946 to be used as a Jewish recreation center for boys, and their Palo Alto home is now a Catholic center,
and a registered architectural landmark.

In the dead-end Sierra Court just off the freeway, Kenneth Patchen
lived his last years. As his degenerative spinal condition grew progres-
sively worse, pain and cortizone treatments combined to rob Patchen of
much creative energy, but he produced almost forty books and many
drawings and paintings. One of his many outspoken remarks was once

turned into a poster (most suitable for display over the poetry sections in bookstores): "People who say they love poetry and never buy any are a bunch of cheap sons-of-bitches."

Stanford University has seen many writers come and go — John Steinbeck attended classes over a period of six years, from 1919 to 1926. In 1947 Wallace Stegner founded the Creative Writing Center at Stanford, and taught there until 1971. The University grants a Stegner Fellowship to promising young writers. Stegner, who now lives in Los Altos, won a Pulitzer Prize in 1972 for *Angle of Repose*, and the National Book Award in 1977 for *The Spectator Bird*. The *Big Rock Candy Mountain* of 1943, however, is still his most famous work. Robert Stone is a graduate of the writing program; and Denise Levertov comes every year to teach in it. On the faculty now are poets Juan Felipe Herraro and Chilean immigrant Fernando Alegria, both of them active in progressive Latin American causes.

Palo Alto resident Al Young is one of the Bay Area's brightest talents — as poet, teacher, novelist, and screenwriter. Born in Ocean Springs, Mississippi, Young moved from Detroit in 1960 to Berkeley, where he wrote poetry and played guitar at Robbies while earning a degree in Spanish at U.C. After a year as a Stegner Fellow, he was Jones Lecturer in Creative Writing at Stanford, a post he describes as "a euphemism for Serf." Since then he has taught variously at Berkeley, Colorado College, University of Washington, at Rice (where he was a Distinguished Professor of Humanities), and most lately at U.C. Santa Cruz where he led a community studies course. Young has written for films like "Bustin' Loose," and scripts for Sidney Poitier, Bill Cosby, Richard Pryor and other black actors — until roles for blacks began to disappear from the screen in the 1970s. Among his books are *Dancing, Snakes, The Blues Don't Change, Bodies and Soul*, and *Sitting Pretty* (for which he also wrote the screenplay).

Ken Kesey came to Stanford from Oregon in 1958 on a creative writing fellowship. He and several other writers lived on Perry Lane near the college, a street that was razed in 1963 when the campus expanded. Kesey wrote *One Flew Over the Cuckoo's Nest* there in 1960-61, basing it on his experience as a night orderly in the psych ward of a hospital in nearby Menlo Park. The character of the Indian, Chief Broom, came to Kesey in an L.S.D. vision after he had volunteered to test experimental drugs for $75 a day in the Veterans Hospital in Menlo Park the winter of 1959-60, becoming one of the first counter culture heroes to drop acid.

Following route 84 toward the sea from Palo Alto you'll come to the rural community in and around:

4 LA HONDA Ken Kesey began his second novel, *Sometimes a Great Notion*, in Perry Lane, but finished it after moving fifteen miles away to a home along route 84, beyond Cahill Ridge in La Honda. Here the people who had gravitated to the parties he'd thrown on Perry Lane (including Neal Cassady, always on top of the current scene) metamorphosized on acid into the anarchic Merry Pranksters, counter culture frontrunners of the 1960s. When Kesey's new novel was published in 1964 he put aside writing and began experimenting with more immediate means of expression—wiring the woods for sound, mixed media, film, all leading toward the Acid Tests. Cassady, given the Prankster name "Speed Limit," inspired the group: "I saw that Cassady did everything a novel does," Kesey said, "except that he did it better because he was living it and not writing about it."

Cassady drove the 1939 schoolbus they bought and painted dayglo psychedelic. The destination sign read "Further" and on the back it said "Caution: Weird Load." The Pranksters drove around the country filming an epic movie, and threw acid parties in La Honda to which Allen Ginsberg, the Hell's Angels and Hunter S. Thompson, and countless others came—all recounted in Tom Wolfe's documentary *The Electric Kool Aid Acid Test* (1969).

South of Palo Alto along 280 you'll reach the city of:

5 ATHERTON   Occasionally you'll met someone who thinks this city was named after novelist Gertrude Atherton, but the honor goes to her father-in-law. The rancher Faxon Dean Atherton built a home known as Valparaiso Park in the 1860s on land near Menlo Park—his property was sub-divided numerous times as the land was developed and the town of Atherton sprang up. His original house (now gone) occupied a site near the present location of the Menlo Circus Club, and is of literary interest as a home of Gertrude Franklin Horn, the young wife of Faxon's son George Atherton. Gertrude wrote in her *Adventures of a Novelist* (1932): "I do not think I have ever met a family so completely satisfied with themselves, with their condition, with life itself, as the Athertons. They were well born, well bred, had always known wealth. . . ." She scandalized Society when a well-known alcoholic heiress appeared as a character in her first novel *The Randolphs of Redwoods*, published anonymously in the *Argonaut:* "Poor George was frantic. At any moment the truth might come out, and the name of Atherton be forever disgraced."

At the foot of the Peninsula you'll enter the vast urban sprawl of:

6 SAN JOSE At 432 8th Street you'll find the Edwin Markham home, now a state historic site. Here Markham wrote his sensationally popular poem "The Man With the Hoe," published in the *Examiner* January 15, 1899. In the next three decades he earned $250,000 for reprintings of this one poem. Markham had been a school teacher in Oakland and other Bay Area cities, but this protest poem against the harsh treatment of farm laborers made him an international celebrity and populist spokesman. *Literary San Francisco* notes that "In 1922, over a hundred thousand persons came to hear him read 'Lincoln' at the dedication of the Lincoln Memorial, broadcast on radio nationwide."

W. C. Morrow, whose tales of the Civil War and contemporary horror influenced strongly the later short fiction of Ambrose Bierce, worked as a reporter for the San Jose *Mercury* from 1881 to 1884 and then worked as deputy county clerk in the San Jose court house, while his many short stories were appearing in San Francisco newspapers and magazines. The Weekly *Wasp* for January 24, 1891, alluded to Morrow's terrific reputation as a horror writer in an editorial note: "Thinking of San Jose one is necesarily reminded of a former resident of the place, W. C. Morrow, who writes stories which make one feel as if a stream of electrified lizards from ice were streaking it up his back. . . ." The *Wasp* goes on to recount how a prominent spiritualist has been seen wandering at night near a spot where the ghastly spectre of the bandit Vasquez has been reported. Asked if he isn't afraid to be out in such an area, the spiritualist replies: "I have one of Morrow's infernal ghost stories in my pocket, and I don't dare to go where there's light enough to read it!"

The "big old house" at 1047 East Santa Clara Street in San Jose was home for Neal and Carolyn Cassady after they left Russian Hill in San Francisco. With his wages from Southern Pacific Neal bought this home, where Kerouac visited them off and on in the 1950s, staying for a few months when he was also working on the rails.

From San Jose the Cassadys moved southwest, down Highway 17 to the city of:

7 LOS GATOS where Carolyn Cassady wrote her long account of life with Neal Cassady and her relationship with Jack Kerouac, of which *Heart Beat* (1976) is an excerpt. Kerouac breezed through here with Lew Welch, Lenore Kandel, and company en route to Ferlinghetti's cabin in Bixby Canyon, Big Sur, in 1960. In the late 1970s another prominent figure of the Beat days in North Beach, "Big Daddy" Eric Nord, a founder of the hungry i club, moved to Los Gatos.

North of Los Gatos in the adjoining town of Monte Sereno you'll find a place where John Steinbeck lived on Greenwood Lane—and south of the city, in the hills above the road to Santa Cruz, a second Los Gatos area home for Steinbeck.

A most significant literary site is found a few miles north of the city limit of Montalvo off Highway 9 in Saratoga: Villa Montalvo. This summer home of James Duval Phelan, San Francisco mayor and U.S. Senator, was a major attraction for writers. Gertrude Atherton was often a guest, and she mentions that in addition to entertaining the politically powerful and the wealthy, Phelan gave literary luncheons attended by "Charles Caldwell Dobie and Sanborn Young, who came with his wife, Ruth Comfort Mitchell. Charles and Kathleen Norris drove over from their ranch in the hills and Mr. and Mrs. Fremont Older from theirs. Peter B. Kyne and his handsome wife; Charmian London; the budding poet, Dorothe Bendon; those already distinguished poets, Charles Erskine Scott Wood and Sara Bard Field; Ednah Aiken; George Sterling, until his tragic death. Generally the luncheon was given to some visiting celebrity, on one occasion to Richard Halliburton, on another to Philip Guedalla." Sterling wrote the poem "At Villa Montalvo" on one of his many visits; the original manuscript is sometimes on display in the mansion.

The villa was built in 1912 and left in trust after Phelan's death in 1930, "to be used as far as possible for the develoment of Art, Literature, Music, and Architecture" according to the plaque, complete with bas-relief bust of Phelan, set next to the side entrance. If you follow the path uphill to the nature trails that run along the hills you'll find busts of Joaquin Miller and Edwin Markham flanking the paved pathway—and at the top of the path is a bust of John Muir. Other interesting statues are scattered about the elaborate grounds, which feature an outdoor theatre behind the large villa. A large sign on the highway points the way to this estate. The grounds are open and there is also a botanical garden. The mansion itself is open only in connection with gallery showings of art—for a current calendar write Montalvo Association, P.O. Box 158, Saratoga, CA 95071 or phone (408) 867-3421 or 867-3586.

Following Highway 17 south-west over the mountains you'll come to:

8 SANTA CRUZ   The dean of American science fiction writers, Robert A. Heinlein, whose books include *Stranger in a Strange Land, The Moon Is a Harsh Mistress*, and dozens of others—has lived on Bonny Doon Road above Santa Cruz for several years. George Hitchcock, poet & editor of *Kayak*, lives on this road too. Peter S. Beagle—*I See by My Outfit, The Last Unicorn*—lives in Watsonville. William Everson, fine printer, and a poet influenced by Robinson Jeffers, now teaches at U.C. Santa Cruz; he lives close by, near Davenport. As a member of the Dominican order from 1951-1969 he wrote books—such as *The Residual Years* (1958)—under the name Brother Antoninus.

The first Acid Test was held in 1965 in Soquel outside Santa Cruz at Kenneth Babbs' place. Babbs was an original Prankster who dubbed himself "The Intrepid Traveler." Among the celebrants were The Grateful Dead, who played, and Stewart Brand, who was inspired by the "test" to organize the Trips Festival in Longshoreman's Hall the following January.

In the days of stagecoaches and carriages, before coastal railroad lines connected the two cities, a trip south from San Francisco to Monterey required an overnight stop, and one of the most popular places to stay midway along the route was:

9 SAN JUAN BAUTISTA This small town with its historic adobes and church tower (used by Alfred Hitchcock in "Vertigo") still makes an interesting side excursion today, when the trip south requires only about three hours on the freeway. Exit off Highway 156 into Monterey Street and follow that to Second Street, then right until you reach the expansive town square—one of the sites most evocative of the days of Spanish California. The literary point which provides an excuse for this trip is Breen's Tavern on the corner of Second and Washington, built about 1825 by General José de Castro and purchased in 1849 by Patrick Breen—a survivor of the snowbound Donner Party—for use as a hostelry. Tradition has it that it was here that Helen Hunt Jackson wrote the opening chapters of her hugely popular novel about the vanishing California Indians, *Ramona* (1884). This tradition also has it that the man Breen had put in charge of the inn ordered Jackson off the premises when he learned that she was not a Catholic. (Yet another tradition holds that Jackson dashed off the entire novel in one dynamic surge while holed up in the Berkeley Hotel in New York City.)

From San Juan Bautista travel on directly down Highway 1 to:

10 MONTEREY This city and the adjoining town of Pacific Grove feature Cannery Row and a number of John Steinbeck residences, detailed in the chapter on Steinbeck (which includes a map for this area). Charles Warren Stoddard, who founded the original Monterey Artists' colony with Jules Tavernier, returned in his old age, surrounding himself with exotic memorabilia accumulated in his travels.

Alice B. Toklas often visited Monterey at the turn of the century; Harriet Lane Levy in *920 O'Farrell Street* (1947) mentions the dramatic change in dress this trip south brought about, for "At a period when street dress was bright and decorative, Alice wore only gray. A severe tailored suit, the long coat buttoned from collar to hem, a cloth turban of the same color, gave to her slender figure the appearance of a furtive nun." Yet when she came each spring as a paying guest to the "lovely old adobe home known as Sherman's Rose . . . the nun's garb was discarded for a brilliant red mandarin coat." Toklas returned to Monterey in 1935 with Gertrude Stein on their grand tour of America; they stayed in the Hotel Del Monte.

Among other writers who have lived in this city is Stanton Coblentz, a longtime resident. His first poetry collection appeared in 1923, and he edited *Wings: A Quarterly of Verse* from 1933 until 1960. Coblentz died in Monterey in 1982.

The star literary attraction in Monterey is found at 530 Houston, a one-block-long street between Pearl and Webster to the north and south, and Tyler and Abrego to the west and east, the:

11 ROBERT LOUIS STEVENSON HOUSE   Here "the tall gaunt Scotchman," Robert Louis Stevenson, stayed most of the four months from his arrival August 31, 1879, until shortly before Christmas, when he moved to 608 Bush Street in San Francisco. He had met Mrs. Fanny Van de Grift Osbourne at Grez in France the summer of 1876. They fell in love, and when her husband demanded that she return to their Oakland home in the fall of 1878, Stevenson told her he would follow if she asked. Her telegram summoned him halfway across the world to Monterey, where, separated from Sam Osbourne and suffering from nervous disorder, she waited for a divorce — and re-marriage to Stevenson.

This building, home of Don Rafael Gonzales, the first administrator of customs for Alta California, dates from the 1830s, and was bought in 1856 by the pioneer Frenchman, Juan Girardin and his wife, who added several rooms and began to take in boarders. During their tenure it became known as the French House, but Stevenson's international fame has since claimed the place for his memory, though he stayed only briefly in one room here.

The house is open to the public from ten to four, except Wednesdays, with groups of no more than twenty persons escorted on a forty-five-minute tour usually given on the hour. Cost: $1.00; ages six to seventeen years, only 50¢.

If you happen to arrive between tours there are a number of other historic adobes within easy walking distance; you can pick up a free leaflet, Discover Monterey's Shops, Gardens and Adobe Houses, *with a map to the Larkin House, where William Tecumseh Sherman was stationed before his rise to infamy in the War Between the States [three blocks west on Pearl, between Calle Principal and Pacific, "Sherman's Rose" of Toklas and her red mandarin coat], the old Custom House, and others. The De Soto adobe where John Steinbeck lived is only five blocks away; it and the other buildings were described by Richard*

Henry Dana in Two Years Before the Mast: *"The houses here, as every-where else in California, are of one story, built of* adobes, *that is, clay made into large bricks . . . and hardened in the sun."*

Stevenson's widow donated many of his personal belongings for display. In the main room downstairs you will see the large table on which his coffin rested before burial atop Mount Vaea in Samoa — a scratch mars the surface where the coffin slipped in the hands of the pall bearers. Stevenson's second-floor room overlooking the patio has been restored to look much as it would have in 1879.

Here he worked on his never published "dime novel" *Arizona Breckenridge* and wrote the story "The Pavilion on the Links," whose seaside setting is thought by Stevensonians to resemble nearby Pebble Beach as much as the seacoast of Scotland. R.L.S. certainly knew this area well, as witness his essay on Monterey, "The Old Pacific Capitol" (which the Monterey State Park Service, 210 Olivier Street, Monterey, CA 93940, sells as a souvenir booklet.) Stevenson wrote articles on the local scene, unsigned, for the Monterey *Californian* for two dollars a week in this period. "The Pavilion on the Links" appeared in *New Arabian Nights* (1882) — which also features Stevenson's tales of the Suicide Club that inspired Gary Warne to create an adventurer's club of the same name in San Francisco in 1977. Many scholars feel that Stevenson based his map and descripton of "Treasure Island" in his classic adventure novel on the Point Lobos peninsula four miles below Monterey. Roy Nickerson in *Robert Louis Stevenson in California* (1982) points out that Big Dome on Point Lobos closely resembles Spyglass Hill, though "RLS himself said the inspiration came from no one place, but from several, and he had in mind the pirates of the Caribbean. The Caribbean, however, has no sea lions or other such beasts as described, no pines or cypresses, and RLS himself had never been there."

The Stevenson House has a compelling tradition of being haunted by a Woman in Black, who is sometimes seen in the nursery room by people touring the building. Some say the ghost is Fanny Stevenson — others believe she is the spirit of Mrs. Girardin, Stevenson's landlady, who died December 21, 1879, of typhoid while attending her stricken grandchildren. This place certainly does not require the additional glamor of a ghost to make it worth touring, but if you see the rocking chair in the nursery begin to move by no visible means or whiff carbolic acid — used in those days as a sickroom disinfectant — consider it a bonus.

Roughly between the Steinbeck residences at 222 Central and 147 11th Street you'll find 117 9th Street (between Central Avenue and Ocean View Boulevard), a notable site for:

12 PACIFIC GROVE In this neat little house the poet and fantasist Clark Ashton Smith lived after marrying Carol Dorman in 1954, until his death August 14, 1961. Smith wrote little during this period, busying himself carving numerous eidolons and pagan gods out of stone, and receiving visitors. Donald Sidney-Fryer stopped here in

1958 and 1959 gathering information for his massive Smith bibliography, *The Emperor of Dreams*, and the science fiction writer and editor L. Sprague de Camp visited late in July 1961, shortly before the poet's death, getting Smith's comments on a map de Camp had sketched of Smith's fantasy world Zothique.

A couple of miles south of Monterey along Highway 1 you'll find:

13 CARMEL-BY-THE-SEA Famous as a rustic artist's colony for writers weary of city life in San Francisco, Carmel offers many literary sites, such as Robinson Jeffers' Tor House—the most impressive author's home in northern California, and houses once occupied by Mary Austin, Lincoln Steffens, and other writers.

In his 1974 biography of Steffens, Justin Kaplan points out the early 1900s origins of literary Carmel "when a canny real-estate operator, recognizing the promotional value of bohemia, offered house lots to Jack London, the poet George Sterling, Mary Austin, and others. In Carmel's operatic setting, Van Wyck Brooks recalled, the bohemians who elected to spawn there like salmon lived curiously operatic lives, full of passion and drama, before they succumbed to listlessness, beachcombing, and a generalized postcoital tristesse."

Jack London was in Carmel only briefly; it was George Sterling and Mary Austin who put this town on the literary map, though their highly publicized lifestyle scandalized many. The Carmel *Pine-Cone* observed later that "Picnics such as the ones Jimmie Hopper, Mary Austin, George Sterling, Ferdinand Burgdorf and others frequently organized, were regarded as Bacchanalian orgies. The women danced around bonfires with bare feet, their long hair flying. A gallon jug of red wine was in evidence and anyone who stumbled upon these seemingly mad, wild gatherings was deeply shocked and went away thinking Carmel was getting to be as wicked as Paris"—for in those days, respectable women did not show their ankles or let down their hair, and "red wine, very certainly, was in the worst of taste."

Any genuine Bohemian revelry, in fact, was tolerated only in the early days for its promotional value. John Steinbeck in *Travels with Charley* (1962) observed that "If Carmel's founders should return, they could not afford to live there, but it wouldn't go that far. They would instantly be picked up as suspicious characters and deported over the city line." George Sterling, whom Nancy Peters described as "resembling Pan or Peter Pan," was forced out of town by the influx of more conservative Carmelites, outraged by his numerous love affairs, and rumors of a liaison with a teenage girl. The flamboyant, independent Mary Austin was strongly disliked by many members of the community who came to set up shops, and she rarely visited after 1913. Kaplan notes that by the time Lincoln Steffens settled in Carmel in 1927, "Things were more stable. . . . The cult of the great god Pan had declined into gossip, artiness, and a taste for peasant crafts, dirndl outfits, picnics, psychic pnenomena. . . . The promoter's dream had been realized. Carmel was the nucleus of a thriving regional community of plutocrats, socialites, sportsmen, comfortably retired persons, and others who had 'died and gone to heaven,' Steffens said."

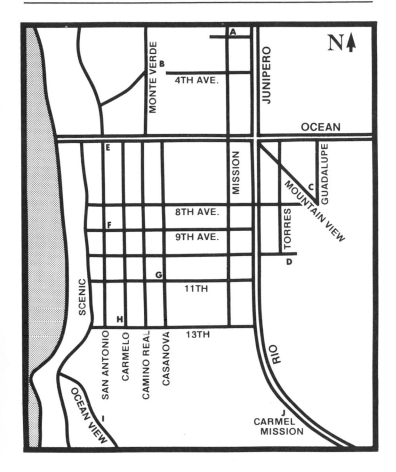

Many authors have lived in Carmel in the intervening years—the poet Ling-Fu Yang with her *Boundless Water and Mountain* of 1927, Harry Leon Wilson, creator of *Ruggles of Red Gap*, artist-writer Jo Mora, "Danny Santiago," Martin Flavin, Ernest K. Gann, David Duncan, archaeologist-writer Roy Chapman Andrews, savage-romance writer Rosemary Rogers—as Carmel has grown increasingly artsy-craftsy.

Exit off Highway 1 into Ocean Avenue, the main street in Carmel leading to the beach. Strong walkers can explore the relatively small area, thirty blocks or so, on foot, or you may drive between sites. There are no street numbers in Carmel; each house is given a name—and directions depend on the compass and number of houses in from the corner. At the north end of town you may start with:

A—PERRY NEWBERRY'S HOUSE On the northwest corner of Vista and Mission, behind a small grape-stake fence, you'll see the house Perry Newberry had built in 1937. Newberry was one of several literary mayors of this city — among other books he co-authored a series of five mystery novels with fellow Carmelite Alice MacGowan in the 1920s, including *Shaken Down* (1925), in which the enigma is solved as the city goes up in flames in the earthquake and fire of 1906. (Many people moved to Carmel, temporarily or permanently, between 1906 and 1912 when San Francisco was rebuilding after the catastrophic fire.)

Mary Austin

B—MARY AUSTIN'S HOUSE is the most difficult to find, hidden in a cui-de-sac. Take the first righthand turn just north of the intersection of Monte Verde and 4th Avenue. At the circular turnaround of this dead-end lane you'll see a wooden footbridge crossing over this undercut. Standing with the bridge to your right, Mary Austin's home is visible through the trees in the upper lefthand corner of the cul-de-sac, the light green house just up a small footpath. You can get another view of it on its small hill as you exit this lane.

Austin's most famous Carmel dwelling was her tree house, "The Wickiup," located near this spot. It was designed by Louis Mulgardt and erected in 1905, but was destroyed in the great winter storm early in 1915. Austin also kept a small writer's or guest cottage. She came here in 1902 to research her romance about Spanish California, *Isidro*, and returned to live a couple of years later, newly famous for her *The Land of Little Rain* (1903) about Owens Valley, the book which established her as a writer and which is still considered her finest work.

In her autobiography *Earth Horizon* (1932) she wrote "There was no town at Carmel then; nothing but a farm or two, one or two graceless buildings, and the wild beach and the sandy dunes. . . . George and I were very much alone in that first year. It was the simplest occupations that gave us the most pleasure. . . . Sterling's greatest pleasures were those that whetted his incessant appetite for sensations — the sting of surf against his body, the pull of the undertow off Carmel beaches. . . . Of all our walks, he loved best the one to Point Lobos; no poet's stroll, but a stout climb, dramatic, danger-tipped, in the face of bursting spray heads torn up from primordial deeps of sea gardens. . . . Interrupting or terminating such excursions there would be tea beside driftwood fires, or mussel roasts by moonlight, or the lot of us would pound abalone for chowder around the open-air grill at Sterling's cabin, and talk, ambrosial, unquotable talk."

C—THE FOREST THEATRE now found on Mountain View between Guadalupe and Santa Rita, was built in 1939 by another literary mayor of Carmel, Herbert Heron Peet, who had founded this prototypical "little theatre" in 1910 with his wife Opal and Perry Newberry. Young Sinclair

Lewis acted in some of the plays and many others took part. During her last full year in town, 1913, Mary Austin produced her play "Fire." In 1941 Robinson Jeffers' "Tower Beyond Tragedy" was staged, with Judith Anderson in the lead role of Clytemnestra.

D—GEORGE STERLING'S CABIN was once found on present-day Torres Street off 10th Avenue, but burned down by the 1930s. Here Sterling sat as the "High Panjandrum" of the artist colony, hosting visitors such as Ambrose Bierce, before the powerful columnist moved on to Washington, D.C., and broke with his poetic protege over Sterling's increasing interest in socialist politics — young Clark Ashton Smith, who at eighteen years was declared "the Keats of the Pacific Coast" when his *The Star-Treader and Other Poems* appeared in 1912 from A. M. Robertson — Van Wyck Brooks, who said that Sterling during his visit in 1911 "had precisely the aspect of Dante in hell" — Upton and Mary Kimbrough Craig Sinclair (Sterling's posthumously published *Sonnets to Craig* of 1927 were love poems to Sinclair's wife) — Jack and Charmian London — Jimmie Hopper, who inherited the cabin when Sterling returned to San Francisco — and the poet Nora May French, who swallowed cyanide here November 14, 1907, beginning the grand suicide march of the Bohemian Circle, and becoming a legend. (In his science fiction novel *Then Beggars Could Ride* Ray Nelson imagines a future society which lives in Carmel, each year re-creating the "golden age" of 1907, with the young women all vying with each other to play the part of Nora May French and swallow cyanide, so their ashes may be scattered from Point Lobos by Sterling, Jimmie Hopper, and other of her suitors.) The second house south of 10th on Torres on the east side of the street is the one Hopper built where Sterling's cabin had stood.

Lincoln Steffens, age sixty-one, retired to Carmel in 1927 to finish writing his Autobiography *(1931), and built:*

E—THE GETAWAY the third house from the southeast corner of Ocean Avenue and San Antonio, marked by a plaque dedicated June 17, 1967, by Sigma Delta Chi, the society of professional journalists, and placed on a stone near the walkway to the house. Steffens' house in his day was the closest construction to the beach — now several more rows of houses have sprung up on the former sand dunes. During their years here his wife Ella edited *The Carmelite* and Steffens contributed a regular column. The famous muckraker had assisted in the 1907 graft prosecution of Eugene Schmitz and Boss Ruef in San Francisco begun by Fremont Older, and had traveled all over America and the world doing his investigative journalism. The Getaway was the first place of his own in sixteen years.

Max Eastman, Steinbeck, Langston Hughes, Edna St. Vincent Millay, and Carl Sandburg stopped in on him here. So did the national aviation hero Charles Lindbergh. Ernest Hemingway stayed in the basement apartment during his visits, as did Gertrude Stein and Alice B. Toklas. Stein, Toklas, composer George Antheil, and sculptor Jo Davidson were all part of the Paris circle Steffens moved in, who visited him in Carmel before his death in 1936.

George Sterling, Mary Austin, Jack London, James Hopper

The nearby beach is a wonderful place—and lines from Sterling's "The Abalone Song" echo along the shore, recalling their roasts years ago: "By Carmel Bay, the people say/ We feed the lazzaroni/ On Boston beans and fresh sardines/ And toothsome abalone." It's said that Opal Heron Peet, Clark Ashton Smith, Michael Williams, and others contributed additional stanzas to this rollicking opus, with Sinclair Lewis penning "Some stick to biz, some flirt with Liz/ Down on the sands of Coney/ But we, by hell, stay in Carmel/ And nail the abalone."

F—JAIME DE ANGULO   lived some four blocks from Steffens' place in 1912-14 in a log cabin at 9th and Carmelo. It's said he rode about Carmel on a black stallion, dressed in black shirt, black chaps, and a black sombrero, his long hair flowing. He moved further south to Big Sur in 1914, where true bohemian lifestyles continued to flourish even as they disappeared from Carmel.

G—ARNOLD GENTHE,   the famous photographer and writer, lived in the second house from the northeast corner of 11th Avenue and Camino Real, on Camino Real. He came to Carmel late in 1905 and described life there in *As I Remember* (1936).

H—THE MacGOWAN SISTERS   Alice MacGowan and Grace Mac-Gowan Cooke, both writers, lived in the huge half-timbered, two-story house with the large gable found two houses up from the northeast corner of San Antonio and 13th Avenue. There were no other buildings in this immediate area when they had it constructed, except for a small cottage (now gone) where their secretaries Sinclair Lewis and William Rose Benét lived. Now it is thoroughly surrounded. Lewis sold Jack London twenty-seven story plots which Lewis "despaired of getting published," for $137.50, during his stay in Carmel. London wrote up five of them. It would be over a decade before Lewis would come into his own with such novels as *Babbitt* and *Main Street*.

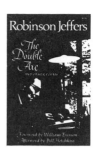

*The greatest literary site in
Carmel, and one of the most
impressive in America, is
found on Oceanview Avenue
between Stewart and Bay
View:*

I—TOR HOUSE   The poet Robinson Jeffers moved to Carmel September 1914, and came to this place on Mission Point in August 1919. He hired a stone mason to help him build one of the smaller houses, then over the years he alone built another house and the colossal tower, dragging boulders up from the beach using pulleys. By the time he came to construct the monumental tower, Jeffers had used most of the stones close by, and had to travel farther and farther for materials. Many of the boulders weigh hundreds of pounds.

Tor House and the Tower are perhaps the only literary sites in this book which will impress *anyone* who stands before them. Other sites depend for their interest on knowing something of the writers who have lived in them, but this place has a primordial power independent of literary association. Even if you have never heard of Robinson Jeffers, it is impossible to stand before the tower without awe. The fact that Jeffers built it *single-handed* makes its construction seem virtually supernatural. It may well stand as a monument to Jeffers generations after his poetry has been forgotten.

Roan Stallion, Tamar and Other Poems (1925), *The Women at Point Sur* (1927), and *Cawdor and Other Poems* (1928) are three of his many volumes of poetry. Jeffers also wrote drama, such as the play *Medea* (1946) in which Judith Anderson starred, *The Cretan Woman* (1954), and others. George Sterling, in some ways mentor to the younger poet, penned one of the first appreciations of Jeffers' work, *Robinson Jeffers: The Man and the Artist*, published the year Sterling died. Jeffers retreated more and more from society after Sterling's suicide. William Everson is one of the later poets influenced by Jeffers; he wrote *Robinson Jeffers: Fragments of an Older Fury* (1968). Today Jeffers is considered a major voice in American poetry by many in academic circles, and by some non-academic poets — Charles Bukowski, for one. But his gloomy cosmic perspective and Biblical symbolism is not for everyone, and in 1948 his collection *The Double Axe and Other Poems* was censored by Random House for its suggestion that America's leaders in World War II were acting in their own interests and were not much better than Hitler or Stalin. Many find Jeffers too depressing — others revel in his dark poetry.

Jeffers did most of his work here in seclusion with his family, though at one point Mabel Dodge — whom the Jeffers had visited in Taos, New Mexico — came to live nearby, in hopes of spiriting him away to *that* artist's colony in the Southwest, apparently as a replacement for D. H. Lawrence, who (according to Lincoln Steffens) had "unfeelingly died." She was unsuccessful. Jeffers died here at the age of seventy-five January 20, 1962.

Tours of Tor House take about an hour, are limited to six people at a time, and cost $5.00. Telephone (408) 624-1813 for an appointment or write Tor House Foundation, Box 1887, Carmel, CA 93921, for more information. Highly recommended. The skull that Jeffers hid behind a secret panel in his living room is only one of the many arcane symbols he worked into these buildings during his long years as the Poet and Stone Mason of Tor House.

On Junipero Street at Lasuen
Avenue, on the way back to
Highway 1, you may stop at:

J—CARMEL MISSION   Father Junipero Serra liked this mission above all the others he founded up and down the California coast, and he requested that his mortal remains be buried here. This place is nicely evocative of that earlier day, and Stevensonians believe that we have Robert Louis Stevenson largely to thank for it. As an anonymous reporter for the *Californian* in 1879 it is thought that R.L.S. came to the Feast day for San Carlos, patron saint for this mission, and that it was he who first suggested that the mission, then falling into ruin, be restored. Restoration work began five years later, and when Gertrude Stein came through in 1935 this was a place she insisted on seeing. (She refused to visit Carmel, saying "I don't like art colonies," and had no interest in meeting Robinson Jeffers, the literary lion of the area— the only men in America she had wanted to meet were Dashiell Hammett and Charlie Chaplin, and she had met both shortly before at a party in Hollywood.)

Continuing south on Highway 1
some forty miles you'll reach:

14 **BIG SUR**   Numerous Beat Generation writers visited Lawrence Ferlinghetti's cabin in Bixby Canyon. Lew Welch wrote in the San Francisco *Oracle*, "I remember a 1959 gathering in Big Sur with Kerouac, McClure, Neal Cassady, me, Lenore Kandel, Kirby Doyle, Ferlinghetti, and all assorted manner of minstrels and painters, their ladies and kids." Kerouac freaked out, reading Stevenson's *Dr. Jekyll and Mr. Hyde* one night when he was alone in the cabin. Kerouac's *Big Sur* (1962) covers that period, with Welch appearing under the name "David Wain," Kandel as "Romona Swartz," Ferlinghetti as "Lorenzo Monsanto," McClure as "Pat McLear," and Philip Whalen as "Ben Fagin."

Jaime de Angulo lived on a ranch on Partington Ridge. His neighbor Henry Miller, who moved permanently to Big Sur in the mid-1940s, described the eccentric anthropologist in *A Devil in Paradise* (1956): "Brown as a walnut, gaunt, slightly bowlegged, he was still handsome, still very much the Spaniard—and still utterly unpredictable . . . Jaime was one of the very few men I ever met of whom I could say that he had a streak of the Devil in him."

Miller was another writer made instantly famous when his first book, *Tropic of Cancer*, issued in Paris in 1934, was banned in all English-speaking countries. The major literary figure associated with Big Sur, he wrote *The Air Conditioned Nightmare*, *Big Sur and the Oranges of Hieronymus Bosch*, and many other renowned books. One anecdote has Miller in Paris at the time Ernest Hemingway was rising to fame, and

Henry Miller

asking Hemingway to autograph some books for him. Miller made a telling critical point— Hemingway stalked angrily away when Miller brought out a set of Mark Twain. Karl Shapiro describes Miller's life here in Big Sur as "a far cry from the bitter isolationism of Robinson Jeffers or even Lawrence. Morally I regard Miller as a holy man, as most of his adherents do— Gandhi with a penis."

In *My Life and Times* Miller wrote "There are some men whose devotion goes beyond the bounds of friendship. Such a man is Emil White. For twenty-five years I've known that I could depend on Emil for anything. . . ." Miller lived atop a ridge near White who brought supplies to him until Miller decided to get a car. He bought an old Cadillac for $100 and spent $1000 a year to keep it running. White had come to Big Sur about three months after Miller did in 1944. He opened a Henry Miller Memorial Library in his home in the 1960s in honor of their forty-year friendship. The library is located on the landward side of Highway 1 about half a mile south of Nepenthe Inn, and it is marked by a large sign over the gate. It houses a complete reference collection of Miller's publications. There is no charge to use the library: call (408) 667-2574 between 11 a.m. and 5 p.m. for an appointment if you plan to be in the area.

The next canyon beyond the Miller Library is named after Harry Lafler who built a cottage there early in the century. Rumor had it that Lafler's cottage was a hideaway for Jack London and Sterling during their Carmel days— and in his wanderings through the area some years ago, Emil White confirmed half the rumor when he found manuscript material by Sterling in the ruins of the house. Even those remains are gone today.

The Esalen Institute, founded by novelist Michael Murphy in 1961, is about eleven miles south of Nepenthe. Best known as an early center for the "human potential" movement, many writers— including Alan Watts— have held seminars here. In the mid-1960s Ken Kesey and the Merry Pranksters came down for a somewhat uneasy meeting with the Esalen contingent: "The Pranksters were friendly, but they glowed in the dark," as Tom Wolfe put it: he described Esalen as "a place where educated middle-class adults came in the summer to get out of The Rut and wiggle their fannies a bit."

Points further south take you into another state of the arts.

JOHN STEINBECK

John Steinbeck at the Pacific Grove Cottage, 1962

"You remember how happy I was to come back here. It really was a home coming. Well there is no home coming nor any welcome. What there is is jealousy and hatred and the knife in the back. . . . Our old friends won't have us back— always except Ed. . . . I hate a feeling of persecution but I am just not welcome here.

"This isn't my country anymore. And it won't be until I am dead. It makes me very sad."

—John Steinbeck in a letter, Spring 1945

From the summers of his childhood in the Salinas Valley and Monterey Bay, and from the region's political and social scene, John Steinbeck created a body of fiction—*The Red Pony*, *Tortilla Flat*, *The Long Valley*, *The Grapes of Wrath*, *Cannery Row*, and *East of Eden*—that gave the California of his youth a new name: Steinbeck Country. These books won him recognition as a great writer, and many awards, including a Nobel Prize in 1962 for his life's work.

Born February 27, 1902, to John Ernst and Olive Steinbeck, John Ernst Steinbeck, Jr. grew up in the family home on Central Avenue in Salinas. He spent summers in the Steinbeck's Pacific Grove cottage, and a few weeks each year on an uncle's farm near King City—the setting for *The Red Pony*. He and his sister Mary explored Pacific tidal pools and played games based on stories of King Arthur, childhood occupations that became abiding interests.

As a boy Steinbeck enthralled companions by telling them ghost stories; by his freshman year of high school he had decided that he would be a writer. He entered Stanford University in 1919, and though he hated the formalities, he got through about three years of classes he felt would benefit his writing. At the same time he worked at a number of jobs—as a longshoreman, farm laborer, manager of field crews in the Salinas Valley, and "chemist," running simple tests on the sugar beets in the Spreckels' refinery in Manteca.

In *The True Adventures of John Steinbeck, Writer* (1984), Jackson J. Benson says,

> Many of the hardest and dirtiest jobs at the sugar mill were done by Mexican laborers. Some have the impression that Steinbeck got much of his information about the Mexican-Americans and *paisanos* second- and third-hand, but he knew them well from childhood on. His friend Max Wagner had lived in Mexico until he was twelve, and together they were friendly with a number of Mexican families in Salinas, especially the Sanchez brothers, with whom Steinbeck ran around in his teens. From his association with the Mexican nationals who worked at Spreckels, he picked up several of the characters and stories that he later used in *Tortilla Flat*: the ex-corporal of Mexican cavalry whose wife is stolen by a captain; the old Mexican who hangs himself for the love of a fourteen-year-old girl; and Sweets Ramirez, who is paid for her favors with a sweeping machine without a motor. This storing of material, not only stories but also metaphors and even phrases, was typical of Steinbeck, and since he did not keep systematic notes, he apparently kept such things in his head for use ten or fifteen years later.

After he left college in 1925, Steinbeck went to New York City to break into the literary world, but he did not sell a single story. By 1926 he had returned to California, supporting himself over the next two years with a number of odd jobs. As caretaker for a homeowner at Lake Tahoe, Steinbeck completed his first novel, *Cup of Gold*, about the pirate Henry Morgan. It was published in 1929 while he was living in San Francisco. Shortly after, he married Carol Henning and they moved south to live in the family cottage in Pacific Grove.

Cup of Gold attracted little attention, nor did Steinbeck's second novel *The Pastures of Heaven* (1932), in which he first turned to the California people and land he knew. (In a letter dated May 8, 1931, Steinbeck said, "I here is, about twelve miles from Monterey, a valley in the hills called Corral de Tierra. Because I'm using its people I have named it *Las Pasturas de Cielo*.") In 1933 *To a God Unknown* and the first parts of *The Red Pony* appeared.

Several publishers refused his next novel, but when *Tortilla Flat* finally saw print in 1935 the response from readers was enthusiastic. Steinbeck, after a decade of struggle, had at last a popular and commercial success in this episodic novel about the *Paisanos* in Monterey's

Mexican ghetto, whose lives and little adventures Steinbeck pictured in the romantic mode and structure of the legends of King Arthur and his Knights of the Round Table. In 1936 *Tortilla Flat* won a medal from the Commonwealth Club of California, establishing Steinbeck as a major regional writer. His next novel *In Dubious Battle* (1936), about striking harvest workers used as pawns by both the Communist Party and the Farmers Association, easily took the Commonwealth Award for 1937.

With money coming in, Steinbeck left the family's summer home to build his own house in Los Gatos, where he wrote the book that put him in the ranks of major American novelists: *Of Mice and Men.* An immediate bestseller in 1939 and selected by the Book-of-the-Month Club, it was quickly adapted into a play that had its world premiere in North Beach at the Green Street Playhouse. Directed in New York by George S. Kaufman, it won the Drama Critic's Circle Award for the fall season. *Of Mice and Men* made Steinbeck a genuine celebrity from coast to coast, but it also brought unwanted attention. Hollywood besieged him with offers, but he resisted working on the screenplay for the film starring Burgess Meredith and Lon Chaney, Jr. — even for $1000 a week. That 1940 movie won an Oscar for Chaney's portrayal of the moronic giant Lenny, and presented Steinbeck's story to the widest possible audience.

Early in 1937 Steinbeck, a reclusive man who valued his privacy, told one of his correspondents, "I was recognized in San Francisco the other day and it made me sick to my stomach." When the phone calls became unbearable, he and his wife fled their home in Los Gatos to travel to New York and Europe. But the pressure of fame was on, and it contributed to wrecking two marriages, and to many moves over the years. Though he could never again be *just* another writer, Steinbeck tried to write what he wanted, without considering the expectations of his public or the critics. He wrote light books such as *The Short Reign of Pippin IV*, wartime propaganda — *The Moon is Down* and *Bombs Away*, original screenplays, and non-fiction on marine biology. He worked as a newspaper correspondent and published a travelogue about his trip around America with his dog — *Travels with Charley.* Steinbeck spent over a decade working on a modern English version of the King Arthur legends.

In 1939, *Grapes of Wrath* took Steinbeck beyond even the national reputation he had earned into world literature: In *Steinbeck: A Life in Letters* (1975) a letter from February 1938 expresses the concerns that led Steinbeck to write this book:

> I must go over to the interior valleys. There are about five-thousand families starving to death over there, not just hungry but actually starving. The government is trying to feed them and get medical attention to them with the fascist group of utilities and banks and huge growers sabotaging the thing all along the line and yelling for a balanced budget. In one tent there are twenty people quarantined for smallpox and two of the women are to have babies in that tent this week. I've tied into the thing from the first and I must get down there and see it and see if I can't do something to help knock these murderers on their heads. Do you know what they're afraid of? They think that if these people are allowed to live in camps with proper sanitary facilities, they will organize and that is the bugbear of the large landowner and the corporation farmer. The states and counties will give them nothing because they are outsiders. But the crops of any part of this state could not be harvested without these outsiders. I'm pretty mad about it. No word of this outside because when I have finished my job the jolly old associated farmers will be after my scalp again.
>
> I guess that is all. Funny how mean and little books become in the face of such tragedies.

The Grapes of Wrath far surpassed *Of Mice and Men* and *Tortilla Flat* as a literary sensation. The saga of the "Okie" Joad family, forced from their land by drought, who make the long trek west to the "promised land" of California, presented an America many readers had never seen—and many wanted to deny. If the nicer elements of Monterey denied that a district such as "Tortilla Flat" existed, then polite society and the money powers in back of it had far more reason to say that Steinbeck's picture of conditions in the migrant labor camps was grossly distorted and that Steinbeck was a Communist, *The Grapes of Wrath* a subversive tract.

When the novel was reported as a nominee in the 1940 Commonwealth Club Awards the jury panel was split by controversy. Founded in 1931 to "provide recognition and encouragement to the art of letters in California," the awards had honored Steinbeck twice in nine years, but political pressure came into play this time. A few weeks before the judges' final decision, *The Grapes of Wrath* won the Pulitzer Prize, and Steinbeck was elected to the National Institute of Arts and Letters. Although Steinbeck won his third, and final, Commonwealth Award for *The Grapes of Wrath* in 1940, one Sacramento newspaper cried that the book "is a public attack on our far-flung Commonwealth, interesting only as showing the extent to which an addlepated bird can go in fouling the nest in which he rattles around."

When asked by Viking to edit out shocking passages, Steinbeck replied that he "tried to write this book the way lives are being lived not the way books are written," and there is no doubt that *The Grapes of Wrath*—mild enough by today's standards—was revolutionary in its day. Some people on the Left suggest that Steinbeck had not been radical enough; in a 1969 interview for *The San Francisco Poets*, Kenneth Rexroth, who was involved in radical politics in the West from 1927 on, mentioned that "I had somebody ask me one time at an anarchist meeting in Italy, 'Is *The Grapes of Wrath* true?' One-eighth is true. In the novel, one guy gets killed. In a Bakersfield cotton strike, to which I took Steinbeck, eight guys get killed."

But there is no question that Steinbeck had "fouled his nest"—his next years in California were made increasingly uncomfortable. Except for the friendship of marine biologist Ed Ricketts, the model for "Doc" in *Cannery Row* and *Sweet Thursday*, Steinbeck's last period in Steinbeck Country was short on warmth. Even the exuberant and non-political Cannery Row novels could not erase the fact that Steinbeck had exposed the underbelly of California's agricultural wealth.

After the 1940s, Steinbeck seldom returned to his native region, but spent the years writing, traveling, and researching Arthurian myths. His final novel, *The Winter of Our Discontent* (1961), showed the power that had made him a major American writer. He made his last home in Sag Harbor, New York, where he died December 20, 1968. He was buried in Salinas.

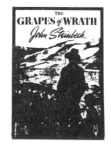

JOHN STEINBECK TOUR
SAN FRANCISCO

John Steinbeck lived in San Francisco for a couple of years in the late 1920s. He had visited the city before, especially when he was at Stanford and brought dates up for a night on North Beach. In 1926, after he had returned from New York to Caliornia, he lived the bohemian life of a struggling young writer, moving from place to place every few months. In *The True Adventures of John Steinbeck, Writer*, Jackson L. Benson notes:

> It is remarkable how many images in memory from this period in San Francisco match those from previous stay in New York. Lloyd Shebley came up to visit Steinbeck that fall and remembers climbing one flight of stairs after another until he came to a small, dark room at the top, a "real garret . . . ." John himself had memories of "a dark little attic on Powell Street. It was in the best tradition [of Bohemian living] with unsheathed rafters and pigeons walking in and out of a small dormer window. Then there was a kind of cave in North Beach completely carpeted wall to wall with garlic." He remembered coming back after a night out, to a "room with narrow bed, straight chair, typewriter and naked electric bulb with two sheets of copy paper pinned around it to shield the eyes." A small room with a cot, a table, chair, and typewriter — whether in Palo Alto, New York, San Francisco, or at Lake Tahoe — had been his lot for a long, long time.

The actual number of Steinbeck's bohemian digs in the city is unknown, the attic on Powell and the cave in North Beach have proven untraceable. A confirmed address for the writer is 1901 Vallejo Street, but the building is gone today. The remaining Steinbeck sites of the city may be found grouped conveniently around Alta Plaza in Pacific Heights — and it is said that Steinbeck often walked and sat in this park, thinking, composing stories.

Begin this walk of about six
blocks on Jackson between
Baker and Broderick at:

1 2953 JACKSON Steinbeck came to the city in 1928 to live. Before he left New York, he had persuaded an old friend from his Stanford days to act as his literary agent. In January 1929, *Cup of Gold* — a manuscript that had been rejected by at least seven other houses — was accepted by Robert M. McBride and Company. The novel had been floating the rounds for four years, and Steinbeck wasn't very happy with it by the time it finally saw print. But he wrote in a letter from this address late in 1929 that "The Morgan atrocity pays enough for me to live quietly and with a good deal of comfort. In that far it was worth selling."

Steinbeck was sharing this place with another writer from Stanford, Carl Wilhelmson, and he wrote that "[we] live in the upper storey of an old house here in S.F. It is a good life and very cheap. . . . We take our efforts to write with great seriousness, hammering away for two years on a novel and such things. . . . We have taken the ordinary number of beatings and I don't think there is much strength in either of us, and still we go on butting our heads against the English Novel and nursing our bruises as though they were the wounds of honorable war."

2953 Jackson is in a series numbered 2953-57, and the entrance to Steinbeck's place was through the alley. In this apartment he was at work on early drafts of his second novel, *To a God Unknown* based on his observation of ranch life in Northern California.

*Follow Jackson east to
Divisadero, go south two
blocks to Clay, and turn east
again until you stand before:*

2 2829 CLAY This building, originally 2833 Clay, is a somewhat earlier Steinbeck residence — and another place he worked on *To a God Unknown.*

*Continue east, and angle
across Alta Plaza. The street
on the eastern border of the
park is Steiner, and another
block east will bring you to
Fillmore where you will find,
near the corner of Jackson:*

3 2441 FILLMORE Perhaps the major reason for Steinbeck's move to San Francisco is the fact that he had fallen in love with Carol Henning, whom he had met at Lake Tahoe in 1927 where he was working as a house-caretaker and putting *Cup of Gold* through final revisions. She had a job in San Francisco, and when his job ended at Tahoe he followed her. By December 1929 he was writing from this address that they planned to get married. They wed early in 1930; that summer they left the city and settled in the Steinbeck cottage in Pacific Grove.

LOS GATOS AREA

John and Carol Steinbeck lived in the family cottage for six years, making do with the relatively small amounts of money earned by his first books, but with the sudden success of *Tortilla Flat* in 1935 they finally could afford a place of their own. On May 27, 1936, Steinbeck wrote to his longtime agent Elizabeth Otis:

> We're putting up a little shack near Los Gatos to escape the nasty summer fogs that hang around here all summer. My wife is building it while I stay here and work.

The "little shack" is found in the township of Monte Sereno, northwest of Los Gatos onHighway 9, the Saratoga-Los Gatos Road. Turn south into Greenwood Road, then angle to the right into Greenwood Lane, following it to where it suddenly switches back to the left. Negotiate the switchback and follow the narrowing road around the shoulder of the hill to:

4 16250 GREENWOOD LANE   Carol Steinbeck supervised construction of this fine large home on two acres in what in 1936 was a rural area. Soon other people began building homes nearby, and Steinbeck—to protect his privacy—built the tall stake fence that still rings the grounds, with the placard on the gate naming the place "Arroyo del Ajo," Garlic Gulch.

In this house Steinbeck completed *Of Mice and Men*, wrote more sections of *The Red Pony*, and began *The Grapes of Wrath*. He wrote to his agent on July 22, 1938, that "This place is getting built up and we have to move. Houses all around us now and so we will get back farther in the country. But next time we'll be in the middle of fifty acres, not two. I can hear the neighbors' stomachs rumbling."

Undoubtedly the unwanted attention and persistent phone calls occasioned by the phenomenal popularity of *Of Mice and Men* contributed to Steinbeck's desire to move away—by standards of the places Steinbeck had lived in San Francisco or Pacific Grove, his house on Greenwood Lane, even with the more modern homes erected in the years since he sold Arroyo del Ajo, is on spacious grounds.

Return to Highway 9. A few miles northwest on this road will take you to Villa Montalvo, James D. Phelan's summer home—well worth visiting if you get to this area. It is ironic that Steinbeck, who would become the only writer to win the Nobel and Pulitzer prizes as well as The Presidential Medal of Freedom (in addition to numerous smaller awards) lost out when he applied for a Phelan Award in 1931 to help get him over the lean years. "Other people get Phelan Awards," he remarked.

*Take Highway 9 southeast
from Villa Montalvo or
Greenwood Road to the
freeway on Route 17 and head
south into the Santa Cruz hills.
A few miles south of Los
Gatos, rising steeply to the
right, Brush Road climbs into
these hills. Follow it up past
woods and open pastures to
the crest of the ridge, where
the road falls down on the
other side. Shortly before you
reach the crest, Old Well Road
turns off to the left. If you
follow it around to the right to
where it deadends at a
homemade basketball court
you can park and look at
Steinbeck's next home across
a field to the right:*

5 THE BRUSH ROAD FARM could have been an ideal retreat for
Steinbeck (though today other homes have gone up nearby, as happened on Greenwood Lane). In the fall of 1938 he and Carol moved into a farmhouse built here in 1852. While he sat in the kitchen of the old house, writing the final draft of *The Grapes of Wrath*, she supervised the building of the green ranch-style home you see today. The original farmhouse stood to the left of the new house; it was destroyed by a fire only three years ago.

In this place Steinbeck's first marriage went to ruin. He spent part of 1940 on a specimen-collecting trip with his friend Ed Ricketts, taking notes for *The Log from the Sea of Cortez*. And in 1940 he met Gwyndolyn Conger, with whom he began living by 1941. A divorce from Carol went through in 1942, and in 1943 he married Gwyn. He lived in this home slightly more than two years.

MONTEREY-PACIFIC GROVE

*Follow 17 south to Highway 1,
and follow the coast road south
to Monterey. Take the first exit
into downtown Monterey. You
may take in the Robert Louis
Stevenson House at 530
Houston Street and Clark
Ashton Smith's last home at
117 9th Street while looking
up the several Steinbeck sites
here and in the adjoining town
of Pacific Grove.*

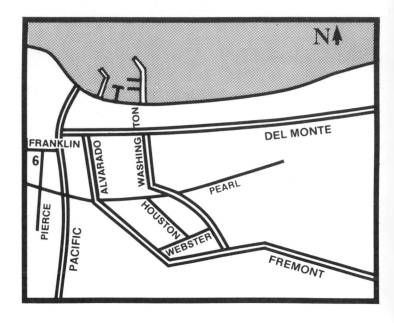

6 THE LARA-SOTO HOUSE This one-story adobe under the gigantic cypress was purchased by Steinbeck in fall 1944 and here he wrote *Cannery Row* (1945).

In 1849 this property was first granted as a town lot to Feliciana Lara and in the 1890s passed into the hands of Manuel Soto and his Indian wife Felicidad—a piece of Old California. It was in this home that Steinbeck began to feel like an outsider in his own land, to feel that "This isn't my country anymore." He left Monterey. When his second marriage failed late in 1948, Steinbeck returned once again to the family cottage in Pacific Grove, but he left California for good in November 1949. He married his third wife, Elaine Scott, in December of the following year, and made his home in New York and Sag Harbor between travels.

From the Soto House take Pacific Street to Lighthouse Avenue and follow the signs to one of the most famous and beloved fictional locales in the country, a place whose appeal Anne-Marie Schmitz in her book In Search of Steinbeck *(1978) evokes when she recalls a 1960 visit to Monterey, and the chance purchase of a paperback book: "Out of the pages of the thirty-five-cent paperback came Ed Rickets, Mac and the Boys, the*

girls of Dora, Mrs. Malloy
sewing her curtains at the door
of the boiler, Western
Biological and the Palace
Flophouse. I did not give the
author a second thought. The
people Steinbeck had
remembered or created were
too much alive for me to ever
think they could have come
from a man's imagination:"

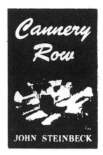

7 CANNERY ROW Originally a stretch of Ocean View Avenue running along Monterey Bay, these few blocks where Monterey's sardine canning industry thrived from shortly before World War I until the close of World War II were named Cannery Row in 1953. In *Steinbeck's Street: Cannery Row* (1980) Maxine Knox and Mary Rodriguez write:

> When Fort Ord was reactivated in 1942, the commanding general placed Ocean View Avenue off limits to the military because of the painted, perfumed prostitutes who paraded on paydays. Under such pressure, city officials had to ban prostitution and force the closing of the previously legal houses of ill repute. The neon lights went out, and the street became strangely silent at night, a portent to old-timers. To others it signaled a new era. With great ceremony, Ocean View Avenue was rechristened "Cannery Row" in 1953 following the great popularity of John Steinbeck's whimsical tale, which he wrote to relax from a war. Cannery Row became as familiar to folks everywhere as their own hometown main streets.

Steinbeck's novel happened to catch a lost age—with the war the prostitutes were removed from the row, and 1945 was the last peak year for the sardine industry as the fingerlings changed their migration patterns. By the 1950s the abandoned or largely inactive canneries were ripe for the installation of expensive restaurants and gentrified shops which have made Cannery Row—like Jack London Square in Oakland—one of the most famous literary shopping centers in the country.

The book by Knox and Rodriguez gives a detailed history of all the buildings along the row—you can get copies from the Monterey Historical Society when you walk the tour of the adobes, though the book doesn't seem to be sold by any of the places along Cannery Row itself. Yet since the guide appeared in 1980 many changes have swept along this street, with more to come. Several of the canneries they describe which once stretched on piers out into the bay have been razed, and construction is well underway on a multi-million-dollar Monterey Bay Aquarium, with some one-hundred tanks displaying the marine life of the coastal waters.

The essential literary sites are found within two blocks along the Row. Begin with the bust of Steinbeck found at the foot of Prescott Avenue, donated by Mr. and Mrs. Merle W. Strauch in 1973. The plaque on the pedestal reproduces the first paragraph of the novel, with Steinbeck's invocation of "Cannery Row in Monterey in California" as "a poem, a stink, a grating noise, a quality of light, a tone, a habit, a nostalgia, a dream. . . ."

From the bust walk northwest toward the aquarium. On the bayside of the street at 800 Cannery Row you'll find a dilapidated wooden building—the lab of Ed "Doc" Ricketts, who first established Pacific Biological Laboratories,Inc. here in 1923. A fire in November 1936 destroyed

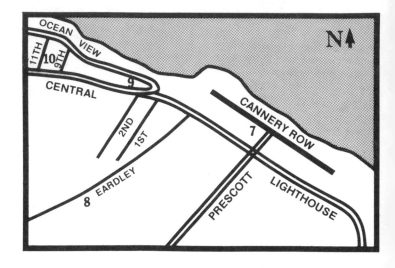

his original lab and living quarters, including an impressive library on marine biology; Rickets worked out of this laboratory until he died in May 1948, after his car was hit by a Southern Pacific train. Steinbeck met Doc in 1930, and in their early years in Pacific Grove his wife Carol worked as an employee in the lab to help pay their bills. With the first great success of *Tortilla Flat* the Steinbecks were free from workaday life, but Steinbeck often assisted Ricketts in his work in the next years, collaborating with him on *Sea of Cortez* (1941). Ricketts' *Beyond Pacific Tides* has gone through several editions, and still is considered the definitive basic work on the subject of local marine biology. Ricketts was used as the model for several characters in Steinbeck's fiction, but is best known from the novels *Cannery Row* and its sequel, *Sweet Thursday*, where he appears under almost no disguise as "Doc," working out of the "Western Biological Laboratories"—this very building. (A group of local businessmen have bought this place to use as a private club, but also to preserve it—don't let its moribund look lead you into thinking they will raze it tomorrow. It is considered a landmark, and the fact that it has not been renovated is deliberate—the exterior of Doc's lab has seen almost no change since the heydays of the 1940s.)

Directly across from the lab Steinbeck lay his "Palace Flophouse and Grill" where characters like Mack and Whitey No. 1 and Whitey No. 2 flopped and drank their wine. Close by at 851 Cannery Row is the site of La Ida's Cafe (and whorehouse), in recent years the home of Kalisa's International Restaurant (just a restaurant). Up the block the Old General Store occupies the site of Wing Chong Market, called "Lee Chong's Heavenly Grocery" in the books.

A look at these places and a ramble through the converted canneries and back alleys, past restaurants such as Steinbeck's Lobster Grotto, will give you the best literary tour that can be made of Cannery Row, which even at the time Steinbeck was writing was quickly becoming "a dream," a fragment of the past.

Steinbeck's three major Pacific Grove sites are within twenty blocks of Cannery Row, just across the town line. On Eardley Avenue between 2nd and Spencer on the south side of the street you'll see:

8 **425 EARDLEY** To be near Ed Ricketts during the period they were working on *Sea of Cortez* and Steinbeck's *Log*, based upon their 1940 specimen-hunting expedition, Steinbeck returned to Monterey with Gwyn Conger, and in 1941 bought this house. Here he wrote his notes for Rickett's book and another work of non-fiction, *The Forgotten Village* (1941), but moved away that summer. Until their return in 1944 to buy the Lara-Soto House the Steinbecks lived in New York—Steinbeck himself spent many months overseas as a war correspondent.

Downhill toward the bay from the Eardley house, on the corner of 2nd Street, is a place Steinbeck helped build— where he was a frequent guest:

9 **222 CENTRAL** According to one set of claims this place is the original summer cottage the Steinbecks kept in Pacific Grove as a place to escape the heat of the Salinas Valley, the place where young John and his sisters summered. His maternal grandmother Elizabeth Hamilton died in this house in 1918, and various old-timers recall the Steinbecks staying here.

To the left of the front entrance a little garden fronts on the street. You'll see a small wing of the house, in effect a separate cottage, built behind this garden. According to the sister of Steinbeck's first wife, Carol, her husband and John Steinbeck built this wing in the mid-1930s as a place for her and her husband to live—after they built an addition to the other Steinbeck house on 11th Street in which John and Carol were staying.

Here Steinbeck came to eat dinner, drink wine, and unwind. Ed Ricketts was a frequent visitor—Steinbeck's sister-in-law recalled that John and Carol were away on a trip to Mexico at the time Doc's first lab burned in 1936, and that Ricketts came to their door early in the morning for solace, with "the sky still red from the burning."

With the construction of the Monterey Bay Aquarium on Cannery Row, plans to open this house to visitors are being made—write The John Steinbeck Studies Foundation, 222 Central Avenue, Pacific Grove, CA 93940 or call (408) 375-4649 for latest information.

A few blocks away you'll find the last Steinbeck home in this area at:

10 **147 11TH STREET** Built by Steinbeck's father, this is the place where the newly-married writer came to live in 1930 and stayed until the move to Los Gatos in 1936. In this house Steinbeck rewrote *To a God Unknown*, wrote sections of *The Red Pony*, and finished *The Pas-*

tures of *Heavey*, *Tortilla Flat*, and *In Dubious Battle*. He began *Of Mice and Men* here, but completed the novel after he and Carol moved north.

The year he came here, he met Ed Ricketts, and it was only a mile or so to Ed's lab and Cannery Row. When his first and second marriages broke up, Steinbeck returned here — and though he lived largely on the East Coast from 1949 on, he returned to this place for short stays.

In the fall of 1932 Steinbeck's mother was ill, and he divided his time between the family cottage on 11th Street and the family home in:

SALINAS

John and his sister Mary on Jill, the red pony

You may follow Highway 68 across country from the Monterey Bay to the valley and downtown Salinas, site of Steinbeck's birth in the large Victorian home at:

11 **132 CENTRAL AVENUE** Built in 1897, this house was purchased by John Ernst Steinbeck, Sr., in 1900; his son was born February 27th two years later and lived here until he left for Stanford University in 1919. Young John Steinbeck occupied the upstairs bedroom under the gable overlooking Central Avenue, and here he told ghost stories to his friends and sent off, unsigned, his first stories to an unknown end. In *East of Eden* (1952) he pictured his home as "an immaculate and friendly house, grand enough but not pretentious . . . it sat inside its white fence surrounded by clipped lawn and roses. . . ."

On weekdays the downstairs rooms are open for luncheons, with servings at 11:45 and 1:15 – part of the efforts to raise funds for the continued upkeep of this house as a major literary and historic site. The reception room is the front bedroom where Steinbeck was born; reservations are required – phone (408) 424-2735.

If you get to Salinas you might lunch in the Steinbeck house and eat dinner in the "East of Eden Restaurant" at 327 Pajaro Street, formerly a First Presbyterian Church – another indicator of Steinbeck's drawing power on his home grounds. And in the Garden of Memories at 768 Abbott you will find Steinbeck's grave under a large oak near Romie Lane.

A trip to this area certainly should include a stop in:

12 **110 WEST LUIS STREET,** formerly the Salinas Public Library, now the John Steinbeck Library. The best time for a literary visit is around the first of August, when the annual Steinbeck Festivals, begun in 1979, are held. They usually last for a week and a half, and feature bus tours of Steinbeck sites, wine tastings, displays of memorabilia, speakers, and the like. Call the library at (408) 758-7311 for more information. The library's Steinbeck Room features permanent exhibits of photos and first editions of the writer's many books, and is open 10 a.m. to 9 p.m. Monday-Thursday, 10 a.m. to 6 p.m. Friday-Saturday, and is closed Sunday. The library also has on file an enormous collection of taped interviews made with locals who knew the man who put Salinas and Monterey on the world literary map, and in the courtyard stands a lifesize statue of the writer, cigarette in hand, watching with bronze eyes over Steinbeck Country.

POINTS NORTH

Kenneth Rexroth in the High Sierra, ca. 1939

North from San Francisco across the Golden Gate Bridge you'll find many literary enclaves scattered through Marin, Mendocino, and Sonoma counties; a Robert Louis Stevenson tour that winds (drunkenly or not) through the Napa Valley wine country; Jack London's spectacular Beauty Ranch and the monumental ruins of Wolf House. There is a wealth of literary sites and associations all the way up to the legend-haunted slopes of Mount Shasta, a source of mystical inspiration for writers from Joaquin Miller to date.

Over the bridge Interstate 101 will take you angling north through Marin County, where many affluent writers move after they've made their mark. Away from the crowding and noise of San Francisco, it is but a short drive from all that the city has to offer. The first exit off the bridge will take you to Vista Point, where you get a great look at the city, Alcatraz, Angel Island, and the Pacific, and the second exit will take you down a long hill into:

Alan Watts

1 SAUSALITO This picturesque small town was home for Alan Watts, who lived part-time on a houseboat moored in the Marina. Watts was a charismatic presence, a terrific, witty speaker — his various lectures and radio talks seem fresh (and as refreshing) today when they are rebroadcast as they did when first aired in the 1950s and 1960s. Watts was a major figure in bringing Eastern religious beliefs and practices to the Western audience, and he wrote many books in addition to his series of lectures.

Daniel O'Connor, author of *Songs from Bohemia* — one of many Bohemian Club members who essayed verse in the 1800s and now are forgotten — lived in Sausalito in a cottage whose site is marked with a granite bench at Harrison and Bulkley. The Beat poet Kirby Doyle, born in Marin County, lived in this city and literary residents include Ron Kovik, author of *Born on the Fourth of July*, an activist with Veterans Against War, and Evan Connell, whose stories set in the Po-Po Club evoke an atmosphere much like that of Sausalito's no name bar — a haunt of Connell, Lew Welch, and other writers.

Heading north out of Sausalito along the bayside road you'll next reach the city of:

2 MILL VALLEY Jack Kerouac is probably one of the few writers who has had to *walk* from San Francisco across the bridge to Mill Valley. In 1956 he was crashing in a cottage here with Gary Snyder until Snyder left the Bay Area for Japan on May 15. Kerouac saw his poet-brother off at the docks, spent the evening drinking in The Cellar, and later found himself stranded with no car fare fifteen miles south of the cabin. He plodded north over the Golden Gate Bridge, across the ridge and down to the cottage which he later described in *The Dharma Bums* (1958). This place, which Snyder called "Marin-An," has since been demolished; it stood on the hill behind 348 Montford Avenue in Mill Valley.

Don Carpenter now lives in Mill Valley. After his novel *The True Life Story of Jody McKeegan* appeared in 1975 he devoted almost five years to writing motion picture screenplays, including an adaptation of Bukowski's first novel *Post Office*, which were never filmed. Carpenter returned to prose with *A Couple of Comedians* (1980), saying he'd "never write for Hollywood again."

Mill Valley resident Robert Byrne, who operates a pool hall, wrote one of the best books to come out of Marin County: *McGoorty; The Story of a Billiard Bum* (1972) — the biography of billiard hustler Danny McGoorty, written from taped reminiscences and dedicated "To Lillian McGoorty — who suffered most." McGoorty was born in San Francisco in 1901 but grew up in Chicago, returning to the city late in life. Short Gordon said, "His control of cueball speed was so beautiful I drool when I think of it," and Bob McCarty stated, "McGoorty was championship timbre, but he gave the dolls and refreshments first call." McGoorty's oral biographical style, wonderfully translated into prose by Byrne, equals the best of Bukowski, as in this representative passage:

> Plenty of times I played for money when I didn't have any, which is called playing on your nerve. When you do that you absolutely have to win. You can't show any mercy, or give the other guy any chance at all. All good hustlers and tournament players have the killer instinct, and the way they get it is by playing on their nerve a few times. A lot of good players never get to the top because when they get ahead in a game they start feeling sorry for their opponent. They ease up on him instead of kicking him when he is down. Players who do that have never had to play for their breakfast. You've got to look at it this way: If you are playing your grandmother a fifty-point game, try to beat her fifty to nothing. Or if you have her forty-nine to three, try to keep her from getting to four. Try to hate her. It helps to hate whoever you are playing, which has never been any problem for me. I don't know how much talent I have, but I have a lot of natural hate. A guy by the name of Rusty Jones told me that a great many players are killers and haters, but with me the hate shows through. "When you bend over that table, McGoorty," he said "you *look* like a killer."

Johnny Dark and Sam Shepard

Sam Shepard has a home near Mill Valley. The author of many hit plays — *True West, Fool for Love* — and the winner of many Obies, Shepard netted a Pulitzer Prize for *Buried Child* in 1979. He's at least as famous as a film star, featured in such movies as "Days of Heaven" directed by Terrence Malik, and "Resurrection." Shepard was nominated for an Oscar for his portrayal of daredevil pilot Chuck Yeager in "The Right Stuff" — a terrific performance, since Shepard himself refuses to fly. His *Motel Chronicles* (1983) contains many scenes with Marin County settings, and is the basis for the Wim Wenders film "Paris, Texas."

Poet James Broughton lives in Mill Valley, and the poet Stanton Coblentz was a resident in the 1950s. The Thompson family lived here in the late 1800s — a period Kathleen Thompson Norris chronicled in her first novel *Mother* (1911). A park at Molina and Wildomar in Mill Valley is named Norris Memorial Park in honor of the prolific novelist. The most popular look into modern Mill Valley and Marin and hot-tub chic is Cyra McFadden's novel *The Serial* (1977), which captures the more vacuous aspects of the Marin lifestyle.

Looking west from Mill Valley you'll see the mountain rising up between the town and the sea; you may follow several routes up to the crest of:

3 MOUNT TAM The Episcopalian Zen philosopher Alan Watts had a home on Mount Tamalpais. On these slopes Jack Kerouac and Gary Snyder hiked in 1956, and the "Golden Gate Trinity" of Ina Donna Coolbrith, Charles Warren Stoddard, and Bret Harte hiked here almost a century earlier. Here Coolbrith and Joaquin Miller gathered laurel boughs in 1874 for Miller to place on Lord Byron's neglected grave. A year later Ambrose Bierce walked these trails after he moved to San Rafael, and Coolbrith read her poem "California" ("The sunset purple slipped from Tamalpais/ And bay and sky were bright with sudden stars") here in 1896 before a gathering of the Pacific Coast Women's Press Association. Coolbrith, Sterling, Stoddard, Edward Rowland Sill, and many other poets have been inspired to commemorate Mount Tam. Gertrude Atherton wrote part of her novel *Tower of Ivory* while staying in a mountaintop inn here circa 1908.

Sir Arthur Conan Doyle and his family visited Mount Tam during their week in San Francisco in 1923, and also explored Muir Woods at the mountain's foot. Naturalist and author John Muir, after whom Muir Woods National Monument was named when it was created in 1908, had only limited connections with this place, though of course he visited this magnificent park after its opening — and his efforts on behalf of Yosemite and the creation of the Sierra Club justly entitle him to more names in *honorarium* than anyone else in the history of California's excellent park system. On the offtrail side of one of Muir Woods' giant redwoods — ask a ranger to point out the tree — a plaque was placed in honor of Ralph Waldo Emerson's one-hundredth birthday on May 25, 1903. Lincoln Fairley in his article "Literary Associations With Mt. Tamalpais," *California History*, summer 1982, writes that "Bailey Millard, historian of the Bay Region, presided. Present were Jack London, George Sterling (poet), Edward B. Taylor (later mayor of San Francisco), Herman Scheffaur (writer), Austin Lewis (writer), and Mr. and Mrs.

Morrison F. Pixley of Corte Madera. . . . Messages were read from John
Muir and from Emerson's son, Edward Waldo Emerson. Emerson had
been in San Francisco on a lecture tour in April and May, 1871, but
there is no record of his going to Redwood Canyon" — now Muir Woods,
whose mighty trees the poet John Masefield in 1937 described as:
"They were more like gods than anything I have ever seen."

*Writers have lived in many of
the other cities dotted about
Marin County. In:*

4 SAN ANSELMO   The mystery writers Joe Gores (*Hammett, Interface*) and Martin Cruz Smith (*Gorky Park*) have homes in the Sleepy
Hollow area.

And in:

5 TIBURON   Sterling Silliphant has resided here for eight years. Silliphant writes mystery-action novels about John Locke, an adventurer
who sails the South Seas on a forty-foot ketch (the author has a seventy-
six-foot ketch on which he sails several months each year). Silliphant is
better known for his many movie scripts and teleplays, which total some
four-hundred hours of screentime — the "Route 66" series, "The Swarm,"
the "Shaft" films, and the San Francisco-based movies "The Enforcer,"
starring Clint Eastwood, and "The Towering Inferno."

The town of:

6 FAIRFAX   is where Alan Paton stayed for a few days with Aubrey
and Marigold Burns in late 1946 and early 1947 when he was finish-
ing *Cry, the Beloved Country* in the Hotel Somerton on Geary Street.
They lived at 127 Cypress Drive in a house Paton described as built
around four redwood trees that rose "through holes cut in floors and
ceiling. The trees were young but were over a hundred feet high. . . ."

In the 1940s nearby:

7 SAN ANSELMO   was home for poet Eric Barker and his wife, the
dancer Madelynne Greene, where Clark Ashton Smith often visited.
The three roamed the hills above the town. On one of their last walks
and picnics they rested beneath an enormous oak tree, and Madelynne
placed a small pagan god she had made of clay into its boughs as an
offering. In 1966 Barker wrote of those days: "We had a favorite hill that
Ashton named the Hill of Dionysus. It is the name of his last cycle of love-
lyrics that he dedicated to Madelynne. . . . Only a few days ago Madelynne
and I drove up there, the first time in years. Now a paved road leads to
the top and we stopped by the Hill of Dionysus. Most of it is occupied by
a spacious house and garden. Mercifully, the great oak is still there.
Madelynne's pagan image must long since have succumbed to the
elements. Ashton has gone too, but the hill and the tree are in his
poems. And by poetry's ancient incontestable right the hill is still ours —
sans house, sans garden. An ownership — no — a heritage shared by
three — two poets and a dancer. For all time."

On the coast you'll find:

8 STINSON BEACH Gina Berriault lived in this seaside town for many years, and uses the familiar Marin coast and its settlements in her story collection *The Lights of Earth* (1984). This collection has won wide acclaim, as has the earlier collection *The Infinite Passion of Expectation* (1982), of which Bay Area novelist Wright Morris said: "Gina Berriault is at home with the emotions that do our living for us, enlarge us and deflate us, nourish and exhaust us, and in the fullness of time betray our extravagant expectations."

*Further north along the Pacific
shore you'll come to:*

9 BOLINAS Locally famous for its wooden sidewalks, dirt roads, and inbred slang ("Bo Bo Land," "pud," "rad"). In a sense the Haight Ashbury scene of 1967 just moved north across the bridge: you can always see a stoned hippie in Bolinas. This small town has sheltered part of the Bay Area's small press movement, such as Donald Allen's Grey Fox Press and Michael Wolfe's Tombouctou Books. In *Literary San Francisco* Ferlinghetti points out the huge number of writers who've been in and out of Bolinas: "Among writers who have lived there for at least a month since 1969, the better known are Bill Berkson, Tom Clark, Lewis Warsh, Richard Brautigan, Joanne Kyger, Robert Creeley, Ted Berrigan, David Meltzer, Ebbe Borregaard, Aram Saroyan, Gerard Malanga, Lewis MacAdams, Philip Whalen, Peter Warshall, Orville Schell, Kenneth Lamont, Bobbie Louise Hawkins, Alice Notley, Jim Carroll, Jim Koller, Margot Patterson Doss, Duncan McNaughton, Charles Fox." It was in his three-story frame house at 6 Terrace Street that Brautigan's body was discovered October 25, 1984, a month after his Hemingwayesque suicide.

*You'll come to Sonoma County
north of Marin—site of Jack
London's Beauty Ranch in
Glen Ellen (described in the
chapter on London—one of
California's great literary sites).
In the town of:*

10 GLEN ELLEN Novelist M. F. K. Fisher, now in her seventies, lives in a two-room *palazzino* on her friend David Bouverie's ranch. She has written poetry, screenplays, and a novel—*Not Now But Now*, partly set in San Francisco of the 1880s. Called by *Newsweek* "a national treasure," Fisher is best known as a writer on gastronomy—these books have now been collected in *The Art of Eating*. In the late 1940s she published a brilliant translation of Brillat Savarin's *The Physiology of Taste*. In *As They Were* she describes moving from her three-room Victorian house in St. Helena where she had lived many years to: ". . . a ranch on Route 12 in northern California, about two miles from Glen Ellen, where Jack London lived and drank and piled up the reddish volcanic stones of the region into strong clumsy walls, towers, cattle troughs, a dam. . . ."

The Sonoma County town of:

11 SEBASTOPOL is the winter home for Meridel Le Sueur, also in her eighties. Le Sueur organized a women's writing group in the Workers Alliance during the Great Depression, and wrote many stories and novels until the 1940s, when she was blacklisted for her radical political convictions. She published nothing for thirty years, but the modern women's movement has resurrected her fiction with such reprints as *Song for My Time, Women on the Breadlines*, and *Harvest*, and Le Sueur is once more working on fiction. Books such as *Annunciation* (1935) and *Salute to Spring* (1940) prompted Carl Sandburg to say that Le Sueur has "a genius for moving and highly implicative testimony." Nelson Algren wrote, "She is one of the very few revolutionary writers who combine a powerful realism and a deep sense of beauty."

About fifty miles north of San Francisco you'll find a state historic site in:

12 SANTA ROSA Horticulturist Luther Burbank's Santa Rosa home on the corner of Tupper Street and Santa Rosa Avenue, near the center of town, was opened to the public after his death in 1926 as the Luther Burbank House and Gardens, and may be toured today. Here he developed numerous new varieties of plant life, achieving such wide acclaim that he was invited to read one of his *botanical papers* at the Authors Reading to benefit Ina Coolbrith in the Fairmont Hotel, November 27, 1907.

Established by Russian trappers in 1812, the coastal town of:

13 FORT ROSS was where Gertrude Atherton retreated from the "social whirl" of San Francisco to write her novel *The Doomswoman*, which became her first published book in 1893. The latter part of this novel is set in Fort Ross.

Andre Voznesensky visited Fort Ross in 1972 to research the great 1806 love story of the Russian explorer Nicolai Rezanov and the Presidio commander's daughter, young Doña Concepcion Argüello—they vowed to be wed upon Rezanov's return from an expedition home. She waited faithfully, but finally adopted a nun's habit in the third order of Franciscans when he did not return. Forty years later she learned he had frozen to death in Siberia on his way across Russia. Atherton called this tragic episode "the one famous love story of Old California," and wrote of it in her novel *Rezanov* (1906) and in the short story "Concha Arguello, Sister Dominica." Bret Harte also penned a version of the tale.

On the Russian River you'll find the town of:

14 MONTE RIO The famous (or infamous) Bohemian Grove is located near this town—a lodestone for literary San Franciscans in the midsummers before George Sterling's suicide. Monte Rio itself has housed a literary colony similar to that in Bolinas, chronicled in part three of *In America's Shoes* (1983) by Andrei Codrescu, the dissident Romanian poet and essayist.

Cazadero, a small remote village above Monte Rio in the mountains, has been home for the last ten years of Jim Dodge, creator of *Fup* (1984), a crazy tale about an old man and a mystical mallard who's "Duck Fup."

Further north you'll find the town of Mendocino in Mendocino County, a sort of Carmel of the North, with a thriving artists colony with galleries and crafts shows. Many writers have lived here, or come through for readings. Jan Kerouac lived here circa 1969, and also lived in Ukiah. Near the town of Boonville the award-winning writer Alice Walker owns a farm — and on a slightly disguised version of the Moonie farm outside Boonville John D. MacDonald set much of the action in The Green Ripper *(1979), one of his series of novels featuring trouble-shooter Travis MacGee. The real-life adventurer and author Leonard Clark owned the S Bar S Ranch in adjoining Lake County, where he raised beef cattle between expeditions to the wilds of the world.*

Napa Valley south of Lake County is much more famous for its wineries than for the writers who have lived here. The town of:

Jessamyn West, 1929

15 NAPA is now home for Jessamyn West, whose *The Friendly Persuasion* (1940) is a great American classic. West was born in Whittier, and (like Richard Nixon, for irony) graduated from Whittier College, a Quaker. She later attended U.C. West worked on the filmscript of *The Friendly Persuasion*, and wrote many other books: *A Mirror in the Sky, The Massacre at Fall Creek, To See the Dream, South of the Angels, A Matter of Time.* Her novel *The Life I Really Lived* (1979) is about a writer who eventually follows her faith-healer brother to California, and supports him through the course of a sensational trial for murder.

Of the hundreds of thousands of people who pass it every year on their tour of the wine country, how many are aware that the Schramsberg Winery, founded in 1862, was a place where Ambrose Bierce, a friend of owner Joseph Schram, is said to have visited, or that Robert Louis Stevenson devoted a chapter to it in The Silverado Squatters?

ROBERT LOUIS STEVENSON

Stevenson had a remarkable impact on California for someone who spent less than a year here. He has more public memorials in this state than any author except Jack London. The Stevenson House in Monterey, the plaque on 608 Bush, the monument in Portsmouth Square, all represent his first starveling months in northern California, when he tried unsuccessfully to support himself by writing, and waited to marry Fanny Osbourne. Napa Valley marks the end of his stay. On their honeymoon excursion, the couple drove up to Silverado where Stevenson—suffering from tuberculosis—recuperated in the warm, dry climate from May until July, 1880. Upon his return to Scotland he wrote the great classics *Treasure Island, Dr. Jekyll and Mr. Hyde, A Child's Garden of Verse*, and many others. His every move has been studied in dozens of books and hundreds of articles, and Stevensonians still burn with curiosity to know the wording of the telegram Fanny sent to Stevenson that brought him rushing around the world and across the plains.

An effective Stevenson tour in Napa Valley begins in the town of St. Helena on Highway 29, where you'll find located in the library at 1490 Library Lane:

RLS in San Francisco. 1879

16 **THE SILVERADO MUSEUM** Open daily except Sundays, Mondays and holidays from noon until 4 p.m., phone (707) 963-3757, this museum displays one of the world's largest collections of Stevensonian memorabilia. Founded sixteen years ago, it provides tangible reminders of Stevenson's stay in this area and offers a brochure, *Stevenson in Napa Valley*, pointing out the various places R.L.S. stopped or mentioned.

Unfortunately, most of the buildings he knew are gone now. You can tour the Schramsberg Winery north of St. Helena—some four miles before you reach Calistoga—where the original house and vinting building still stand as Stevenson would have seen them. Visits are by appointment only; call (707) 942-4558. For the centennial celebration of R.L.S.'s Silverado days this winery released a commemorative bottling of Napa Gamay with Stevenson's picture on the label. The nearby Alta Vineyard is also mentioned in *Silverado Squatters*.

*Eighteen miles north of St.
Helena on Highway 29, high
on Mount St. Helena (an
elevation named for the
Empress of Russia by an
exploration party from Fort
Ross, who placed a plaque on
the summit in 1841) you'll find:*

17 **ROBERT LOUIS STEVENSON STATE PARK**   This literary site
was dedicated as a park in 1911. The bunkhouse of the abandoned
silver mine where the honeymooners stayed is marked by a bust of
Stevenson in a clearing today. If architectural remains are missing,
however, the geography at least is little changed from Stevenson's
description: "We looked forth into a great realm of air, and down upon
the treetops, and far and near on wild and varied country." You can hike
about a mile up the trail from the parking area to the clearing. A reading
of *Silverado Squatters* will add greatly to a visit to this park, which lacks
the overwhelming grandeur of Muir Woods or the more personal appeal
of actually entering a building where R.L.S. lived, as in the Stevenson
House in Monterey. If you are in the wine country it is worth a side trip —
and combining stops at the museum, Schramsberg Winery, and this
park on a northward drive along Highway 29 will help evoke Stevenson's
still influential spirit.

*On the northeast side of San
Francisco Bay a thousand
miles of inland waterways seep
north toward Sacramento and
east to Stockton:*

18 **THE DELTA**   has served as a place of entertainment for several
boating authors. In July 1909, when Jack and Charmian London
returned from their famous South Sea voyage of over two years aboard
the *Snark*, they prepared to go sailing again on a yachting and duck
hunting trip in the Delta aboard the rented sloop, the *Phyllis*. Charmian,
suddenly seized with a residual attack of tropical malaria, was unable to
join her husband and his great friend George Sterling. Sterling's wife
Carrie and a Canadian visitor at London's Glen Ellen ranch, Louis
Augustin, made up the rest of the party. This expedition lasted from
October 16th to November 10th. Sterling wrote a series of letters to Herbert Heron and Opal Peet of Carmel, posted at various towns on their
course, which have been collected as *Give a Man a Boat He Can Sail*
(1980); the poet reported that: "Jack ordered dead loads of beer and
whiskey" and "On that beautiful Sacramento River, two miles above
Walnut Grove, and headed north against a head wind, the current
slightly against us, and the vile Wolf [Sterling's nickname for London]
two games ahead at pedro" and "Damn these streams! We were able,
the wind absent, to make only such advance as the ebb-tide permitted,
which meant about ten miles a day. We'd still be up-river had not the
Wolf, rendered desperate by inaction and the final consumption of all
the whiskey on board, induced the owner of a naptha launch to tow us
as far as Black Diamond."

In summer 1963 Erle Stanley Gardner, made wealthy by his fictional
lawyer Perry Mason, established a headquarters on Bethel Island in the

Delta. He kept five housetrailers to accommodate himself, his secretaries to whom he dictated his books, and visiting friends, as well as "a flotilla of two houseboats, one cruiser, and three smaller boats, the fastest used to scoot for mail when he was exploring the sloughs," according to his biographer Dorothy B. Hughes. He wrote three travel volumes in appreciation of this region: *The World of Water* (1964), *Gypsy Days on the Delta* (1967), and *Drifting Down the Delta* (1969). In the decade of the 1960s the prolific Gardner completed five other travel books, twenty Perry Mason novels, ten mysteries under his pen name "A. A. Fair," sixty-two articles, and miscellaneous writings for newspapers, with plenty of leisure time to enjoy roaming the state's deserts, the Delta, and Baja California.

En route to the state capitol in
Sacramento you might stop
off at:

19 **U.C. DAVIS** This campus is used as the setting for Diane Johnson's novel *Lying Low* (1978). Johnson has taught at Davis for several years, and recognizably transmutes it into "Orris" in the book:

> The beautiful old houses on Ashby Path are too big for single families any more and have been converted to lodgings for students at the University of California at Orris. . . . Nice gingerbread Victorian houses of Midwestern design, with sleeping porches, furnished with sagging wire-sprung beds, neatly covered with thin chenille bedspreads of washed-out green or coral, bare mattresses underneath awaiting students with sheets.

North on Interstate 80 will
bring you into:

Steffens mansion

20 **SACRAMENTO** The capital has several literary sites worth noting, and is the scene for an earlier novel by Diane Johnson, *The Shadow Knows* (1974), which portrays a divorced woman called "N." and her four children, who live in a housing project owned by the city: "Last week our lives were all right here. . . . But now we are going to be murdered. Just like that. It's not what you'd expect living quietly in North Sacramento."

The Old Town area of the city on the Sacramento River will give you an idea of what the town was like in the days when Mark Twain was writing articles for the Sacramento *Union* in 1866, and persuaded the editors to send him as a travel writer to the Sandwich Islands. He lampooned the city by calling it the City of Saloons instead of its usual appellation the City of the Plains, writing "I have not found any plains here, yet, but I have been in most of the saloons, and there are a good many of them. You can shut your eyes and march into the first door you come to and call for a drink, and the chances are that you will get it."

The Victorian Governor's Mansion at 16th and H Streets in downtown Sacramento was built for Albert Gallatin in 1877, and in November 1903 Governor George C. Pardee moved in with his family. Thirteen other governors lived here until 1967, when Ronald Reagan found this beautiful house "too drafty" and had a more modern mansion built for himself. In the interim between its construction and the coming of the politicians, this was home for young Lincoln Steffens, who was born in San Francisco but grew up here. This house where he spent his youth is open to the public.

Herb Caen, after the great Ambrose Bierce San Francisco's most famous newspaper columnist, the self-proclaimed "Sacramento Kid," grew up in 1631 26th Street at Q Street in the years 1922 to 1936 — a "neighborhood that has changed so little in sixty years."

North on Highway 80 from Sacramento you'll find:

Clark Ashton Smith, 1953

21 AUBURN This town sprang up quickly after Claude Chana discovered gold in the area May 16, 1848. A huge concrete statue of Chana forever pans for nuggets at the entrance to the historic old town district, just off the freeway, and a quick whirl about the city will present a surprising number of literary associations for such a small town.

Buds, Blossoms and Leaves, the first book of poetry by a woman in California, appeared in 1854 from Mary Eulalie Shannon, a native of Kentucky. Her husband, John Shannon Jr., published a newspaper here in whose pages her poems ran under the single name "Eulalie." She became known as "The Auburn Poetess" and gave popular readings of her verse before audiences of the miners, who were greatly saddened when she died not long after her book was published. Her gravestone, bearing the single word "Eulalie," may be found today in the old Auburn cemetery at Nevada Street and Fulweiler Avenue.

Also in this graveyard is the tombstone of Richard H. Barter, a.k.a. "Rattlesnake Dick," the notorious gold rush bandit who terrorized Auburn, Nevada City, and Weaverville. Auburn native Robert B. Elder wrote Dick's "true story in novel form," *Rattlesnake Dick* (1954), covering Barter's eventful nine-year career as a desperado in California, until he received the fatal bullet July 11, 1859.

The western writer Jackson Gregory was also an Auburn native— his wife Susan Myra Gregory was a poet. Esther Birdsall Darling too was born here, though she became known for writing later done in Alaska in the tradition of Jack London— her dog stories Baldy *of Nome and* Navarre of the North *were hugely popular.*

Bret Harte visited here in his rambles about mining country, using Rattlesnake Bar south of the town as the setting for his poem "Crotalus," and Ambrose Bierce often visited, since Auburn's climate provided relief from his worrying asthma. Bitter Bierce set several of his weird tales in this area.

At the age of eighteen, Clark Ashton Smith of Auburn climbed to the peak of literary fame with *The Star-Treader and Other Poems* (1912). Front-page reviews in the San Francisco press proclaimed Smith "the Boy Genius of the Sierras" and "the Keats of the Pacific Coast." In 1918 the prestigious Book Club of California published a deluxe edition of his *Odes and Sonnets*, with an introduction by his mentor George Sterling. By 1922 Smith would have to publish his next collection, *Ebony and Crystal*, himself.

Rhymed, metered, Romantic verse was down, if not out— Clark Ashton Smith continued to write his exquisite poetry until his death in 1961, ignoring the fashion of the age. His long poem "The Hashish-Eater" from *Ebony and Crystal* was called by H. P. Lovecraft "the greatest imaginative orgy in English literature," but Smith might well be forgotten today had not Lovecraft suggested that he direct his talents to writing stories for the newly-created horror and science fiction pulp magazines. Earlier Jack London had transmuted the cosmic-astronomic imagery in *The Star-Treader* into prose form in *The Star Rover* (1915), a novel some London *aficionados* consider his best, unquestionably influenced by Smith's poems.

Both Ray Bradbury and Harlan Ellison have said that reading Smith's novelette "The City of Singing Flame" in their teens inspired them to become science fiction writers. Lovecraft himself thought that Smith was the greatest writer of their weird circle; their reputations have carried, like that of Edgar Allan Poe, to Europe, where they were admired by the Surrealists and others.

Most of Smith's tales occur in other dimensions, in the far future or pre-mythological past, though he sets a very few in San Francisco and Auburn. The old public library on Pine Street, frequented by Smith during the years 1908-1954, is where Philip Hastane encounters the sorcerer Jean Averaud in "The Devotee of Evil." The house Averaud inhabits is found shrouded behind trees in a large yard at 153 Sacramento Street in old town Auburn.

Following Sacramento south beyond the fairgrounds, you'll come to the roughly forty-acre tract where Smith's father built a cabin in 1902. Today the area is a typical suburban development, but for all of Smith's life only a footpath led off the road to his home in the blue oaks. Turning left into Carolyn Street you'll pass Smith Court to the left and Poet Smith Drive to the right. At the end of the street you'll see a church; turn right and go to the dead-end of the block. To your right, surrounded on two sides by the new houses and still open to the country on two sides, is the one acre left of the original Smith property. His cabin stood on the rocky area in the middle of this tract until it burned in 1957. Here he wrote his fantasy tales, often composing them outside at a table under the trees.

A few years after his death Smith's ashes were taken from their urn and buried next to a large boulder — an unmarked natural tombstone — in the growth of trees ringing the western edge of the cabin site.

(Slightly over a mile southwest of the intersection of Sacramento and Maidu Drive on the Auburn-Folsom Road you'll find mail box No. 1320 — a more modern house stands to the left; the older house to the right is where Smith was born January 13, 1893.)

The number of literary associations this far north of San Francisco is remarkable. Up from Auburn, on modern Highway 80 in Grass Valley, Mary Hallock Foote wrote and illustrated her novels of the West, such as *The Ground-Swell* (1919). Her many letters to Catherine Mapes Bunnell of Berkeley have been collected as *A Victorian Gentlewoman in the Far West* (1972) — and her experiences as a woman from an established Quaker family following her husband, a mining engineer, to the gold fields of California, and the traumatic death of her seventeen-year-old daughter in 1904 when Foote was at the peak of her success as a novelist, inspired Wallace Stegner to write *Angle of Repose*, his Pulitzer Prize-winning novel of 1971 — adapted as an opera in 1976.

Gary Snyder

Gary Snyder has lived for many years at Kitkitdizze, his ranch near Nevada City, an area he frequently uses in his poetry, as in *Turtle Island* (1974), which won the Pulitzer for poetry the next year. Here on a visit Lew Welch hiked off into the mountains in 1971 to an unknown end.

Even Oroville further north has its writers and associations: Erle Stanley Gardner lived there as a teenager; Gertrude and George Atherton tried, without success, to run a grape farm in the early years of their mismatched marriage; and Ishi the last wild Indian came, starving, into civilization to become a living symbol of a lost America.

Alan Lau lives in Paradise, a small town near Oroville. Dustbooks makes its headquarters here, too.

Gary Snyder has said: "The backcountry surrounds the country." The social and political implications of that maxim are vast — so too are the mountains, rivers, retreats, history, legends, and mythology of northern California, surrounding San Francisco and inspiring her writers.

PHOTO CREDITS

By Page Number:

1, 7, 14 (top), 17, 52, 58, 62, 73, 75, 79, 98, 148, 178, 180, 208, 210. Courtesy, The Bancroft Library, University of California, Berkeley.

10, 41 (Photograph by Willard Van Dyke), 69, 93, 98, 124, 167, 176. Courtesy, San Francisco Public Library.

8, 13, 14 (bottom), 37 (top), 39, 43, 51, 68, 80, 82, 83, 94, 96, 100, 102, 106, 110, 114, 116, 121, 123, 130, 156, 182, 194. Photographs by Nancy J. Peters.

18. Photograph by James Oliver Mitchell.

19, 20, 50, 125. Photographs by Lawrence Ferlinghetti.

21 (Photograph by Clem Albers), 65, 111, 54 (Photograph by R. Allen), 187, 213, 230, 234, 236. Private / Authors' Collections.

25. Courtesy, Museum of Modern Art.

29. Courtesy, The Bettman Archive.

34, 37 (bottom. Photographs by Mary Sporer.

38. Courtesy, John's Grill.

40. Photograph by Johan Hagemeyer. Courtesy, Tillman Place Bookshop.

49, 65, 175, 202. Photographs by Don Herron.

61. Photograph by Roger Ressmeyer.

65, 66. Courtesy, Carolyn Cassady.

70. Courtesy, Nanda Pivano.

77, 86, 95, 141, 147, 174, 222. Photographs by Chris Felver.

84. Photograph by Jim Hatch. Courtesy, Donald M. Allen.

95. Photograph by Ira Nowinski.

96. Photograph by Kim McCloud.

113. Courtesy, Henri Lenoir.

132. Photograph by Alejandro Stuart.

137. Photograph by Felicia Liu.

143. Photograph by Larry Keenan.

157. Photograph by Sydney Goldstein.

161. Photograph by Judy Olausen.

162. Photograph by Jeffrey Blankfort.

163, 172. Courtesy, Russ Kingman, Glen Ellen.

168, 169, 170, 171, 174. Photographs by Jack London. Courtesy, Estate of Irving Shephard.

177, 197, 204, 221, 222, 227. Photographs by Bill Kostura.

193. Photograph by Gui de Angulo.

195. Courtesy, Collection of American Literature, The Beinecke Rare Book and Manuscript Library, Yale University.

220. Photograph by Karen Marcroft.

214, 216. Courtesy, The John Steinbeck Library, Salinas, California.

228. Photograph by Marie Kass Rexroth. Courtesy, Albert Huerta, S.J. °1984.

229. Courtesy, Estate of Alan Watts.

230. Courtesy, Johnny Dark.

239. Photograph by George F. Haas.

241. Courtesy, Donald M. Allen.

INDEX

Abbott, Steve 135
Adams, Alice 57, 105, 157-58
Aiken, Ednah 202
Alarcón, Francisco 139
Alegria, Fernando 138, 199
Allen, Woody *55*, 115
Anderson, Poul 190
Andrews, Roy Chapman 207
Angelou, Maya 116
Angulo, Jaime de 103, 191, 210, 212
Asher, Don 115-16
Atherton, George 77-*79*, 200, 241
Atherton, Gertrude 4, 6, 10, 13, 15,
    24, 53-54, 55, *75*, 77-79, 97,
    101, *148*, 183, 184, 192, 200,
    201, 231, 234, 241
Auden, W. H. 150, 155
Austin, Mary 124-25, 184, 197, 206,
    208, 209, *210*

Baker, Louise 196
Bancroft, Hubert Howe 15, 141, 184
Barker, Eric 103, 232
Beagle, Peter S. 202
Bender, Albert "Mickey" 24, 125
Benediktsson, Thomas 48
Benet, George 56, 85
Benét, William Rose 148, 210
Benson, Jackson J. 215, 218
Berkson, Bill 233
Berriault, Gina 233
Bessie, Alvah 115
Bierce, Ambrose 4, 9, 10, 13-*14*, 22,
    47, 50, 58, 60, 62, 74, 124, 129,
    146, 178, 183, 192, 201, 209,
    231, 235, 240
Biggers, Earl Derr 44, 128-29
Bishop, Elizabeth 150
Black Bart 17, 60
Bland, Henry Mead 97
Bogan, Louise 150
Bohemian Club 10, 46-49, 53, 68,
    69, 125, 229, 234
Boucher, Anthony 25, 188-89, 190
Boyle, Kay 136, 148, 155
Boyles, Tiny 27
Bradley, Marion Zimmer 190
Brand, Stewart 85, 117, 202
Brautigan, Richard 100-01, *105*, 147,
    158, 233
Breiding, G. Sutton 69, 159
Brilliant, Ashley 147, 152
Brooks, Van Wyck 209
Broughton, James 145, *187*, 196,
    231
Brown, Helen Gurley 44
Brown, Jerry 24
Brown, Rita Mae 105
Browne, J. Ross 47, 89
Browning, Frank 140
Bruce, Lenny 115

Bryant, Dorothy 120, 136-*37*, 191-92
Bukowski, Charles 44, 211
Burbank, Luther 54, 234
Burgess, Gelett 4, 8-9, 11, *58*, 60,
    62, 63, 68, 74, 81, 107, 124, 125
Burroughs, William S. 108, 109
Busch, Niven 17, 48
Byrne, Robert 230

Caen, Herb 16, 55-56, 69, 82, 105,
    114-15, 123, 239
Caldwell, Erskine 48, 56
Callenbach, Ernest 17
Cardenal, Ernesto 138
Carpenter, Don 27, 84-85, 119, 141,
    144, 155, 191, 229
Carr, Terry 182
Carroll, Jim 233
Carson, Bob 85
Cassady, Carolyn 20, 43, 58, 65-66,
    109, 201
Cassady, Neal 20, 43, 58, 65-*66*,
    72, 85, 109, 110, 115, 118, 139,
    154, 187-88, 199-200, 201, 212
Castaño, Wilfred 139
"Caxton," see Rhodes, William Henry
Cha, Bernadette 158
Chan, Jeff 155
Chandler, Raymond 29, 56
Chapel, Steve 140
Chaplin, Charlie 13, 195, 212
Charters, Ann 109
Chen, Yuan-Tsun 127
Cherkovski, Neeli 5, 102
Chin, Frank 127, 130
City Lights 101-02, 103, *106*, 110-12
Clark, Leonard 155-56, 235
Clark, Tom 109, 233
Cleaver, Eldridge 178-79, 187
Clemens, Samuel L., see Twain, Mark
Cobb, Irving 44
Coblentz, Stanton 203, 231
Codrescu, Andrei 235
Collins, Mary 58, 63
Connell, Evan S. 26, 229
Conrad, Barnaby 82, 114
Conrad, Joseph 82-83
Cooke, Grace MacGowan 210
Coolbrith, Ina Donna 4, 46, 47, 53-45,
    58, 61, *62*, 64-65, 90, 94, 164,
    183, 184, 231, 234
Coppel, Alfred 178
Coppola, Francis 43, 66, 83, 117
Corso, Gregory 85, 97, *100*, 102,
    108, 113, 117
Cowley, Malcolm 150
Crawford, F. Marion 11
Creeley, Robert 120, 233
Crumb, R. 146
Cruz, Victor Hernandez 139
Cunningham, Eugene 156

Dana, Richard Henry 82, 134, 204-05
Dark, Johnny 115, *230*
Darling, Esther Birdsall 240
Davidson, Avram 190
Davis, Grania 190
Davis, Kenn 16
Dawson, Emma Francis 9
de Camp, L. Sprague 206
De Cles, John 190
deFord, Miriam Allen 16-17, 22, 137-38
Delano, Alonzo "Old Block" 128
Delehanty, Randolph 112
De Marco, Gordon 12-13, 43, 140
Dennis, Gene 85
"de Quille, Dan" 88-89
Dick, Philip K. 189, 190
diPrima, Diane 136, 144
Dobie, Charles Caldwell 4, 62, 69, 74, 201
Dodge, David 99, 157
Dodge, Jim 235
Doohan, Brian 102
Dooner, Pierton W. 128
Dos Passos, John 156
Doss, Margo Patterson 58, 233
Doyle, Arthur Conan 45, 79, 231
Doyle, Dr. C. W. 129
Doyle, Kirby 108, 117, 212, 229
Dreiser, Theodore 153
Duncan, David 207
Duncan, Isadora 46, 180, 181
Duncan, Robert 72, 109, 110, 135, 139, 144, 145, 155, 181, 186, *187*
Dylan, Bob 115

Eastman, Max 209
Elder, Robert B. 239
Englehart, Stephen 7
Erdman, Paul 48
"Eulalie" 239
Everson, William 108, 145, 186, 202, 211

Faas, Ekbert 186
Fairley, Lincoln 231
Ferlinghetti, Lawrence 5, 41, 44, 59, 69, 86, 102, 103, 108, 109, 110-12, 114, 115, 117, 119, 138, 139, 152, 201, 212, 233
Fernández, Magaly 139
Field, Charles K. 54
Field, Sara Bard 59-60, 69, 202
"Finnegan, Robert" see Ryan, Paul William
Fisher, M. F. K. 233
Flavin, Martin 207
Flint, Homer Eon 7
Foley, Charles 128
Foote, Mary Hallock 241
Forbes, Kathryn 141, 198
Ford, Leslie 55
Forster, E. M. 187
Fox, Ken 85
Foye, Raymond 102
Frankel, David 56

Fraser, Kathleen 136, 150
French, Nora May 54, 98, 209
Friedman, Mickey 16
Frost, Robert 8, 15, 191

Gaines, Ernest J. 155, 158
Gann, Ernest K. 86, 207
Gardner, Erle Stanley, 76, 129, 182, 237-38, 241
Gardner, Leonard 196
Garnett, Porter 11, 69, 125
Garrett, Randall 190
Genthe, Arnold 210
Gentry, Curt 48
George, Henry 47, 101, 137-38
Ginsberg, Allen 20, 28, 44, 57, 61, 71-72, 73, 85, 108, 109, 110, 111, 115, 116, 117, 139, 147, 151, 152, 161, 187, 188, 200
Gleason, Madeleine *187*
Gleason, Ralph J. 43, 85, 152
Goforth, Polly Lamb 101
Gold, Herb 48, 58, 60-*61*, 105, 114, 116, 135
Gold, Mike 136
Goldman, Emma 134-35, 136
Gonick, Larry 140
Goodis, David 66, 99
Gores, Joe 26, 27, 34, 36, 39, 41, 66, 104, 189, 232
Gotanda, Philip 158
Grahn, Judy 144
Greenleaf, Stephen 27
Greer, Maretta 152
Gregory, Jackson 240
Gregory, Susan Myra 240
Grieg, Michael 120
Griffin, Susan 136, 191
Grogan, Emmett 146-47
Gross, Ronald 22
Grossman, Jeffrey 117
Guedalla, Philip 202

Hagedorn, Jessica Tarahata 127, *161*
Hailey, Arthur 48
Hall, Austin 7
Hall, Carroll D. 12
Halliburton, Richard 202
Hammett, Dashiell 4, 13, 15, 17, 19, 22, 26, 27, 28, *29*-39, 41, 43, 50, 54, 57, 73, 82, 98, 126, 128, 129, 142, 184, 212
Hart, Howard 102
Hart, James D. 79, 185
Harte, Bret 12, 16, 48, 50, 60, 61, 65, 90, 93, 107, 123, 128, 140, 178, 183, 184, 185, 196, 231, 234, 240
Hartmann, Sadakichi 124, 126
Hawkins, Bobbie Louise 233
Hayakawa, S. I. 155
Heggens, Thomas 57
Heinlein, Robert A. 202
Hejinian, Lynn 144
Hellman, Lillian 31-32, 39
Hemingway, Ernest 44, 87, 115, 209, 212-13

Herbert, Frank 16, 140
Herrera, Juan Felipe 139, 199
Hilton, James 44
Hinckle, Warren 37, 105, 142
Hirshman, Jack 117
Hitchcock, George 202
Hoffer, Eric 22, 28, 83-84, 86, 145, 153, 185
Hopper, Jimmy 54, 124, 206, 209, 210
Hughes, Dorothy B. 76, 238
Hughes, Langston 209

Irwin, Wallace 108
Irwin, Will 63, 107
Ishi 151, 186
Issler, Anne Roller 181
Iverson, Roderick 117

Jackson, Helen Hunt 60, 203
Jackson, Joseph Henry 190
Jarrell, Randall 150
Jayo, Norman 127, 178
Jeffers, Robinson 184, 191, 202, 206, 209, 211-12, 213
Jenkins, Joyce 135
Johnson, Diane 27, 58, 238
Johnson, Robert Barbour 99, 101
Jones, Idwal 48, 50, 68, 196

Kael, Pauline 110
Kageyama, Yuri 127, 158
Kamstra, Jerry 139
Kandel, Lenore 147, 201, 212
Kaplan, Justin 206
Kaufman, Bob 102, 108, 113, 115, 117
Kees, Weldon 120
Kerouac, Jack 14, 18, 20, 43, 58, 65, 66, 73, 85, 108-10, 113, 114, 115, 118, 120, 131, 139, 145, 146, 179, 187-88, 191, 201, 212, 229, 231
Kerouac, Jan 145, 235
Kesey, Ken 41, 43, 85, 118, 147, 187, 199-200, 202, 213
Kim, Elaine 185
Kingman, Russ 164, 167, 176
Kingston, Maxine Hong 177, 196
Kipling, Rudyard 10, 15
Koller, Jim 233
Kovic, Ron 116, 162, 229
Krich, John 179
Kroeber, A. L. 151, 185, 186, 191
Kroeber, Theodora 151, 186, 191
Kudaka, Geraldine 127
Kwock, C. H. 129-30
Kyne, Peter B. 86, 202

Lafler, Harry 98, 124, 125, 213
Lamantia, Philip 66, 69, 96, 101, 102, 108, 110, 141, 145, 186
L'Amour, Louis 44
Lardner, Ring 44
Lau, Alan Chong 127, 241
Laurie, Annie 63, 69
Lawson, William 179
Lee, C. Y. 130

Leffland, Ella 105, 162, 177, 192
Legaspi, Joaquin 127
LeGuin, Ursula K. 186
Leiber, Fritz 14-15, 16, 21, 22, 25, 28, 35, 39, 142, 160, 189
Leider, Emily 53, 79
Lenoir, Henri 112-13, 114-15
Leong, George 127, 129
Le Seuer, Meridel 136,.234
Levy, Harriet Lane 1-2, 25, 26, 203
Lewis, Austin 231
Lewis, Oscar 12, 185
Lewis, Sinclair 44, 209, 210-11
Lim, Genny 127, 158
Literary parks and museums 17, 39, 64, 68-69, 82-83, 92, 125-26, 134, 167, 174-76, 183-84, 192-96, 201-02, 204-05, 211-12, 213, 223-24, 225, 226-27, 234, 236-37, 239
Literary plaques 8, 19, 37, 46, 48, 49, 50, 68-69, 79, 104, 125-26, 138, 141, 152-53, 183, 209, 223, 229, 231, 237
London, Charmian 69, 174, 175, 176, 202, 209, 237
London, Jack 4, 14-15, 19, 28, 46, 47, 54, 73, 82, 104, 108, 140, 146, 150, 163-76, 177, 181, 182, 183, 184, 206, 209, 210-11, 213, 228, 231, 233, 236, 237, 240
Lowell, Robert 150
Ludlow, Fitzhugh 123
Lupoff, Richard A. 190, 191
Lynn, Elizabeth 190
Lyon, Dana 99

MacAdams, Lewis 233
MacDonald, John D. 235
MacDonald, Ross 97
MacGowan, Alice 208, 210
MacNichol, Kenneth 101
Malanga, Gerard 233
Mallia, Max 85
"Marco, Count" 16, 56
Margolin, Malcolm 191
Markham, Edwin 42, 61, 183, 184, 201, 202
Martinez, Xavier 69, 124, 125, 173
Masefield, John 232
Mason, David 140, 159-60
Matz, Martin 102
Maugham, Somerset 131
Maupin, Armistead 65, 99, 105, 142
May, Antoinette 77
McCabe, Charles 16, 99-100, 119
McCarthy, Mary 44
McClure, Joanna 70, 72, 147
McClure, Michael 70, 72, 108, 109, 116, 139, 144, 147, 151, 212
McCunn, Ruthanne Lum 129
McDonough, Kaye 100, 117
McFadden, Cyra 231
McGoorty, Danny 230
McHugh, Vincent 120, 129
McKuen, Rod 147

McLaren, John 69, 152, 153
McNally, Dennis 58, 66, 131
McNaughton, Duncan 135-36, 233
Meltzer, David 136, 140, 146, 233
Mencken, H. L. 44, 47-48, 108
Mersereau, John 98
Miles, Josephine 136
Millay, Edna St. Vincent 44, 209
Miller, Henry 113, 191, 212-*13*
Miller, Joaquin 47, 54, 123, 124,
    183-85, 196, 202, 228, 231
Mills, Herb 85
Milne, Robert Duncan 9, 13
Mirikitani, Janice 127, 136, 158
Mitchell, Ruth Comfort 201
Mitford, Jessica 178
Montandon, Pat 16, 67
Moore, Daniel 181
Moore, Richard 145
Mora, Jo 48, 207
Morris, Wright 233
Morrow, W. C. 4, 9, 13, 74, 124, 201
Moskowitz, Sam 9
Mott, Gertrude 184
Mueller, Jack 117
Muir, John 47, 177, 184, 192-94,
    202, 231
Mulford, Prentice 47, 49, 123, 196
Murayama, Milton 127
Murguía, Alejandro *132*, 139
Murphy, Michael 213
Myrtle, Minnie 123, 184

Nelsen, Brian 85
Nelson, Ray Faraday 69, 189-90, 209
Newberry, Perry 124, 125, 208
Nickerson, Roy 126, 205
Nin, Anais 150, 186
Nishikawa, Lane 158
Noguchi, Yone 11, 183
Nolan, William F. 27, 39
Notley, Alice 233
Nord, Eric "Big Daddy" 112, 115, 201
Norris, Charles 124, *148*, 184,
    198, 201
Norris, Kathleen 107, 124, 147-*48*,
    182, 184, 198, 201, 231
Norris, Frank 4, 47, 62, 72, *73*, 74,
    108, 124, 148, 150, 160, 178,
    183, 184
Norse, Harold 117, 135

O'Brien, Robert 9, 16, 125
O'Connor, Daniel 229
Offord, Lenore Glen 63-64
Older, Fremont 209
Olsen, Tillie 136, 143, 145
O'Neill, Eugene 54-55, 57, 177, 194-*95*
Orlovsky, Peter 71-72, 115, 139
Oyama, Richard 127, 158

Palmer, Michael 136
Palóu, Fr. Francisco 134, 184
Parker, Pat 136
Parkinson, Thomas 145, 185, 186
Parton, Margaret 98

Patchen, Kenneth 111, 118, 186,
    198-99
Patler, Lois 136
Paton, Alan 45, 232
Paxson, Diana 190
Pease, Howard 57, 99, 157
Peet, Herbert Heron 298, 237
Petaja, Emil 142
Peters, Nancy, 47, 69, 101, 102, 134,
    206
Phelan, James D. 24, 42, 53-54, 61,
    201-02, 220
Plummer, William 118
Polk, Willis 4, 11, 53, 60, 62, 64, 68,
    125, 161
Pommy-Vega, Janine 57
Porter, Bruce 8-9, 11, 60, 63, 67-68,
    125
Price, E. Hoffman 178, 198

"Quin, Mike" see Ryan, Paul William

Randall, Marta 182
Rath, Virginia 58, 63
Rather, Lois 187
Reed, Ishmael, 161, *170*, 185
Reich, Charles 58
Rexroth, Kenneth 72, 108, 109, 111,
    118, 119-20, 139, 140, 145-46,
    161, 186, 188, 190-91, 217, *228*
Rhodes, William Henry 9, 58, 60
Rice, Anne 158-59
Rice, Stan 155
Richards, Janet 123, 140
Richman, Al 136
Rigsby, Howard 99
Robertson, A. M. 42, 46, 48, 69
Robinson, Frank M. 141-142
Robles, Al 127-28
Robles, Margarita 139
Roethke, Theodore 150
Rogers, Rosemay 207
Ronan, Stephen 191
Rukeyser, Muriel 145
Runyon, Damon 44
Russell, Bertrand 45
Ryan, Paul William 13

Sales, Grover 110
Sandburg, Carl 209, 234
"Santiago, Danny" 207
Saroyan, Aram 233
Saroyan, William 12, *41*, 55, 123, 131,
    139, 149, 155, 159, 197
Scheffauer, Herman 54, 231
Schell, Orville 233
Schmitz, Anne-Marie 222
Schneck, Stephen 7
Schorer, Mark 185
Shapiro, Karl 213
Shelton, Gilbert 146
Shepard, Sam 105, 115, *230*-31
Shilts, Randy 105
Shumate, Albert 97
Sidney-Fryer, Donald 69, 142, 205
Siefkin, David 44, 45, 131

Sill, Edward Rowland 47, 184, 231
Silliphant, Sterling 232
Silverberg, Robert 182
Sinclair, Upton 13, 43, 209
Smith, Clark Ashton 24, 28, 43, 49,
    103, 142, 198, 205-06, 209, 210,
    232, *239*, 240-41
Smith, Julie 105, 186
Smith, Martin Cruz 232
Snyder, Gary 24, 57, *84*-85, 108, 109,
    110, 119, 120, 131, 139, 141, 144,
    147, 152, 188, 229, 231, *241*
Soloman, Ruth Freeman 58
Spender, Stephen 150
Spicer, Jack 109, 110, 119, 187
Spillane, Mickey 7-8, 44
Stanley, John 16
Starr, Kevin 16, 24, 47
Steel, Danielle 75
Steffens, Lincoln 12, 13, 206, 209, 239
Stegner, Wallace 199, 241
Stein, Gertrude 26, 55, 144, 179,
    180-81, 184, 187, 209, 212
Steinbeck, John 73, 80, 81, 86, 123,
    184, 199, 201, 203, 204, 206,
    209, 214-227
Sterling, George 4, 12, 14-15, 22, 28,
    40, 41, 43, 47-48, 49, 54, 60, 61,
    68-69, 73, 82, 98, 107, 108, 124,
    125, 126, 140, 153, 161, 171, 173,
    175, 182, 183, 184, 202, 206, 208,
    209, *210*, 211, 213, 231, 234,
    237, 240
Stevenson, Robert Louis 6-7, 11, 17,
    44, 50-51, 52, 60, 68, 97, 123,
    125, 181, 184, 204-05, 212, 228,
    235, *236*-37
Stewart, George R. 98, 151, 162,
    185-86
Stoddard, Charles Warren 4, 6-7, 42,
    47, 54, 61, 90, 97, 124, 184,
    203, 231
Stone, Irving 104
Stone, Robert 41, 118, 147, 199
"Stripteasdale," Sarah 120
Stroud, Robert 97
Sui Sin Far 129
Swaim, Lawrence 6, 27, 140
Syquia, Luis 127, 158

Tagamai, Jeff 127
Tate, Allen 150
Taylor, Edward Robeson 53
Taylor, Samuel W. 19, 198
Teilhet, Darwin and Hildegarde 55
Temko, Allan 113
Thayer, Ernest L. 15
Thomas, Dylan 113, 150, 191
Thomas, Ross 43
Thompson, Hunter S. 143, 150-51,
    153, 200
Toklas, Alice B. 26, 55, 180, 203,
    204, 209
Tsui, Kitty 127
Twain, Mark 6, 12, 60, 65, *87*-94,
    107, 123, 124, 184, 213, 238

Valaoritis, Nanos 155
Vance, Jack 182
Vargas, Roberto *132*, 138
Vawter, Mike 85
Verne, Jules 2
Voznesensky, Andrei 102, 234

Wainio, Ken 56
Walden, Tisa 117
Waldrop, Una 54, 69
Walker, Alice *154*, 162, 235
Walker, Franklin 15, 61, 65, 88, 89,
    178
Ward, Artemus 89, 90, 91, 123
Warsh, Lewis 233
Warshall, Peter 233
Watts, Alan 147, 188, 213, *229*, 231
Weiss, Ruth 25, 136
Welch, Lew 5 *1*-85, 108, 119, 141, 144,
    147, 201, 212, 229
Weidman, Jerome 48, 75
Weiner, Michael 102
West, Jessamyn *235*
Wieners, John 71
Whalen, Philip *84*-85, 108, 109, 119,
    141, 144, 212, 233
Whitaker, Herman 171, 173
White, Edward Stewart 198
White, Emil 213
Wiggin, Kate Douglas 140
Wilcox, Collin 161
Wilde, Oscar *10*, 123, 129
Willeford, Charles 16
Williams, Tennessee 44
Williams, William Carlos 150, 191
Wilson, Edmund 29, 136
Wilson, Harry Leon 207
Witt-Diamant, Ruth 150, 155
Wolf, Leonard 155
Wolfe, Burton H. 55
Wolfe, Tom 200, 213
Woo, Merle 127, 129, 191
Wood, Charles Erskine Scott 59-60
    202
Woollcott, Alexander 148
Wong, Jade Snow 130
Wong, Nellie 127, 191
Wong, Shawn 127, 179
Wong, Victor 127, 129
Wouk, Herman 98

Yamamoto, Doug 127
Yang, Ling-Fu 207
Yarbro, Chelsea Quinn 25, 190
Yat-sen, Dr. Sun 124, 129
Yee, Nelson 130
Yep, Lawrence 94
Yevtushenko, Yevgeny 43, 102
Young, Al 179, 199
Young, Norm 85
Young, Sanborn 201

Zeigler, Mel 58
Zimmer, Paul Edwin 190